For Gerald N. Grob: brilliant scholar,
talented teacher, inspiring colleague,
and compassionate friend.

Library of Congress Cataloging in Publication Data

Billias, George Athan, 1919–   ed.
  The American Revolution.

  Includes bibliographical references.
  1. United States—History—Revolution, 1775–1783—
Addresses, essays, lectures. 2. United States—
History—Revolution, 1775–1783—Historiography—
Addresses, essays, lectures. I. Title.
E297.B54   1980   973.3′1   80–16521

ISBN 0–03–054761–X

Printed in the United States of America

0 1 2 3   059 9 8 7 6 5 4 3 2 1

Third Edition

The American Revolution

How Revolutionary Was It?

Edited by
GEORGE ATHAN BILLIAS
Clark University

Holt, Rinehart and Winston

New York • Chicago • San Francisco • Atlanta
Dallas • Montreal • Toronto • London • Sydney

The American Revolution

PREFACE

Views of the American Revolution by historians have changed considerably over the past 200 years. The selections in this anthology range from the writings of contemporaries—the Loyalists—to those of the current generation of "new social historians." Confronted with conflicting interpretations regarding the nature, causes, and consequences of the Revolution, readers will learn to appreciate the complexity of history and to question any simplistic explanation of the event.

Americans have long felt that their Revolution belonged not only to them but to the world. With that idea in mind, two new sections have been added to this edition—"Comparative Views" and "The Revolution and the Modern World." The selections in these sections emphasize the need for studying the Revolution within the context of comparative history and global history. Given the major role assumed by the United States in world affairs in recent times, it has become increasingly important to approach American history from a broad international perspective rather than from a narrowly nationalistic point of view.

I am grateful to the following, who read the manuscript and made valuable suggestions: Milton Klein, University of Tennessee; Ronald Petrin of Clark University; and Gerald N. Grob of Rutgers University to whom this volume is dedicated.

GEORGE ATHAN BILLIAS

CONTENTS

The American Revolution

INTRODUCTION

The American Revolution represents the single most important event in our nation's history. Within two decades—1763–1783—Americans rejected Britain's monarchical system, waged a war of independence, created states out of colonies, and established a central government based on the principles of popular rule, republicanism, and nationalism. These changes took place with remarkable rapidity, but was the transformation itself sweeping enough to justify the term "revolutionary."? Did the new United States differ that much from the former colonies? Did the laws, institutions, and traditions of the American republic, for example, constitute a sharp break with the British heritage? Was American society radically reshaped and restructured as a result of independence? Was there a dramatic change in the ideas, attitudes, and perceptions of most Americans regarding the relationship between individuals and their government, their society, and one another? These issues within the context of our national history may be reduced to a single question: How revolutionary was the Revolution?

Many scholars have argued, moreover, that the Revolution was significant in world history and ranks with the French, Russian, and Chinese revolutions as an epic event in modern times. The Revolution, they claimed, gave greater impetus to certain principles that influenced other people in different parts of the globe. It set a precedent for other colonies to follow in striking for independence—in Latin America in the nineteenth century, in places such as Ireland before World War II, and throughout Asia and Africa in the post-World War II era. It helped to accelerate the global movement toward extending more political power to broader electorates in the past two centuries. The Revolution also led to the greater use of two mechanisms in government—written constitutions, and constitutional conventions—through which the sovereign power of the people could be exercised. These scholars raised the same question, this time within a world-wide context, of how really revolutionary the Revolution was.

When dealing with this question in terms of our national history, writers have pursued two lines of inquiry. One approach has been to evaluate the character of the Revolution by examining its causes. Why was there a Revolution? Was it an illegal rebellion against legitimate rulers, as some Loyalist writers claimed? Or were the oppressed Americans justified in rebelling against a tyrannical king, as Patriot historians argued? Were the leaders of the revolutionary movement unselfish, liberty-loving ideologues who hoped to defend

1

American rights and liberties? Or was the revolutionary movement led mainly by American merchants and businessmen who were pursuing their self-interest as they sought to escape what they believed to be repressive measures of the British mercantilist system? Did the Revolution assume a deeply conservative character as it aimed to preserve the existing social order in America? Or was it a more radical ideological movement—one involving a great change in how Americans viewed themselves—thus making the colonists feel in their newly discovered self-image that they could no longer achieve their destiny as a republican people within the British empire?

A second approach has been to judge the nature of the Revolution in terms of its consequences. Was the Revolution solely a colonial rebellion directed only at gaining the limited goal of independence from Britain? Or was it accompanied by a genuine "internal" revolution—a class conflict—as the radicalized lower classes sought to achieve a greater degree of democracy?

In examining the causes of the Revolution, the most appropriate place to begin is with those contemporaries actually involved in the event. Peter Oliver, a leading Massachusetts Loyalist, is representative of those who opposed the Whigs—as the Patriots were called. Oliver pictured the Revolution in Massachusetts as a political power struggle between good and evil men. The good were men of reason who upheld law and order—Thomas Hutchinson, the last civilian royal governor whose sister-in-law Oliver married, Governor Francis Bernard, and, of course, Peter Oliver himself. The evil-doers were James Otis, Jr., Samuel Adams, and John Hancock—self-seeking scoundrels who plotted the downfall of the royal government to satisfy their lust for power. Massachusetts Whig leaders were unprincipled demagogues—men who deliberately aroused the passions of the populace—causing the people to abandon reason and to rise up against the colony's legitimate rulers. Oliver saw the Revolution as revolutionary in character because it marked the collapse of the society in which he had prospered—as an iron manufacturer, merchant, and the last chief justice of the Massachusetts Superior Court. The first selection of this volume is drawn from Oliver's history.

Despite the writings of Loyalist historians, the patriotic version of the Revolution was the one overwhelmingly accepted in the late eighteenth century and thereafter. In the generation following that of the Founding Fathers, the same fierce nationalism prevailed. Throughout most of the nineteenth century, scholars accepted uncritically the main underlying assumption of that era— that the major theme of American history was the quest for liberty. Within this context, the Revolution was viewed as a struggle between American liberty and British tyranny.

George Bancroft, one of the greatest historians of the nineteenth century, best illustrates this point of view. To Bancroft the Revolution represented one step in God's grand design for the march of all mankind toward a future golden age of greater human freedom. America, in his eyes, symbolized the forces of liberty and progress in this master plan; Britain, those of tyranny and reaction. Bancroft's heroes were the Patriots because they founded a nation based on the principles of liberty and equality. His villain was King George III, a tyrant who was seeking to limit freedom. Like Oliver, Bancroft saw the Revolution as radical in character, but for a different reason—it speeded the advance of mankind toward the forthcoming millennium.

With the spirit of nationalism widespread throughout much of the nineteenth century, it is not difficult to understand why Bancroft wrote as he did. He intuitively produced the kind of history that met the needs of the American people at that time. During many of the decades between the 1830s and the 1870s—the period when Bancroft published his magisterial ten-volume work—the country was divided. America was split by the bitter party battles of the Jacksonian era and the bloody military conflict of the Civil War. Bancroft's portrait of the Revolution as a spirited patriotic rebellion against Britain's political repression was intended to remind Americans that they had once fought as a united people for the beliefs they held in common. A selection from Bancroft's history is the second in this volume.

By the end of the nineteenth century, a reaction set in against Bancroft's highly nationalistic interpretation for several reasons. After Britain and America resolved many of their differences by signing the Treaty of Washington in 1871, hatred of the former mother country began to die down. Developments on the domestic scene such as the Populist and Progressive movements of the 1890s and early 1900s also affected the outlook of certain scholars. Concerned with the mass reform movements which challenged the growing concentration of power and wealth in the hands of a few financial and business leaders in industrial America, some historians began to interpret the Revolution in a similar light. They viewed the movement as an uprising of the democratic lower classes against the aristocratic upper classes. Finally, the appearance of numerous professional academic historians trained in graduate schools after the 1880s caused scholars to explore the Revolution from different perspectives.

The scholars who revised Bancroft between the 1890s and World War II fell into two broad groupings. One group—the imperial school—insisted that political and constitutional issues were crucial to an understanding of the Revolution. The other—the Progressive historians—held that the primary causes were social and economic in nature. Although both groups disagreed with Bancroft on the precise causes of the Revolution, they were often in accord with his conclusion that the movement was revolutionary in character.

The imperial school, founded in the 1890s, held that the Revolution could not be viewed solely within the narrow confines of national history. To be properly understood, the Revolution had to be seen in a broader context; it had to be considered as an integral part of the story of the British empire as a whole. Approached from this wider perspective, Britain's colonial policies did not appear as unjust as Bancroft had insisted. Imperial historians concluded that the colonists prospered under a system that was liberal and enlightened, that the benefits of Britain's Navigation Laws outweighed the burdens, and that the mother country was justified in taxing Americans after 1763 because largely British arms and money had defended the colonies during the French and Indian War. Historians of the imperial school, it should be noted, began writing at about the time America itself became a "mother country." The United States began facing problems posed by the overseas empire acquired after the Spanish-American War.

But if Britain's policies were so benevolent, why did the Americans rebel? Most imperial historians answered the question by arguing that constitutional issues lay behind the dispute. Charles M. Andrews, in the third selection, claimed that by the eve of the Revolution, Americans had arrived at a new conception of empire. They envisaged the colonies as self-governing units within an empire held together by a common allegiance to the king. The British considered the American theory a radical departure from their ideas of empire—one composed of dependent colonies. To Andrews the dispute, while constitutional in nature, represented the very essence of revolution. It revealed a deep-seated conflict between two incompatible societies—one static and the other dynamic—that had been developing along divergent lines for some time. These differing notions of the British empire, according to Andrews, placed the colonies and the mother country on a collision course and a clash was inevitable.

The Progressive school of historians, on the other hand, took a different view. They were firmly convinced that social and economic issues constituted the main causes of the Revolution. They emphasized the economic rift caused by growing competition between the colonies and mother country, and the ongoing conflict between upper and lower classes within colonial America.

That the Progressive historians viewed the Revolution in terms of class conflict was hardly surprising. Many of these scholars were sympathetic to the Progressive reform movements and interpreted their own era as a struggle by the common people to free themselves from the grip of large corporate monopolies and trusts. Hence they tended to read back into the Revolution of the 1770s the same conflict between the masses and upper classes that seemed to be raging around them in the Progressive era of the early 1900s.

The emergence of the Progressive school led also to a greater emphasis on the role of economic forces in history. Scholars of this persuasion believed that materialistic forces—not constitutional or ideological factors—were the most important historical determinants. Many accepted a qualified economic determinism, and assumed that human beings were motivated mainly by economic self-interest. They insisted that any political or constitutional ideas which individuals professed were dictated largely by economic considerations. To their way of thinking, pocketbook interests, not patriotism, motivated the leaders whom Bancroft had portrayed as heroes.

Some Progressive historians subscribed to the idea of not one American Revolution but two. The first was an "external" revolution—the colonial rebellion from Britain—produced by the clash of economic interests between the colonies and mother country. The second was an "internal" revolution—a conflict between social groups in America to decide whether the upper or lower classes would rule once the British had departed. Carl L. Becker, one of the leading Progressive historians, first postulated this thesis of "two revolutions" in his book, *The History of Political Parties in the Province of New York, 1760–1776*, published in 1909. New York politics prior to the Revolution, he wrote, revolved around two questions: the "question of home-rule", and the "question . . . of who should rule at home."

The idea that the Revolution arose from deep-seated economic differences between the colonies and mother country, as well as from class conflict and sectional divisions within the colonies, was spelled out further by Arthur M. Schlesinger Sr., another influential Progressive historian. Economic interests—the threat to merchants in the northern and middle colonies from the mother country's new commercial regulations—and the desire of southern planters to escape the enormous debts they owed to English creditors—led America's upper classes to resist Britain's colonial policies after 1763. Within the colonies themselves, there were also divisive forces at work. Population clusters in colonial America were located in two broad regions. One ran along the eastern seaboard which was divided into a commercialized North and an agrarian South. The other lay in the West whose frontier was peopled by democratic farmers, often at odds with the more aristocratic conservative East. The combined forces of democratic farmers in the interior and working class mechanics in the coastal cities formed the backbone of the radical revolutionary movement. Schlesinger, like most Progressive historians, pictured colonial America in terms of conflict —conflict between polarized groups: aristocratic versus democratic; rich versus poor; and East versus West. The next selection is from an article Schlesinger published in 1919 setting forth his interpretive framework.

The most extreme economic interpretation of the Revolution came from Louis M. Hacker, who presented a Marxist viewpoint. Hacker depicted the Revolution as a twofold struggle: an economic confrontation between two sets of capitalists—British and American—for control of various sectors of the colonial economy; and, at the same time, an internal clash between the upper and lower classes within colonial America. Economic causes and class conflict both on the imperial and local level, then, were the major determinants of events in the 1760s and 1770s. Since economic forces represent the classic ingredients of a Marxist revolution, there was no doubt in Hacker's mind that the American Revolution was revolutionary.

Significantly enough, Hacker's article was written during the dark days of the Great Depression, when some Americans began doubting whether capitalism would survive. Hacker's position was the most radical taken by an American historian. Although his views changed considerably in later years, the next selection, Hacker's article published in 1937 in the *Marxist Quarterly*, reflects his position at that time.

After the end of World War II, the direction of American historical writing changed dramatically. During the late 1940s and 1950s, a group of historians called the Neo-conservatives appeared on the scene to revise the Progressive point of view. They were labelled "Neo-conservatives" in part because they seemed to hark back to the position taken by Bancroft. Like Bancroft, they emphasized the unity of the American people during the Revolution.

The Neo-conservatives also reflected the sober mood within the country after the Second World War. During the Cold War era, America felt its security endangered as the nation assumed the awesome responsibility of leading the struggle against Communism. It was understandable, therefore, that some scholars either consciously or unconsciously, presented an image to the rest of the world of an America that had been strong and united throughout most of its history. Hence these historians minimized internal tensions in American history and emphasized consensus rather than conflict in the country's past.

Neo-conservative scholars saw American colonial society in very different terms from those of the Progressive historians. America was essentially a democratic society, they claimed. Property-holding was widespread, and most colonists could be considered as belonging to the middle class. Since voting rights depended upon property ownership, political democracy flourished. Small farmers invariably owned enough land to qualify for the franchise, and the majority of adult white males could vote. Colonial America was a fluid, open-ended society in which there was considerable mobility. Most people were satisfied with their status; they felt no urge to precipitate a class conflict to achieve a greater degree of democracy, as the Progressive scholars had argued.

If the colonists were content, why was there a Revolution? The answer given by some Neo-conservatives was that Britain's imperial policies after 1763 endangered the middle-class democratic way of life which Americans had created during the colonial era. Robert E. Brown wrote a case study of Massachusetts which sought to demonstrate that Progressive historians were wrong in their assumption about colonial society being undemocratic because property qualifications prevented many persons in the lower classes from voting. In the next selection, Brown asserted that the people of Massachusetts rose in rebellion to defend a social order that was already democratic—not to change it. To Brown the Revolution was not revolutionary; its purpose, indeed, was to preserve the status quo.

During the decades of the 1960s and 1970s, the view of the Revolution changed once again. One group of scholars was inspired by the work of the Harvard historian, Bernard Bailyn, who saw the Revolution primarily as an ideological movement of a radical nature. Bailyn took the position that ideas constituted the major determinants of history. Ideas themselves acted as controlling forces during the revolutionary era, causing changes in the beliefs, attitudes, and perceptions of the colonists.

To Bailyn the Revolution represented, above all, an ideological transformation—a radical change in the way most Americans looked at themselves and their relationship to Britain and the rest of the world. The true revolution took place within men's minds more than in the political and social sphere. This mental revolution constituted a complete transformation in the colonists' image of themselves. Before the Revolution, Americans saw their divergences from the norms of British society as shortcomings. The colonists experienced feelings of inferiority because they lacked the features of a mature society, including a titled aristocracy, a cosmopolitan culture, and an established church along national lines. As the Revolution drew near, Americans began to recognize these divergences as good; not bad, as virtues and not vices, and as advantages rather than defects. This changed perspective led the colonists to believe that they could no longer achieve their destiny as an unspoiled republican people within the British empire. The mother country was corrupt, luxury-loving, and had presumably engaged in a conspiracy to rob Americans of their liberties. The next selection is drawn from Bailyn's book, *The Ideological Origins of the American Revolution,* published in 1967.

Some scholars held that Bailyn had carried the implications of an "idealist" interpretation too far in stressing the important role of ideas. Gordon Wood, writing in the mid-1960s, presented a searching critique of the ideological interpretation. The rhetoric of the revolutionaries—the expression of their political thought and ideas—could not be studied in isolation from their behavior, which was often motivated by materialistic, social, and economic considerations. According to Wood, both modes of analysis had to be applied—the idealist and the behavioral approach—if historians were to gain a full explanation of the Revolution. Progressive scholars, to be sure, had limited their understanding of the Revolution by refusing to acknowledge sufficiently the power of ideas. But by the same token, students of intellectual history in viewing the Revolution had not adequately taken into account the materialistic forces at work. Wood, whose article is included in the next selection, called for a combination of the idealist and behavioral approaches to achieve a better understanding of the Revolution.

The second major trend among historians in the 1960s and 1970s was a development along lines more oriented toward an analysis of the lives of common people. This tendency manifested itself in the appearance of two separate groups of scholars—the "New Left" historians and the "new social historians." Although these scholars were generally interested in the mass of people and their activities, their approaches, perspectives, and methodologies differed markedly.

The "New Left" historians regarded the Revolution as a radical movement, and searched for its causes among the lower classes. Many of the "New Left" school of scholars studied specific groups of poor or underprivileged people to understand why they protested against the established order. One of the most outspoken of these scholars was Jesse Lemisch. He argued that the history of the Revolution had too often been written "from the top down"— that is, from the point of view of leaders like Washington, Jefferson, and John Adams. Such a historical perspective was blind to the concerns of the average person and the inarticulate masses. History, according to Lemisch, should be written "from the bottom up." Seizing upon the grievances of American sailors who protested British impressment—a practice of little or no concern to the middle class—Lemisch sought to show, in the next selection, that the Revolution was more radical and characterized by greater class conflict than the Neo-conservatives realized.

Like their predecessors, the "New Left" historians were influenced by the social and political concerns of their own times. They brought to the study of the Revolution a renewed awareness of the important role played by minority and disadvantaged groups throughout American history. The protest movements of the 1960s and 1970s—by blacks, Indians, women, and the poor— made these scholars more sensitive to the claims of other social groups that had been oppressed in the past. Moreover, the social protest associated with the anti-war movement during the Vietnam crisis also sensitized these historians to the importance of conflict rather than consensus in America's past.

The "new social historians," on the other hand, had somewhat different aims. They sought to recreate the lives of the inarticulate mass of ordinary folk by employing new methodologies. Instead of relying on traditional literary sources to document their histories, they turned to a different set of records. By using genealogies, registers of births and deaths, church and town records, tax lists, and wills and deeds, they hoped to reconstruct conditions of community life in bygone days. Through the use of statistical methods and the aid of computers, they gathered and recorded detailed information and drew conclusions based upon quantifiable data to support their findings.

American scholars interested in the "new social history" that appeared in the 1960s and 1970s were influenced also by external factors. Some were affected by French scholarship—the so-called *Annales* school—that had developed in the 1930s. The aim of these French scholars was to apply a more interdisciplinary approach in order to create a better understanding of the totality of human activity within a given society or geographical region. Others were influenced by developments in the social and behavioral sciences. Finally, the increased use of computers and quantitative techniques brought about a greater emphasis upon scientifically measurable data in the field of history. The selection from Robert A. Gross, included later in this volume, represents many of these developments in the "new social history."

So much for the causes of the Revolution, what about its consequences? To return to the second line of inquiry employed by historians: How revolutionary was the Revolution in terms of its results? The answer to this question depends largely upon the period in which the historian was writing, and upon the approach taken to the problem.

If the Revolution was really revolutionary in nature, as the Progressive scholars claimed in the early decades of this century, then the lower classes should have made significant democratic gains. In what ways did they do so? J. Franklin Jameson, a Progressive historian writing in the 1920s, stressed these advances in the next selection. Jameson emphasized those social and economic reforms that improved the lot of the common man at the expense of America's prewar aristocracy. Economic democracy was promoted by the redistribution of property that accompanied the Revolution. Large Loyalist estates were confiscated and broken up into small parcels for sale to yeomen farmers; vast domains controlled by the Crown and proprietary families before the war passed into the hands of state legislatures, which threw these lands open to settlement; and state laws put an end to the aristocratic practices of primogeniture and entail. Social democracy made similar strides. Slavery and the slave trade were abolished in some states; the Anglican church was disestablished in certain areas; and property qualifications for voting and office holding were lowered. Indeed, Jameson's book, *The American Revolution Considered as a Social Movement,* was hailed as a landmark in the historiography of the Revolution when it was published.

What about political gains? Merrill Jensen, a scholar who continued the Progressive tradition in his selection published in the 1950s, argued that the Revolution made for a more democratic America. He maintains that when framing the Declaration of Independence, Americans stressed the democratic idea that government should rest on the consent of the governed. The central government under the Articles of Confederation was made more democratic by granting it fewer powers over the states than the British had enjoyed over the colonies. When writing their state constitutions, Americans showed the same penchant for greater political democracy: they emphasized the lower house as the dominant branch of government, reduced the powers of the governors, and insisted that more state officials be elected than appointed. The Revolution, Jensen insisted, had unintentionally moved America in the direction of greater democracy, even though democracy had not been a conscious goal of the revolutionary movement at the outset.

In the next selection, Daniel J. Boorstin, a Neo-conservative historian writing in the Cold War era of the 1950s, took quite a different view of the consequences of the Revolution. He underscored the nonrevolutionary character of the Revolution on the imperial level. Prior to the Revolution, he pointed out, the colonists had enjoyed many traditional rights and liberties under the British constitution. When Parliament introduced changes in the government of the empire after the French and Indian War, Americans protested against these innovations on the grounds that they were contrary to the British constitution. After pleading in vain with Parliament to stop exercising powers unwarranted by constitutional precedents, the colonists finally rebelled. But American Patriots proved to be "reluctant rebels," according to Boorstin. They remained loyal to British institutions and practices even while they fought the mother country. Once the Americans gained their independence, they carried over to the new nation those traditional rights of Englishmen that they prized so highly—trial by jury, freedom of speech and assembly, the right to petition, and the concept of no taxation without representation. Boorstin believed that Americans were fighting to maintain old freedoms, and not to achieve new rights.

The final selection regarding the consequences of the Revolution is from a book written in the 1970s by Robert A. Gross—the "new social historian" mentioned previously. Gross' work was an intensive study of a single American community—Concord, Massachusetts—and represented an attempt to capture the impact of the Revolution on the townspeople. Much of his research reconstructed life in the town from less traditional sources: genealogies, tax lists, church records, wills, deeds, petitions, and minutes of town meetings. Rather than making sweeping statements about the Revolution as a social movement, as Jameson had done fifty years earlier, Gross showed how the event directly affected the lives of individuals. He concluded that the people had gone to war not to promote change, but to stop it. To Gross, Concord's Minutemen were driven to rebellion by the desire to defend their traditional way of life from encroachment by the British and other outside forces. Ironically, the Revolution opened the way to innovations which profoundly changed the town. Although the local revolutionary movement had not begun that way, it produced revolutionary consequences.

How have scholars treated the Revolution when writing within the context of world history rather than national history? For the most part, they have raised a wholly different set of questions. Was the Revolution a unique event—one that had little or no relationship to revolutions in other parts of the world? Or did it help trigger the long series of revolutions that have shaken Western civilization since 1776? How aware was the rest of the world of the American Revolution, and did it serve as a model for other colonial peoples bent on achieving independence? And what has been the attitude of the American people themselves toward their Revolution? Have they been proud of their revolutionary heritage and applauded when other people followed their example? Or have Americans grown less enthusiastic about the idea of revolution as the United States has achieved the status of a great world power and has increasingly sought to promote stability and order throughout the globe?

The next selection is from Robert R. Palmer's two-volume work, *The Age of Democratic Revolution,* published in the late 1950s and early 1960s. Palmer insisted that there was but one great revolutionary epoch stretching from 1770 to 1848 which affected both sides of the Atlantic, and that the American Revolution was part of this broad phenomenon. Thus, the American Revolution was set within a world-wide context—an "age of democratic revolution"—that affected much of Western civilization at the time.

Palmer, more specifically, compared the American Revolution to the French Revolution. He observed that though the American Revolution had some unique features, it was, like the French Revolution, a violent social upheaval. In comparing these revolutions, Palmer noted that in at least two respects—the number of emigrés who fled the two countries, and the amount of personal property confiscated—the revolution in the New World appeared to be more radical than that in the Old. But in other ways, Palmer found the American Revolution to be less revolutionary than the one in France because of what it tried to conserve. The American Revolution, he concluded, was ambivalent because it was both conservative and revolutionary at one and the same time.

The relationship of the Revolution to modern anti-colonial movements was explored on a comparative basis by another scholar, Thomas C. Barrow. Anti-colonial movements, according to Barrow, represent a different category of revolutions—those aimed at gaining national independence through colonial wars of liberation. The leaders of such movements often looked to the American Revolution as an example or precedent to follow. Barrow concluded that there were, indeed, certain common characteristics between America's colonial war of liberation and those waged in the twentieth century.

Barrow's selection, published in the late 1960s, represented another recent trend among certain historians. These scholars were influenced by the social and behavioral sciences and were interested less in describing historical events as separate and discrete developments than in illuminating past episodes with sophisticated conceptualization and analysis to make them relevant to the problems of our own time. In doing so, these scholars tended to view history more as a social science than as a discipline in the humanities.

Richard B. Morris, on the other hand, used a more traditional comparative history approach in his work. He was interested in learning whether America's experience in the Revolution had influenced the emerging new nations of Asia, Africa, and Latin America in the twentieth century. In the revolution-conscious world of the 1950s and 1960s, some countries breaking away from Europe's disintegrating empires employed many of the same methods the United States had used in gaining its independence. Published in 1970, the Morris selection shows in numerous ways, how the American Revolution served as a model for emerging new nations.

Finally, Sung Bok Kim, writing also in the 1970s, sought to demonstrate the impact America's revolutionary heritage has had on the modern world. The legacy of our Revolution was somewhat limited, he argued, because the American model of revolution focused primarily upon civil liberties, whereas the Jacobin model of the French Revolution was concerned more with social questions such as poverty, scarcity, and the unequal distribution of wealth. With the coming of industrialization, it was the French model that proved more relevant to social revolutionaries in different parts of the globe.

Kim claimed also that a remarkable reversal took place in America's attitude toward its own revolutionary heritage. The Founding Fathers had had high hopes for the spread of republicanism and were sympathetic to revolutionary movements that sought to overthrow monarchs. Throughout much of the nineteenth century, Americans continued to support the idea of revolution. But in the twentieth century, Americans increasingly adopted an anti-revolutionary stance. Revolutionary movements were often associated, rightly or wrongly, with the idea of Communism, and were viewed as threats to world order and stability. America, being a rich country, a great world power, and a nation with huge overseas investments, seemed interested in maintaining the status quo than in pursuing the old ideas of its revolutionary heritage.

This review of conflicting interpretations shows that our conception of the Revolution has undergone constant changes. In terms of our national history, each age seems to have rewritten the history of the Revolution to suit its own needs. Bancroft's generation, marked by sectional strife that produced the Civil War and the nationalism that resulted from that conflict, saw the Revolution as a national struggle for freedom. The imperial school of historians, writing when the country began facing the problems of an American empire, interpreted the event as part of the broader story of the British empire. Becker's generation, coping with the complex problems of an industrialized America in the Progressive era, regarded the Revolution as an internal conflict to determine the fate of democracy. During the Great Depression, a few historians interpreted the event as a Marxist revolution. The generation of Neo-conservative historians after World War II may have stressed a consensus among the American people during the Revolution in order to unify the nation in its struggle against Communism. The "New Left" historians of the 1960s, may likewise have been reflecting the problems and predilections of the period in which they lived. And the "new social historians" of the 1970s have demonstrated a greater interest in the inarticulate masses and common people because we live in an age when society has demonstrated a greater sensitivity toward certain deprived social groups that had often been over-looked by scholars dealing with America's past.

When writing about the Revolution in terms of world history, scholars were agreed that the event had exercised a profound impact. But when they began comparing the American Revolution to other revolutions, historians often disagreed on precisely what that effect was. Nor did scholars always agree whether the attitude of the American people toward the Revolution had changed or remained the same over the years.

Historians will continue to study the Revolution in the future because it gave birth to the United States. If in the child may be seen the emerging adult, then much of what is unique in America's subsequent development may be traced back to its origins. Locked within the answer to the question "How revolutionary was the Revolution?" lies the meaning of what America was and is.

PETER OLIVER (1713–1791), was one of the more famous American Loyalists. He, his brother, Andrew, and Thomas Hutchinson represented three of the most important politicians in Massachusetts in the 1770s, and held the highest offices in government. Driven from his political posts and out of the Bay Colony by the Patriots, Peter Oliver took his revenge by writing a vitriolic history of the Revolution. What is his explanation of the origins of the Revolution? Compare Oliver's description of Massachusetts society with that of Robert E. Brown in this volume. Does Oliver support Brown's view of that society and the coming of the Revolution?*

Peter Oliver

An Eighteenth-Century Loyalist View

I shall, with all due Deference to those who have already given their Opinions upon the *immediate* Cause of this Rebellion, assign an earlier Date than that which hath been affixed to it. It is the Year 1761 from whence I shall begin my Progress; for as I was intimate to the Transactions of that Æra, so I imagine I can see a concatenation of Incidents, wch. conduced to the ushering in this memorable Event; which Time itself can never efface from the Records of New England perfidy.

Towards the latter End of the Year 1760, *Stephen Sewall*, Esqr., Chief Justice of the Province of *Massachusetts Bay*, died. As their are generally Candidates for such Posts, . . . *James Otis Esqr.* claimed the Palm; pleading the Merit of Age, long Practice at the Bar, & repeated Promises of a former Governor. Mr. *Otis* was one, who in the early Part of his Life, was by Trade a Cordwainer. But as the People of the Province seem to be born with litigious Constitutions, so he had Shrewdness enough to take Advantage of the general Foible, & work'd himself into a Pettifogger; which Profession he practised in, to the End of his Life. He had a certain Adroitness to captivate the Ear of Country Jurors, who were too commonly Drovers, Horse Jockies, & of other lower Classes in Life. He also, for many Years, had been a Member of the lower House of Assembly, too great an Ingredient of which Composition con-

*From *Peter Oliver's Origin & Progress of the American Rebellion*, Douglass Adair and John A. Schutz, eds. (Stanford, Stanford University Press, 1961), pp. 27–45 and 145–146. Reprinted by permission of the Henry E. Huntington Library and Art Gallery.

sisted of Innkeepers, Retailers, & yet more inferior Orders of Men. . . . [H]is Son was a Lawyer of superior Genius to his Father. He was also a Member of the Assembly for the Town of *Boston*; & while the Appointment of a Judge was in Suspence, this Son . . . swore, *"that if his Father was not appointed a Justice of the superior Court; he would set the Province in a Flame if he died in the Attempt."*

The People of the Province, in general, not coinciding with the Judgment which the Father had formed of his own Merit, & thinking, that Integrity was an essential Qualification of a Judge, expressed a jealous Fear of such an Appointment; the surviving Judges of the Bench also, not willing to have an Associate of such a Character to seat with them, applied to Mr. *Bernard*, the then Govr., who had the Nomination to that Office, asking the Favor to have such a Colleague with them, that the Harmony of the Bench might not be interrupted; & accordingly proposed Mr. *Hutchinson*, the then Lieut. Governor of the Province; Mr. *Bernard* most readily acquiesced, & had already, before requested, determined on the Appointment. Mr. *Hutchinson* was also applied to, by the Judges, to take a Seat with them; but he refused, 'till he could be informed of the general Sentiment; *that* was for him, & he was prevailed upon to accept the Office of Chief Justice: upon which the two *Otis's*, the eldest of whom had for many Years before almost idolized him, now exerted theirselves, . . . to revenge their Disappointment, in Mr. *Hutchinson's* Destruction. . . .

Mr. *Otis*, ye. Son, understanding the Foibles of human Nature, although he did not always practise upon that Theory, advanced one shrewd Position, which

seldom fails to promote popular Commotions, vizt. *that it was necessary to secure the black Regiment*, these were his Words, & his Meaning was to engage ye. dissenting Clergy on his Side. . . .

As I have introduced several Persons of the Drama, I shall begin to comply with the Promise I made, at first setting out, of giving a Sketch of their Portraits; those who have now offered to sit I shall begin with; the rest will be taken in their Turns. Perhaps these Sketches may throw some Light on the more interesting Scenes. I shall begin with the late Govr. *Hutchinson.* . . .

Mr. *Hutchinson* was a Gentleman on whom Nature had conferred, what she is very sparing of, an Acumen of Genius united with a Solidity of Judgment & great Regularity of Manners. He descended from Ancestors who conferred Honor on the Roll of Magistracy in the Colony & ye. Province of the *Massachusetts Bay*—so early as at 12 Years of Age he was matriculated into *Harvard College in Cambridge*, & here he bore the Palm of classick Learning. After he had been graduated, he quitted a Collegiate Life, & trod the mercantile Walk; & his Steps were directed by fairness and Punctuality in Dealing & with Success in his Schemes. . . .

Mr. *Hutchinson's* Ancestors in their political Principles, were no Friends to Democracy; & he himself judged it necessary to support the Prerogative, that it might hold the ballance of Power in such Equilibrio, that it might not sink into Republicanism, upon the Verge of which many of the colonial Systems of Government were erected. Notwithstanding his Sentiments upon Government were universally known, yet his Candor, Integrity, & Capacity were so well established, that he very early caught the publick Eye. . . .

Mr. *Hutchinson* not only has sustained many publick Offices, dependant upon the Sufferages of the People, but he was appointed by the Crown, in 1757, Lieut. Governor; & in 1771 Governor & Commander in Chief of the Province of the *Massachusetts Bay*. . . .

He was also, where the Power of the Crown was united with the Nature of this provincial Legislature, appointed *Judge of Probate* for the County of *Suffolk*, the most important County of the Province; & afterwards, *Chief Justice* of the Province as also one of his Majesty's Council. . . .

In short, in all the various Departments of Life, he behaved with that Dignity which was ornamental to each of them; & when he left his native Country & retired to *England*, his Character was so fully established, that he was particularly noticed by the greatest Men in the Kingdom; & by his *Majesty* himself, who was too sensible of the Merits of his Service, not to distinguish him by particular Marks of his royal Favor. . . .

After 7 years Residence in *England*; from the Transition from a very active to an almost inactive Life; from a Reflection on the Miseries of his native Country, & from a Combination of other Causes, he sunk into a chronical Disorder which hurried him out of Life. . . .

Perhaps Sir! you will ask me why I have been so diffuse upon Mr. *Hutchinson's* Character? Let me tell you then, that the Distinction of Applause which attended him, roused the Envy & Malice of the Leaders of the Faction, who dipped their shafts in more than infernal Gall, & made him the Butt to level them at. He exerted every Nerve to save his Country; they were determined to ruin him, tho' they plunged their Country & theirselves too, into absolute Destruction.

It vexed them to find an Antagonist who was superior to them, with their united Understanding; but I will relieve you by several Contrasts; in which you will see human Nature in her various Attitudes, & you may then judge, whether to dwell upon her Beauties or Deformities is the most agreeable.

The first Character of. the Contrast which I shall exhibit will be young Mr. *Otis*, as he was the first who broke down the Barriers of Government to let in the *Hydra* of Rebellion; agreeable to the already mentioned Stygian Oath which he had taken, of "setting the Province in a Flame."

Mr. *Otis* was designed, by Nature, for a Genius; but it seemed as if, by the Impetuosity of his Passions, he had wrested himself out of her Hands before she had complemented her Work; for his Life seemed to be all Eccentricity. He passed through a Collegiate Education, & then entred upon the Study of the Law. . . . [H]e made great Progress in it, & would have been of distinguishing Figure in it had he not have mistaken a contemptuous Pride for a laudable Ambition; & given too loose a Rein to the Wildness of his Passion. He seemed to have adopted that Maxim which *Milton* puts into the Mouth of one of his Devils, vizt.

"Better to reign in Hell than serve in Heaven."

And his whole Life seemed to be a Comment on his Text. He carried his Malevolence to so great Length, that being often thwarted in his Opposition to Government, he took to the Course of Dram drinking, & ruined his Family, with an amiable Wife at the Head of it, who had brought him a Fortune, & who, by his bad Conduct, became disordered in her Mind. . . . By drinking, & other

Misconduct, he grew so frantick, that he was frequently under the Guardianship of the Law, & confined; & the last I heard of him was, that he seemed to be a living Monument of the Justice of Heaven, by his being a miserable Vagabond, rolling in the Streéts & Gutters, the laughing-Stock of Boys & the Song of the Drunkard. Even in his best Estate, he was indelicate in his Manners, & rough in his Conversation. He was devoid of all Principle; & would, as a Lawyer, take Fees on both Sides, in which he had been detected in open Court. . . .

I shall next give you a Sketch of some of Mr. *Samuel Adam's* Features; & I do not know how to delineate them stronger, than by the Observation made by a celebrated Painter in *America*, vizt. "That if he wished to draw the Picture of the Devil, that he would get *Sam Adams* to sit for him:" & indeed, a very ordinary Physiognomist would, at a transient View of his Countenance, develope the Malignity of his Heart. He was a Person of Understanding, but it was discoverable rather by a Shrewdness than Solidity of Judgment; & he understood human Nature, in low life, so well, that he could turn the Minds of the great Vulgar as well as the small into any Course that he might chuse; perhaps he was a singular Instance in this Kind; & he never failed of employing his Abilities to the vilest Purposes. He was educated at *Harvard College*; and when he quitted that Scene of Life, he entered upon the Business of a Malster, the Profits of which afforded him but a moderate Maintenance; & his Circumstances were too well known for him to gain a pecuniary Credit with Mankind.

He was so thorough a *Machiavilian*, that he divested himself of every worthy Principle, & would stick at no Crime to accomplish his Ends. He was chosen a Collector of Taxes for the Town of *Boston*; but when the Day of Account came, it was found that there was a Defalcation of about £1700. Sterling. He was apprized of it long before, & formed his Plans accordingly. . . .

[I]n Order to extricate himself, he duped Mr. *Hancock*, by persuading him to build Houses & Wharves which would not bring him 2 p ct. Intrest for his Mony. This Work necessarily engaged a Variety of Artificers, whom *Adams* could prefer. This secured these Orders of Men in his Interest; & such Men chiefly composed the Voters of a *Boston* Town Meeting. At one of their Meetings the Town voted him a Discharge and 2/3d of his Debt, & Mr. *Hancock* & some others, into whose Graces he had insinuated his balefull Poison, subscribed to a Discharge of the other Third—thus was he set at large to commit his Ravages on Government, untill he undermined the Foundations of it, & not one Stone had been left upon another. He soon outrivalled Mr. *Otis* in popularity. . . .

It may not be amiss, now, to reconnoitre Mr. *Otis's* black Regiment, the *dissenting Clergy*, who took so active a Part in the Rebellion. The congregational perswasion of Religion might be properly termed the established Religion of the *Massachusetts*, as well as of some other of the *New England* Colonies; as the Laws were peculiarly adapted to secure ye Rights of this Sect; although all other Religions were tolerated, except the *Romish*. This Sect inherited from their Ancestors an Aversion to Episcopacy; & I much question, had it not been for the Supremacy of the British Government over them, which they dared not openly deny, whether Episcopacy itself would have been tolerated. . . .

The Clergy of this Province were, in general, a Set of very weak Men; & it could not be expected that they should be otherwise, as many of them were just relieved, some from the Burthen of the Satchel; & others from hard Labor; & by a Transition from those Occupations to mounting a Desk, from whence they could overlook the principal Part of their Congregations, they, by that mean acquired a supreme Self Importance; which was too apparent in their Manners. . . . The Town of *Boston* being the Metropolis, it was also the Metropolis of Sedition; and hence it was that their Clergy being dependent on the People for their daily Bread; by having frequent Intercourse with the People, imbibed their Principles. . . .

. . . Among those who were most distinguished of the *Boston* Clergy were Dr. *Charles Chauncy,* Dr. *Jonathan Mayhew* & Dr. *Samuel Cooper*; & they distinguished theirselves in encouraging Seditions & Riots, untill those lesser Offences were absorbed in Rebellion. . . .

I have done Sir! for the present, with my Portraits. If you like them, & think them ornamental for your Parlour, pray hang them up in it; for I assure You, that most of them justly demerit a *Suspension*. . . .

We have seen a Set of Men favored with the Liberty & Charter Grant of an extended Country, under ye. Auspices of the english Government; & protected by it; but under an Obligation to conform to such Regulations as should be made by its Authority. We have seen these new Settlers, for a long Series of Years, paying all due Deference to those Regulations, as stipulated in their Charter. We have seen them also rising, by easy Gradations, to such a State of Prosperity & Happiness as was almost enviable, but we have seen them also run mad with too much Happiness, & burst into an open Rebellion against that Parent, who protected them (upon their most earnest Entreaties & humble Solicitations) against the Ravages of their Enemies. This, in private Life would be termed, base Ingratitude; but Rebellion hath sanctified it by the Name of, Self Defence—and why is the sudden Transition made, from Obedience to Rebellion, but to gratifye the Pride, Ambition & Resentment, of a few abandoned Demagogues, who were lost to all Sense of Shame & of Humanity? The generality of the People were not of this Stamp; but they were weak, & unversed in the Arts of Deception. The Leaders of the Faction deceived the Priests, very few of whom but were as ignorant as the People; & the Wheel of Enthusiasm was set on going, & its constant Rotation set the Peoples Brains on Whirling; & by a certain centrifugal Force, all the Understanding which the People had was whirled away, as well as that of the Clergy; & a Vacuum was left for *Adams*, & his *Posse* to crowd in what Rubbish would best serve their Turn.

GEORGE BANCROFT (1800–1891), historian, diplomat, and politician, like most nineteenth-century scholars, adopted the view that history was essentially the story of liberty. For Bancroft, the Revolution was a nationalistic rebellion of liberty-loving American yeomen against a tyrannical and oppressive British government. His famous *History of the United States of America,* whose first volume appeared in 1834, shows the Revolution in its broadest context, as part of an epic struggle to gain greater freedom for all mankind. Why was freedom able to flourish in America and not in England?*

George Bancroft

A Nineteenth- Century Nationalist Overview

The American Revolution, of which I write the history, essaying to unfold the principles which organized its events, and bound to keep faith with the ashes of its heroes, was most radical in its character, yet achieved with such benign tranquillity that even conservatism hesitated to censure. A civil war armed men of the same ancestry against each other, yet for the advancement of the principles of everlasting peace and universal brotherhood. A new plebeian democracy took its place by the side of the proudest empires. Religion was disenthralled from civil institutions; thought obtained for itself free utterance by speech and by the press; industry was commissioned to follow the bent of its own genius; the system of commercial restrictions between states was reprobated and shattered; and the oceans were enfranchised for every peaceful keel. International law was humanized and softened; and a new, milder, and more just maritime code was concerted and enforced. The trade in slaves was branded and restrained. . . . The equality of all men was declared; personal freedom secured in its complete individuality; and common consent recognised as the only just origin of fundamental laws: so that in thirteen separate states, with ample territory for creating more, the inhabitants of each formed their own political institutions. By the side of the principle of the freedom of the individual and the freedom of the separate states, the noblest work of human intellect was consummated in a federative union; and

*From George Bancroft, *History of the United States of America from the Discovery of the Continent* (6 vols.; Boston: Little, Brown and Company, 1876), vol. III, pp. 9–13.

that union put away every motive to its destruction, by insuring to each successive generation the right to better its constitution, according to the increasing intelligence of the living people.

Yet the thirteen colonies, in whom was involved the futurity of our race, were feeble settlements in the wilderness, scattered along the coast of a continent, little connected with each other, little heeded by their metropolis, almost unknown to the world; they were bound together only as British America, that part of the western hemisphere which the English mind had appropriated. England was the mother of its language, the home of its traditions, the source of its laws, and the land on which its affections centered. And yet it was an offset from England, rather than an integral part of it; an empire of itself, free from nobility and prelacy; not only Protestant, but by a vast majority dissenting from the church of England; attracting the commoners and plebeian sects of the parent country, and rendered cosmopolitan by recruits from the nations of the European continent. By the benignity of the law, the natives of other lands were received as citizens; and political liberty, as a birthright, was the talisman that harmoniously blended all differences, and inspired a new public life, dearer than their native tongue, their memories, and their kindred. Dutch, French, Swede, and German renounced their nationality, to claim the rights of Englishmen.

The extent of those rights, as held by the colonists, had never been precisely ascertained. Of all the forms of civil government of which they had ever heard or read, no one appeared to them so well calculated to preserve liberty, and to secure all the most valuable advantages of civil society, as the English; and of this happy constitution of the mother country, which it was usual to represent, and almost to adore, as designed to approach perfection, they held their own to be a copy, or rather an improvement, with additional privileges not enjoyed by the common people there. The elective franchise was more equally diffused; there were no decayed boroughs, or unrepresented towns; representation, which was universal, conformed more nearly to population; for more than half the inhabitants, their legislative assemblies were chosen annually and by ballot, and the time for convening their legislatures was fixed by a fundamental law; the civil list in every colony but one was voted annually, and annually subjected to scrutiny; appropriations of money often, for greater security against corruption and waste, included the nomination and appointment of the agents who were to direct the expenditures; municipal liberties were more independent and more extensive; in none of the colonies was there an ecclesiastical court, and in most of them there was no established church or religious test of capacity for office; the cultivator of the soil was, for the most part, a freeholder; in all the continent the people possessed arms, and the able-bodied men were enrolled and trained to their use: so that in America there was more of personal independence, and far more of popular power, than in England.

CHARLES M. ANDREWS (1863–1943), one of the leading colonial scholars of his day, taught at Yale University and wrote *The Colonial Background of the American Revolution*. In his presidential address to the American Historical Association in 1925, Andrews summarized the position of the "imperial school" he had helped found: if the American Revolution is to be seen in its proper perspective, it must be viewed as an integral part of the history of the whole British empire. Taking issue with Bancroft's view that the Revolution was caused by British tyranny, Andrews claims instead that it was the consequence of a long historical process during which two different societies developed along divergent lines. The imperial school is usually identified as being pro-British. Does this selection have a pro-British bias?*

Charles M. Andrews

The Imperial School Approach

You will not, I trust, take it amiss if, on this the occasion of our annual meeting, I select as my topic the familiar subject of the American Revolution. Quite apart from the pleasure that comes from harping on an old string, there is the conviction, which I hold very strongly, that no matter how familiar a subject may be, it can always be re-examined with profit and viewed not infrequently from such points of vantage as to set the scene in quite a new light. The writing of history is always a progressive process, not merely or mainly because each age must write its own history from its own point of view, but rather because each generation of scholars is certain to contribute to historical knowledge and so to approach nearer than its predecessor to an understanding of the past. No one can accept as complete or final any rendering of history, no matter how plausible it may be, nor consider any period or phase of the past as closed against further investigation. Our knowledge of history is and always will be in the making, and it has been well said that orthodox history and an orthodox historian involve a contradiction in terms.

The explanations of history have been characterized as a rule by overmuch simplicity. So wrote Maitland of the history of England and so with equal justice might he have written of the history of America. As with natural phenomena in the pre-Copernican days of celestial me-

*Charles M. Andrews, "The American Revolution: An Interpretation," *American Historical Review*, XXXI (January, 1926), pp. 218–232. Reprinted by permission of the *American Historical Review*.

chanics, when the world believed that the sun moved and the earth was flat, so it has been at all times with historical phenomena, that what to the superficial observer has appeared to be true has been accepted far too often as containing the whole truth. Among these pre-Copernican convictions, for example, widely held in America to-day, is the belief that the American Revolution was brought about by British tyranny. Whatever explanation of that great event comes to be accepted by competent historians and their intelligent readers as a near approach to the truth, it is quite certain that it will not be anything as easy and simple as all that. There was nothing simple about the Balance of Power or the Balance of Trade, even when construed in terms of such vulgar commodities as fish, furs, and molasses, and particularly when one must give due consideration to the doctrine, as seriously held in some quarters today as it was in the eighteenth century, that colonial possessions are the natural sources for home industries. Our history before 1783 was a much more complex and cosmopolitan affair than older writers would have us believe, for they have failed to account for many deep-lying and almost invisible factors and forces which influence and often determine human action and are always elusive and difficult to comprehend.

Recent writers have approached the subject with a full recognition of the complexity of the problems involved. They have found many and varied conflicting activities making for disagreement and misunderstanding between the mother country and her offspring, giving rise to impulses and convictions, ideas and practices, that were difficult, if not impossible, of reconciliation. Such scholars have expressed their conclusions in many different forms. Some have seen a struggle between two opposing historical tendencies—one imperialistic and expansive, the other domestic and intensive; others, a clash of ideas regarding the constitution of the British empire and the place that a colony should occupy in its relations with the mother country. Some have stressed the differences that were bound to arise between an old and settled country and one that was not only dominated by the ideas and habits of the frontier, but was opposed also to the continued supremacy of a governing authority three thousand miles away. Others have explained the situation in terms of an antagonism between the law and institutions of England and those, growing constantly more divergent, of the Puritan and non-Puritan colonies in America. All of these explanations are sound, because they are based on an understanding of the deeper issues involved; and taken together, they are illuminating in that they enable a reader to broaden his point of view, and to break away from the endless controversies over immediate causes and war guilt that have hitherto tended to dominate the American mind.

But elucidating as these explanations are, no one of them seems quite sufficient to resolve so complex a subject as the causes of the American Revolution. To-day we conjure with such words as evolution and psychology, and look for explanations of acts on the part of both individuals and groups in states of mind produced by inheritance and environment. Fielding, acknowledged expert in the study of human experience, can say that for a man "to act in direct contradiction to the dictates of his nature is, if not impossible, as improbable as anything which can well be conceived." The philosophers tell us that mind can be more resistant even than matter, and that it is easier to remove mountains than it is to change the ideas of a people. That the impact of convictions is one of the most frequent causes of revolution we must acknowledge; and I believe that we have not considered sufficiently the importance of this fact in determining the relations of England with colonial America. If I may, by way of illustrating my point, I should like to show that certain differences existing between England and her colonies in mental attitudes and convictions proved in the end more difficult to overcome than the diverging historical tendencies or the bridging the three thousand miles of the Atlantic itself.

The American Revolution marks the close of one great period of our history and the beginning of another of even greater significance. It is the red line across our years, because by it was brought about a fundamental change in the status of the communities on the American seaboard—a change from dependence to independence. We sometimes hear that revolutions are not made but happen. In their immediate causes this is not true—for revolutions do not happen, they are made, in that they are the creatures of propaganda and manipulation. But, in reality, revolutions are not made. They are the detonations of explosive materials, long accumulating and often long dormant. They are the resultants of a vast complex of economic, political, social, and legal forces, which taken collectively are the masters, not the servants, of statesmen and political agitators. They are never sudden in their origin, but look back to influences long in the making; and it is the business of the modern student of the subject to discover those remoter causes and to examine thoroughly and with an open mind the history, institutions, and mental past of the parties to the conflict. In pursuit of my purpose let me call to your attention certain aspects of that most important of all periods of our early history, the years from 1713 to 1775.

The middle period of the eighteenth century in England, resembling in some respects the mid-Victorian era of the next century, was intellectually, socially, and institutionally in a state of stable equilibrium. The impulses of the Revolution of 1689 had spent their force. English thought and life was tending to become formal, conventional, and artificial, and the English mind was acquiring the fatal habit of closing against novelty and change. The most enlightened men of the day regarded the existing order as the best that could be conceived, and in the main were content to let well enough alone. Those who held the reins of power were comfortable and irresponsible, steeped in their "old vulgar prejudices," and addicted to habits and modes of living that were approved by age and precedent. The miseries of the poor were accepted as due to inherent viciousness; class distinctions were sharply marked, and social relations were cast in a rigid mould; while, as far as the mass of the poor was concerned, the vagrancy laws and the narrow policy of the corporate towns made free movement in any direction practically impossible. Life at large was characterized by brutality and widespread sense of insecurity. Little thought was given to the education of the poor, the diseases of poverty and dirt, the baneful effects of overcrowding in the towns, or the corrupting influence of life in tenements and cellars. Excessive drinking and habitual resort to violence in human relations prevailed in urban sections; and while it is probably true that in rural districts, where life was simple and medieval, there was greater comfort and peace and less barbarity and coarseness, nevertheless, it is equally true that the scenes of English country life in the eighteenth century, that have come down to us in literature and painting, are more often conventional than real. Vested interests and the rights of property were deemed of greater importance than the rights of humanity, and society clung tenaciously to the old safeguards and defenses that checked the inrush of new ideas. There was a great absence of interest in technical invention and improvement. Because the landed classes were in the ascendant, agriculture was the only national interest receiving attention—drainage, rotation of crops, and the treatment of the soil being the only practical activities that attracted capital. The concerns and welfare of those without the right to vote were largely ignored; and it is no mere coincidence that the waste of human life, which was at its worst in London between 1720 and 1750, with the population of England declining during that period, should not have been checked until after 1780. The age was not one of progress in government, social organization, or humanitarianism; and it is important to note that the reconstruction of English manners and ways of living, and the movement leading to the diminution of crime, to sanitation, the greater abundance of food, and amelioration of living conditions—particularly in the towns and among the poorer classes—came after and not before, the American Revolution.

The state of mind, to which were due the conditions thus described, permeated all phases of British life and government, and determined the attitude of the ruling classes toward the political, as well as the social, order. These classes were composed in a preponderant degree of landed proprietors, whose feeling of feudal superiority and tenacious adherence to the ideas and traditions of their class were determining factors in political life both in Parliament and the country. They believed that their institutions provided a sufficient panacea for all constitutional ills and could not imagine wherein these institutions needed serious revision. They were convinced that the existing system preserved men's liberties better than any that had gone before, and they wanted no experiments or dangerous leaps in the dark. They not only held as a tenet of faith that those who owned the land should wield political power, but they were certain that such an arrangement had the sanction of God. They revered the British system of government, its principles and philosophy, as the embodiment of human wisdom, grounded in righteousness and destined by nature to serve the purpose of man. They saw it admired abroad as the most enlightened government possessed by any nation in the world, and so credited it with their unprecedented prosperity and influence as a nation. They likened its critics to Milton's Lucifer, attacking "the sacred and immovable mount of the whole constitution," as a contemporary phrased it, and they guarded it as the Israelites guarded the ark of the covenant. Woe to him who would defile it!

Nor were they any less rigid in their attitude toward the colonies in America. Colonial policy had developed very slowly and did not take on systematic form until well on in the eighteenth century; but when once it became defined, the ruling classes regarded it in certain fundamental aspects—at least in official utterance—as fixed as was the constitution itself. At first England did not take her colonies seriously as assets of commercial importance, but when after 1704 naval stores were added to the tobacco and sugar of Virginia and the West Indies, and it was seen that these commodities enabled England to obtain a favorable balance of trade with European countries, the value of the plantations in British eyes increased enormously. However, it was not until after 1750, when a favorable balance of trade was reached with the colonies themselves, that the mercantilist deemed the situation entirely satisfactory; and from that time on for twenty years—epochal years in the history of England's relations with America—the mercantilist idea of the place that a colony should occupy in the British scheme of things became fixed and unalterable. Though the colonies were growing by leaps and bounds, the authorities in Great Britain retained unchanged the policy which had been adopted more than half a century before. They did not essentially alter the instructions to the Board of Trade in all the eighty-six years of its existence. They created no true colonial secretary, even in 1768, and no department of any kind at any time for the exclusive oversight of American affairs. They saw no necessity for adopting new methods of managing colonial trade, even though the colonial situation was constantly presenting new problems for solution. Manufacturing was undoubtedly more discouraged in 1770 than it had been in 1699, when the first restrictive act was passed; and the idea that the colonies by their very nature were ordained to occupy a position of commercial dependence to the advantage and profit of the mother country was never more firmly fixed in the British mind than just before our Revolution. In fact, that event altered in no essential particular the British conception of the status of a colony, for as late as 1823, Sir Charles Ellis, undoubtedly voicing the opinion of his day, could say in Parliament that the colonial system of England had not been es-

tablished for the sake of the colonies, but for the encouragement of British trade and manufactures. Thus for more than a century England's idea of what a colony should be underwent no important alteration whatever.

Equally unchangeable was the British idea of how a colony should be governed. In the long list of commissions and instructions drawn up in England for the guidance of the royal governors in America, there is to be found, with one exception only, nothing that indicates any progressive advance in the spirit and method of administration from 1696 to 1782. Year after year, the same arrangements and phraseology appear, conforming to a common type, admitting, it is true, important modifications in matters of detail, but in principle undergoing at no time in eighty-six years serious revision or reconstruction. These documents were drawn up in Whitehall according to a fixed pattern; the governors and councils were allowed no discretion; the popular assemblies were confined within the narrow bounds of inelastic formulae, which repeated, time after time, the same injunctions and the same commands; while the crown reserved to itself the full right of interference in all matters that were construed as coming under its prerogative. These instructions represented the rigid eighteenth-century idea of how a colony should be retained in dependence on the mother country. And what was true of the instructions was true of other documents also that had to do with America. For instance, the lists of queries to the governors, the questionnaires to the commodore-governors of the Newfoundland fishery, and the whole routine business of the fishery itself had become a matter of form and precedent, as conventional and stereotyped as were the polite phrases of eighteenth-century social intercourse. Rarely was any attempt made to adapt these instructions to the needs of growing communities such as the colonies were showing themselves to be; and only with the Quebec instructions of 1775, issued after the passage of the Quebec Act and under the guidance of a colonial governor of unusual common-sense, was there any recognition of a new colonial situation. In this document, which appeared at the very end of our colonial period, do we find something of a break from the stiff and legalistic forms that were customary in the earlier royal instructions, some appreciation of the fact that the time was approaching when a colony should be treated with greater liberality and be allowed to have some part in saying how it should be administered.

Without going further with our analysis we can say that during the half-century preceding our Revolution English habits of thought and methods of administration and government, both at home and in the colonies, had reached a state of immobility. To all appearances the current of the national life had settled into a backwater, and as far as home affairs were concerned was seemingly becoming stagnant. At a time when Pitt was breaking France by land and sea, and men on waking were asking what new territories had been added during the night to the British dominions, occurrences at home were barren of adventure, either in society or politics. Ministers were not true statesmen; they had no policies, no future hopes, no spirit of advance, no gifts of foresight or prophecy. In all that concerned domestic interests, they were impervious to suggestions, even when phrased in the eloquence of Pitt and Burke. They wanted no change in existing conditions; their eyes were fixed on traditions and precedents rather than on the obligations and opportunities of the future. Their tenure of office was characterized by inactivity, a casual handling of situations they did not understand and could not control, and a willingness to let the ship of state drift for itself. As a modern critic has said, they were always turning in an unending circle, one out, one in, one in, one out, marking time and never going forward.

To a considerable extent the narrow point of view and rigidity of attitude exhibited by the men who held office at Whitehall or sat in Parliament at Westminster can be explained by the fact that at this time officials and members of Parliament were also territorial magnates, lords of manors, and country squires, who were influenced in their political life by ideas that governed their relations with their tenantry and the management of their landed estates. It is not necessary to think of them as bought by king or ministers and so bound and gagged against freedom of parliamentary action. In fact, they were bound and gagged already by devotion to their feudal privileges, their family prerogatives, and their pride of landed proprietorship. They viewed the colonies somewhat in the light of tenancies of the crown, and as they themselves lived on the rents from their estates, so they believed that the king and the kingdom should profit from the revenues and returns from America. The point of view was somewhat that of a later Duke of Newcastle, who when reproached for compelling his tenants to vote as he pleased said that he had a right to do as he liked with his own. This landed aristocracy reflected the eighteenth-century spirit. It was sonorous, conventional, and self-satisfied, and shameless of sparkle or humor. It clung to the laws of inheritance and property, fearful of anything that might in any way offend the shades of past generations. In its criticism of the manners of others it was insular and arrogant, and was mentally so impenetrable as never to understand why any one, even in the colonies, should wish things to be other than they were or refuse to accept the station of life to which by Providence he had been called.

A government, representative of a privileged social and political order that took existing conditions as a matter of course, setting nature at defiance and depending wholly on art, was bound sooner or later to come into conflict with a people, whose life in America was in closest touch with nature and characterized by growth and change and constant readjustments. In that country were groups of men, women, and children, the greater portion of whom were of English ancestry, numbering at first a few hundreds and eventually more than two millions, who were scattered over many miles of continent and island and were living under various forms of government. These people, more or less unconsciously, under the influence of new surroundings and imperative needs, were establishing a new order of society and laying the foundations of a new political system. The story of how this was done—how that which was English slowly and imperceptibly merged into that which was American—has never been adequately told; but it is a fascinating phase of history, more interesting and enlightening when studied against the English background than when construed as an American problem only. It is the story of the gradual elimination of those elements, feudal and proprietary, that were foreign to the normal life of a frontier land, and of the gradual adjustment of the colonists to the restraints and restrictions that were imposed upon them by the commercial policy of the mother country. It is the story also of the growth of the colonial assemblies and of the education and experience that the colonists were receiving in the art of political self-government. It is above all—and no phase of colonial history is of greater significance—the story of the gradual transformation of these assemblies from the provincial councils that the home government intended them to be into miniature parliaments. At the end of a long struggle with the prerogative and other forms of outside interference, they emerged powerful legislative bodies, as self-conscious in their way as the House of Commons in England was becoming during the same eventful years.

Here was an *impasse,* for the British view that a colonial assembly partook of the character of a provincial or municipal council was never actually true of any assembly in British America at any time in its history. From the beginning, each of these colonial bodies, in varying ways and under varying circumstances, assumed a position of leadership in its colony, and exercised, in a manner often as bewildering to the student of to-day as to an eighteenth-century royal governor, a great variety of executive, legislative, and judicial functions. Except in Connecticut and Rhode Island, requests for parliamentary privileges were made very early and were granted year after year by the governors—privileges that were essentially those of the English and Irish Houses of Commons and were consciously modelled after them. At times, the assemblies went beyond Parliament and made claims additional to the usual speaker's requests, claims first asked for as matter of favor but soon demanded as matters of right, as belonging to representative bodies and not acquired by royal gift or favor. One gets the impression that though the assemblies rarely failed to make the formal request, they did so with the intention of taking in any case what they asked for and anything more that they could secure. Gradually, with respect to privileges, they advanced to a position of amazing independence, freeing themselves step by step from the interfering power of the executive, that is, of the royal prerogative. They began to talk of these rights as ancient and inherent and necessary to the orderly existence of any representative body, and they became increasingly self-assertive and determined as the years passed.

Nor was this the only change affecting the assemblies to which the eighteenth-century Englishman was asked to adapt himself. The attitude of the assemblies in America found expression in the exercise of powers that had their origin in other sources than that of parliamentary privilege. They adopted rules of their own, that were sometimes even more severe than those of Parliament itself. They regulated membership, conduct, and procedure; ruled against drinking, smoking, and profanity, against unseemly, unnecessary, and tedious debate, against absence, tardiness, and other forms of evasion. They punished with great severity all infringement of rules and acts of contempt, and defended their right to do so against the governor and council on one side and the courts of the colony on the other. Nor did they even pretend to be consistent in their opposition to the royal prerogative, as expressed in the instructions to the royal governors, and in their manoeuvres they did not follow any uniform policy or plan. They conformed to these instructions willingly enough, whenever it was agreeable for them to do so; but if at any time they considered an instruction contrary to the best interest of a particular

colony, they did not hesitate to oppose it directly or to nullify it by avoidance. In general, it may be said that they evaded or warded off or deliberately disobeyed such instructions as they did not like. Thus both consciously and unconsciously they were carving out a *lex parliamenti* of their own, which, evolving naturally from the necessity of meeting the demands of self-governing communities, carried them beyond the bounds of their own membership and made them responsible for the welfare of the colony at large.

The important point to remember is that the plan of governmental control as laid down in England was never in accord with the actual situation in America; that the Privy Council, the Secretary of State, and the Board of Trade seem not to have realized that their system of colonial administration was breaking down at every point. Their minds ran in a fixed groove and they could construe the instances of colonial disobedience and aggression, which they often noted, in no other terms than those of persistent dereliction of duty. Either they did not see or else refused to see the wide divergence that was taking place between colonial administration as they planned it and colonial administration as the colonists were working it out. Englishmen saw in the American claims an attack upon an old, established, and approved system. They interpreted the attitude of the colonists as something radical and revolutionary, menacing British prosperity, British political integrity, and the British scheme of colonial government. Opposed by tradition and conviction to new experiments, even at home, they were unable to sympathize with, or even to understand, the great experiment, one of the greatest in the world's history, on trial across the sea. There in America was evolving a new idea of sovereignty, inherent not in ʋrown and Parliament but in the people of a state, based on the principle—self-evident it may be to us to-day but not to the Englishman of the eighteenth century—that governments derive their just powers from the consent of the governed. There was emerging a new idea of the franchise, as a natural right, under certain conditions, of every adult citizen, an idea which theoretically is not even yet accepted in Great Britain. There was being established a new order of society, without caste or privilege, free from economic restrictions and social demarcations between class and class. There was taking shape a new idea of a colony, a self-governing dominion, the members of which were competent to develop along their own lines, while working together with the mother country as part of a common state.

For us to-day with our perspective it is easy to see the conflict approaching and some of us may think perhaps that the British ministers and members of Parliament ought to have realized that their own ideas and systems were fast outgrowing their usefulness even for Great Britain herself; and that their inflexible views of the colonial relationship were fast leading to disaster. Yet we must keep in mind that it is always extraordinarily difficult for a generation reared in the environment of modern democracy to deal sympathetically with the Englishman's point of view in the eighteenth century, or to understand why the ruling classes of that day so strenuously opposed the advance of liberalism both in England and America. The fact remains, however, that the privileged and governing classes in England saw none of these things. They were too close to events and too much a part of them to judge them dispassionately or to

appreciate their real significance. These classes, within which we may well include the Loyalists in America, were possessed of inherited instincts, sentiments, and prejudices which they could no more change than they could have changed the color of their eyes or the texture of their skins. That which existed in government and society was to them a part of the fixed scheme of nature, and no more called for reconsideration than did the rising of the sun or the budding of the trees in spring. If Lord North had granted the claims of the colonists he probably would have been looked on by Parliament as having betrayed the constitution and impaired its stability, just as Peel was pilloried by a similar landowning Parliament in 1845, when he advocated the repeal of the corn laws. One has only to read the later debates on the subject of enclosures and the corn laws to understand the attitude of the British landowners toward the colonies from 1763 to 1776. To them in each instance it seemed as if the foundations of the universe were breaking up and the world in which they lived was sinking beneath their feet.

Primarily, the American Revolution was a political and constitutional movement and only secondarily one that was either financial, commercial, or social. At bottom the fundamental issue was the political independence of the colonies, and in the last analysis the conflict lay between the British Parliament and the colonial assemblies, each of which was probably more sensitive, self-conscious, and self-important than was the voting population that it represented. For many years these assemblies had fought the prerogative successfully and would have continued to do so, eventually reducing it to a minimum, as the later self-governing dominions have done; but in the end it was Parliament, whose powers they disputed, that became the great antagonist. Canning saw the situation clearly when, half a century later, he spoke of the Revolution as having been a test of the equality of strength "between the legislature of this mighty kingdom ... and the colonial assemblies," adding further that he had no intention of repeating in the case of Jamaica, the colony then under debate, the mistakes that had been made in 1776. Of the mistakes to which he referred the greatest was the employment of the deadly expedient of coercion, and he showed his greater wisdom when he determined, as he said, to keep back "within the penetralia of the constitution the transcendental powers of Parliament over a dependency of the British crown" and not "to produce it upon trifling occasions or in cases of petty refractoriness and temporary misconduct." How he would have met the revolution in America, based as it was on "the fundamental principles of political liberty," we cannot say; but we know that he had no sympathy with any attempt to force opinion back into paths that were outworn. That he would have foreseen the solution of a later date and have granted the colonies absolute and responsible self-government, recognizing the equality of the assemblies in domestic matters and giving them the same control over their home affairs as the people of Great Britain had over theirs, can be conjectured only by inference from his liberal attitude toward the South American republics. He stood half-way between the ministers of the Revolutionary period — blind, sensitive, and mentally unprogressive — and the statesmen of the middle of the nineteenth century, who were willing to follow the lead of those courageous and far-sighted Englishmen who saved the empire from a second catastrophe after 1830 and were the founders of the British colonial policy of to-day.

The revolt of the colonies from Great Britain began long before the battles of Moore's Creek Bridge and Lexington; before the time of James Otis and the writs of assistance; before the dispute over the appointment of judges in North Carolina and New York; before the eloquence of Patrick Henry was first heard in the land; and even before the quarrel in Virginia over the Dinwiddie pistole fee. These were but the outward and visible signs of an inward and factual divergence. The separation from the mother country began just as soon as the mercantile system of commercial control, the governmental system of colonial administration, and the whole doctrine of the inferior status of a colonial assembly began to give way before the pressure exerted and the disruptive power exercised by these young and growing colonial communities. New soil had produced new wants, new desires, new points of view, and the colonists were demanding the right to live their own lives in their own way. As we see it to-day the situation was a dramatic one. On one side was the immutable, stereotyped system of the mother country, based on precedent and tradition and designed to keep things comfortably as they were; on the other, a vital, dynamic organism, containing the seed of a great nation, its forces untried, still to be proved. It is inconceivable that a connection should have continued long between two such yokefellows, one static, the other dynamic, separated by an ocean and bound only by the ties of a legal relationship.

If my diagnosis is correct of the British state of mind in the eighteenth century, and the evidence in its favor seems overwhelming, then the colonists were as justified in their movement of revolt as were the Englishmen themselves in their movement for reform in the next century. Yet in reality no great progressive movement needs justification at our hands, for great causes justify themselves and time renders the decision. The revolt in America and the later reforms in Great Britain herself were directed against the same dominant ruling class that in their colonial relations as well as in their social and political arrangements at home preferred that the world in which they lived should remain as it was. Reform or revolt is bound to follow attempts of a privileged class to conduct affairs according to unchanging rules and formulae. The colonies had developed a constitutional organization equally complete with Britain's own and one that in principle was far in advance of the British system, and they were qualified to co-operate with the mother country on terms similar to those of a brotherhood of free nations such as the British world is becoming to-day. But England was unable to see this fact or unwilling to recognize it, and consequently America became the scene of a political unrest, which might have been controlled by compromise, but was turned to revolt by coercion. The situation is a very interesting one, for England is famous for her ability to compromise at critical moments in her history. For once at least she failed. In 1832 and later years, when she faced other great constitutional crises at home and in her colonies, she saved herself from revolution by understanding the situation and adjusting herself to it. Progress may be stemmed for a time, but it cannot be permanently stopped by force. A novelist has expressed the idea in saying: "You cannot fight and beat revolutions as you can fight and beat nations. You can kill a man, but you simply can't kill a rebel. For the proper rebel has an ideal of living, while your ideal is to kill him so that you may preserve yourself. And the reason why no revolution or religion has ever been beaten is that rebels die for something worth dying for, the future, but their enemies die only to preserve the past, and makers of history are always stronger than makers of empire." The American revolutionists had an ideal of living; it can hardly be said that in 1776 the Englishmen of the ruling classes were governed in their colonial relations by any ideals that were destined to be of service to the future of the human race.

ARTHUR M. SCHLESINGER (1888–1905) late professor at Harvard University, was author of *The Colonial Merchants and the American Revolution, 1763–1776*, which won the Justin Winsor Prize of the American Historical Association in 1918. In this article Schlesinger views the Revolution from a Progressive perspective, as a dual revolution: a struggle for independence against Great Britain and an internal class conflict within America to see whether the upper or lower class would dominate. According to Schlesinger, how did conservative merchants deal with the dilemma facing them at home and abroad?*

Arthur M. Schlesinger

The Progressive Perspective

The term "American Revolution" is itself not without difficulties and its use has led to misconception and confusion. In letter after letter John Adams tried to teach a headstrong generation some degree of exactness in the use of an expression whose meaning they had knowledge of only by report. "A history of the first war of the United States is a very different thing from a history of the American Revolution," he wrote in 1815. ". . . The revolution was in the minds of the people, and in the union of the colonies, both of which were accomplished before hostilities commenced. This revolution and union were gradually forming from the year 1760 to 1776." And to another correspondent he wrote: "But what do we mean by the American

Revolution? Do we mean the American war? The Revolution was effected before the war commenced. The Revolution was in the minds and hearts of the people."

This distinction is not only valid in point of fact but it offers a helpful avenue of approach for a consideration of the facts of the nation's birth. If the period from 1760 to 1776 is not viewed merely as a prelude to the American Revolution, the military struggle may frankly be regarded for what it actually was, namely a war for independence, an armed attempt to impose the views of the revolutionists upon the British government and a large section of the colonial population at whatever cost to freedom of opinion or the sanctity of life and property. The major emphasis is thus placed upon the clashing

---

*Arthur M. Schlesinger, "The American Revolution Reconsidered." Reprinted without footnotes with permission from *Political Science Quarterly*, vol. 34, no. 1 (March, 1919), pp. 63–75.

of economic interests and the interplay of mutual prejudices, opposing ideals and personal antagonisms—whether in England or America—which made inevitable in 1776 what was unthinkable in 1760. . . .

With this brief view of affairs in Great Britain it is now possible to consider the situation in America. Conditions there were both simpler and more complex than the traditional accounts represent. In place of thirteen units of population thinking alike on most public questions, there were in fact two or possibly three major groupings of population, differentiated by physiographical conditions, economic interests and political ideals. The communities on the coastal plain from New Hampshire to Pennsylvania constituted one of these divisions; the settlements of the tidewater regions from Maryland to Georgia formed another; and the third, less clearly outlined geographically, consisted of the western sections of many of the provinces. These three divisions represented modes of living and attitudes of mind much more fundamental than those indicated by arbitrary political boundaries.

The first area may conveniently be called the commercial section because the dominant economic interest of the people was the carrying trade and shipbuilding. Here great mercantile families had grown up, who had gained their wealth through smuggling with the West Indies or else through legitimate trading enterprises that embraced the entire world. The merchants were keenly alive to the golden benefits which membership in the British empire had always yielded; and like the business interests of any generation or clime, they might be expected to combat any effort to tamper with the source of their profits. For the merchants the unfolding of the new imperial program involved a very serious interference with their customary trading operations; and during the decade from 1764 to 1774 their constant aim was to effect a restoration of the commercial conditions of 1763. As a class they entertained neither earlier nor later the idea of independence, for withdrawal from the British empire meant for them the loss of vital business advantages without corresponding benefits in a world organized on a basis of imperial trading systems. They strove to obtain the most favorable terms possible within the empire but not to leave it. Indeed they viewed with no small concern the growth of republican feeling and leveling sentiment which the controversy occasioned.

The great ports of the north—Boston, New York, Philadelphia, Newport—bore eloquent testimony to the prosperity of the mercantile class; and on the continuance of this prosperity depended the livelihood of the mechanics and petty shopkeepers of the towns and, to a lesser degree, the well-being of the farmers whose cereals and meats were exported to the West Indies. This proletarian element was not inclined by temperament to that self-restraint in movements of popular protest which was ever the *arrière pensée* of the merchant class; and being for the most part unenfranchised, they expressed their sentiments most naturally through boisterous mass meetings and mob demonstrations.

In the southern coastal area colonial capital was invested almost exclusively in plantation production; and commerce was carried on chiefly by British mercantile houses and their American agents, the factors. The only town in the plantation provinces that could compare with the teeming ports of the north was Charleston; and political life was focused in the periodical meetings of the great landed proprietors in the assemblies. Under the wasteful system of marketing, which the apparent plenty of plantation life made possible, the planters found themselves treading a morass of indebtedness to British merchants from which it seemed that nothing less than virtual repudiation could extricate them. In the last twenty-five years of colonial dependence the assemblies passed a succession of lax bankruptcy acts and other legislation prejudicial to nonresident creditors; but these laws nearly always ran afoul the royal veto. This fact, together with the sturdy sense of self-determination which the peculiar social system fostered, made the plantation provinces ready to resent any new exercise of parliamentary authority over the colonies, such as the new imperial policy involved. Georgia, as the youngest colony, not yet self-sustaining, and dependent on the home government for protection against a serious Indian menace, was less a part of this picture than the other provinces of the group.

On the western fringe of the coastal communities lay an irregular belt of back-country settlements whose economy and modes of thought were almost as distinctive as those of the two tidewater regions. Certainly the western sections of many of the provinces had grievances in common and resembled each other more than they did the older sections with which they were associated by provincial boundaries. These pioneer settlements extended north and south, up and down the valleys between the fall line of the rivers and mountains, from New England to Georgia. Outside of New England the majority of the settlers were of non-English strains, mostly German and Scotch-Irish; but throughout the long frontier the people cultivated small isolated farms and entertained democratic ideas commensurate with the equalitarian conditions to which their manner of living accustomed them. In many of the provinces they had long been discriminated against by the older settlements in the matter of representation in the assemblies, the administration of justice and the incidence of taxation; and they were thus familiar, of their own experience, with all the arguments which the Revolution was to make popular against non-representative government and unjust taxation. Being self-sustaining communities economically, their zeal for popular rights was in no wise alloyed by the embarrassment of their pocketbooks. Although out of harmony with popular leaders of the seaboard in both the commercial and plantation provinces on many matters of intracolonial policy, they could join forces with them against the new imperial policy; and they brought to the controversy a moral conviction and bold philosophy which gave great impetus to the agitation for independence.

The history of the American Revolution is the story of the reaction of these three sections to the successive acts of the British government and of their interaction upon each other. The merchants of the commercial colonies were the most seriously affected by the new imperial policy and at the outset assumed the leadership of the colonial movement of protest. They were closely seconded by the planters of the south as soon as enough time had elapsed to make clear to the latter the implications of the issue of home rule for which the merchants stood. The democratic farmers of the interior, more or less out of contact with the political currents of the seaboard, were slower to take part; and it is largely true that their measure of participation varied inversely according to the degree of their isolation. Patrick Henry and his fellow burgesses from the western counties of Virginia began to undermine the conservatism of the tidewater statesmen as early as 1765, but the Germans and Scotch-Irish of Pennsylvania did not make their influence fully felt until the critical days of 1774–1775.

The new British policy of imperial control assumed its first form under George Grenville (1764–1765). The numerous regulations of trade, which need not be analyzed here, injured fair traders and smuggling merchants alike and threatened bankruptcy to the great mercantile houses of Boston, New York and Philadelphia. The prohibition of colonial legal tender added to their woes and indeed made the hard-pressed planters of the south sharers in the general distress. The Stamp Act, with its far-reaching taxes burdensome alike to merchant and farmer, sealed the union of commercial and plantation provinces at the same time that it afforded an opportunity for placing the colonial argument on constitutional grounds; and because of the character of the taxation, it rallied to the colonial position the powerful support of the lawyers and newspaper proprietors. The plan of the British to garrison their new acquisitions in America and to station a few detachments of troops in the older colonies was, in the feverish state of the public mind, envisaged as a brazen attempt to intimidate the colonists into submission. The merchants of some of the ports, intent on restoring the conditions of their former prosperity, adopted resolutions of non-importation; and little recking the future, they aroused the populace to a sense of British injustice, even to the extent of countenancing and instigating mob excesses and the destruction of property.

In the end parliament resolved upon the passage of certain remedial laws (1766), an outcome which, from the standpoint of the more radical colonists, can be regarded as little more than a compromise. The Stamp Act was indeed repealed and important alterations were made in the trade regulations; but the Currency Act, the regulations against smuggling and the provisions for a standing army remained unchanged. In addition the Declaratory Act was passed; and the new molasses duty was an unvarnished application of the principle of "taxation without representation" announced in the Declaratory Act. The rejoicing of the colonists can be explained only on the ground that the merchants of the north dominated colonial opinion; and like practical men of affairs, they were contemptuous, if not fearful, of disputes upon questions of abstract right.

The passage of the Townshend Acts in 1767 was the second attempt of parliament to reconstruct the empire in the spirit of the Grenville experiment. Again the merchants of the commercial colonies perceived themselves as the class whose interests were chiefly imperiled; but sobered by the mob outrages of Stamp Act days, they resolved to guide the course of American opposition in orderly and peaceful channels. They, therefore, began an active agitation for corrective legislation through merchants' petitions and legislative memorials to parliament; and after much questioning of each others' sincerity they succeeded in developing an elaborate system of commercial boycott, which united the commercial colonies in an effort to secure the repeal of the objectionable laws. After a year or so this movement in a much modified form spread to the plantation provinces, where, under the leadership of Washington and other planters, it was employed as a means of preventing the landed aristocracy from falling more deeply into the toils of their British creditors.

Meantime the merchants began to see that in organizing their communities for peaceful resistance to Great Britain they were unavoidably releasing disruptive forces which, like Frankenstein, they were finding it impossible to control. The failure of non-importation to effect swift redress compelled the merchant bodies, as the months passed, to depend more and more upon the tumultuous methods of the proletariat in order to keep wavering merchants true to the cause. Increasing friction between smuggling merchants and customs officers also produced outbreaks of mob violence in many provinces, and led by a broad, smooth road to such distressing affairs as the Boston "Massacre" on the one hand and to the destruction of the revenue cutter *Gaspee* on the other. As the political agitators and turbulent elements gained the upper hand, the contest began to assume more clearly the form of a crusade for constitutional and natural rights; and when word arrived in May, 1770, that parliament had repealed all the Townshend duties except the trifling tax on tea, the merchants found it difficult to reassert their earlier control and to stop a movement that had lost all significance for hard-headed men of business. The merchants of New York, under the leadership of their newly formed Chamber of Commerce, were the first who were able to wrench loose from their enforced alliance with the radicals; and the cancellation of their boycott resolutions was soon followed by similar action in the ports of Philadelphia and Boston. The plantation provinces were coolly left in the lurch notwithstanding that parliament had not receded from its position

of arbitrary taxation, and the movement there soon died of inanition.

The two or three years that followed the partial repeal of the Townshend duties were, for the most part, years of material prosperity and political calm. The merchants had grown to look askance at a doctrine of home rule which left it uncertain who was to rule at home. As a class they eagerly agreed with the merchant-politician Thomas Cushing that "high points about the supreme authority of Parliament" should best "fall asleep." And so—John Hancock as well as Isaac Low—they deserted politics for business, even to the extent of importing dutied tea which people imbibed everywhere except at Philadelphia and New York, where local conditions made it possible for merchants to offer the cheaper Dutch tea to consumers. The sun of the radical had suffered an eclipse; and quietly biding their time, they began to apply to their own following the lessons of organization that they had learned from the "mercantile dons." In the commercial colonies Sam Adams—"that Matchiavel of Chaos"—sought, through the establishment of town committees of correspondence, to unite the workingmen of the port towns and the farmers of the rural districts in political action; and the burgesses of Virginia launched their plan of a provincial committee of correspondence that might give uncensored expression to the political grievances of the southern planters.

In May, 1773, a new tea act was passed by parliament, which stampeded the merchants into joining forces once more with the political radicals and irresponsible elements. This new law, if put into operation, would have enabled the great East India Company to monopolize the colonial tea market to the exclusion of both American smugglers and law-abiding tea traders. Alarmed at this prospect and fearful lest further monopoly privileges in trade might follow from the success of the present experiment, the colonial merchant class joined in an active popular agitation for the purpose of preventing the landing of any of the tea importations of the East India Company. Though their efforts for a vigorous but restrained opposition met with substantial success elsewhere, they were overreached at Boston by the superior management of Sam Adams and the unintelligence of Governor Hutchinson; and the British trading company became the involuntary host at a tea party costing £15,000.

The Boston Tea Party marked a turning point in the course of events both in America and Britain. In both countries it was regarded by the merchants and moderates as a lawless destruction of private property and an act of wanton defiance which no self-respecting government could wisely ignore. Plainly the issue between the colonies and the mother country had ceased to be one of mere trading advantage. Outside of New England, colonial opinion, so far as it expressed itself, greeted the event with a general disapproval and apprehension. In the mother country parliament proceeded to the passage of the severe disciplinary measures of 1774.

The effect of this punitive legislation cannot be overestimated, for it convinced many colonists who had disapproved of the Boston vandalism that the greater guilt now lay on the side of parliament. "They look upon the chastisement of Boston to be purposely rigorous, and held up by way of intimidation to all America . . ." wrote Governor Penn from Philadelphia. "Their delinquency in destroying the East India Company's tea is lost in the attention given to what

is here called the too severe punishment of shutting up the port, altering the Constitution, and making an Act, as they term it, screening the officers and soldiers shedding American blood." From this time on there occurred in the several provinces a contest for the control of public policy between the moderates on the one hand and the radicals or extremists on the other, the former receiving aid and comfort from the royal officials and their circle of friends. This line of cleavage is unmistakable in the case of practically every province.

The moderates as a group wanted to pay for the tea destroyed and to propose to parliament an act of union which should automatically dispose of all controversial questions for the future. The radicals were opposed to compromise and as a class desired a comprehensive and drastic boycott of Great Britain with which to exact from parliament recognition of the colonial claim to complete home rule. Both parties were willing to make a trial of strength in an intercolonial congress; and after bitter contests in each province to control the *personnel* of the irregularly elected delegations, the First Continental Congress assembled in Philadelphia in September, 1774. In this notable gathering the moderates discovered to their dismay that they were outnumbered; and, in the disconsolate phrase of a Maryland merchant, "Adams, with his crew, and the haughty Sultans of the South juggled the whole conclave of the Delegates." Indeed this extralegal body, by adopting the Association, decreed that the merchants of America should sacrifice their trade for the benefit of a cause from which they had come to be alienated; and the radicals in congress provided for spreading a network of committees over the continent to insure obedience to their decree.

In the popular conventions called prior to the First Continental Congress and in the provincial meetings that were held to ratify its doings, the people from the back-country counties of many provinces were, for the first time, admitted to that full measure of representation which had long been denied them by the unjust system of apportionment in the colonial assemblies. Deeply stirred by the political slogans of the tidewater radicals, they ranged themselves by their side and lent momentum to an agitation that was hastening toward independence. In closely divided provinces like Pennsylvania and South Carolina their voice was undoubtedly the decisive factor.

The proceedings of the First Continental Congress were viewed with mixed feelings by the colonists. The moderates who had lingered in the popular movement in order to control it began to withdraw, although it required the outbreak of hostilities at Lexington or even the Declaration of Independence to convince some that their efforts could be of no avail. The merchants perforce acquiesced in the regulations of the Association, which, in the early months, were not without profit to them. The radical committees of the coast towns, formerly controlled by the merchants, began to fall into the hands of the democratic mechanic class. In New York, Boston and Philadelphia alike, "nobodies" and "unimportant persons" succeeded to power; and even in Savannah, Governor Wright declared that "the Parochial Committee are a Parcel of the Lowest People, Chiefly Carpenters, Shoemakers, Blacksmiths, etc. . . . ." Flushed with success, the radical leaders busied themselves with consolidating their following in town and country through the creation of committees of observation and provincial committees and conventions. Little wonder was it that, in this changed aspect of public affairs, a worthy minister of Charleston, S.C., should be dismissed by his congregation "for his audacity in . . . saying that *mechanics* and country *clowns* had no right to dispute about politics, or what kings, lords and commons had done," or that the newspaper account should add: "All *such* divines should be taught to know that mechanics and country clowns (infamously so called) are the real and absolute masters of king, lords, commons and priests. . . ."

Events had reached a stage where the extremists in both countries were in control. What Chatham and Joseph Galloway might have adjusted to their mutual satisfaction could not be rationally discussed by North and Sam Adams. Under the circumstances it was inevitable that the policy of commercial coercion, adopted by the First Continental Congress, should soon be superseded by armed warfare as the weapon of the radicals, and that open rebellion should in turn give way to a struggle for independence.

LOUIS M. HACKER (b. 1899), a scholar who trained and taught at Columbia University, presents here a Marxist interpretation of the causes of the Revolution. Written in the Great Depression of the 1930s, his article reflects the idea of economic determinism that found favor among some American historians of that era. Hacker believes the Revolution was brought about by a fundamental economic clash between British and American capitalists. At the same time, he sees a class conflict within America over economic issues. How does Hacker's interpretation of the relations between the colonies and mother country compare with that of Andrews?*

Louis M. Hacker

A Marxist Conception

At the outbreak of the American Revolution the great majority of the American population—perhaps nine-tenths of it—was engaged on the land. The owning farmers, whether they were planter lords or modest family farmers, were commercial agriculturists: for either they produced cash crops for sale in a market or they developed subsidiary activities to net them a money return. Self-sufficiency, even on the frontier, is impossible under capitalist organization. Cash is needed everywhere, whether it is to pay taxes or for harvesting the crop or to buy salt, iron and a squirrel gun. Hence, the colonial farmer either produced a cash crop or he tried to find employment among a number of occupations that did not interfere with his agricultural activities. He either trapped or hunted; or worked in logging operations; or shipped with a fishing fleet. Often he really obtained his cash from land speculation: that is to say, as the result of constantly mounting land values, the farmer was in a position to sell his improved land and buy a cheaper farm in the frontier areas. Thus, the American farmer was a dealer in land from the very dawn of settlement until 1920, a period of three centuries. When land values began to decline after 1921, the basis of American agricultural well-being was shaken to its foundations.

This need to develop a cash crop made for the production of staples everywhere.

*Louis M. Hacker, "The American Revolution: Economic Aspects," *Marxist Quarterly*, I (1937), pp. 46–67. Reprinted by permission of the author.

By the eighteenth century New England was producing and sending to market beef, cattle and hogs, work animals and corn to be used for stall feeding. The Middle Colonies had become the great granary of the English settlements, and on the big farms of New York and Pennsylvania, where tenants and indentured servants were being employed, wheat was being grown, processed into flour and sold in the towns and the far away West Indies. In the Southern Colonies agriculture was the keystone of the whole economic structure: Virginia and Maryland planters grew tobacco for sale in England; interior farmers grew grains and raised cattle to be used in the West Indian trade; the tidewater planters of the Carolinas and Georgia cultivated and harvested rice, indigo and some cotton. These crops were sent to seaports, put on ships and carried to distant places to furnish those funds which were the basis of the commercial enterprise of the day. . . .

The plantation economy sprang up in colonial Virginia and Maryland, notably, for obvious reasons. The cultivation of a staple like tobacco served excellently the purposes of the Mercantilist System: it did not compete with an important English crop and hence might be grown on a grand scale; it produced a colonial return on the basis of which large English exports might be sent to the Southern Colonies; it furnished opportunities for the investment of English capital—short-term funds for the financing of the crops and long-term funds for the hypothecation of plantation properties; and it created an outlet for England's surplus populations. Thus tobacco cultivation was closely bound to English mercantilist policy. . . .

There was no question that the tobacco market kept on expanding: at the end of the seventeenth century Maryland and Virginia were exporting 35,-000,000 pounds to the mother country; by 1763 the quantity had trebled. On the other hand, the industry was at the mercy of the imperial system. Tobacco was on the enumerated list and could be sent, therefore, only to England; high sumptuary taxes were placed on it; prices were controlled in London and tended to drop periodically below the cost of production. In addition, capital costs of plantation operation continued to mount, due to the high cost of labor (the price of indentured servants and, more particularly, that of slaves went up while their productivity remained constant), the exhaustion of the soil in the older regions, and the necessity on the part of the planters to buy new lands to which they could be ready to transfer their activities. The other charges against operations—of freight costs, insurance, merchants' commissions and profits, interest on borrowings—hung like millstones about the necks of the encumbered planters.

The plantation system was particularly dependent upon credit. The tobacco grower required credit to assist in the acquisition of the labor force; to market his cash crop; to furnish his equipment; and to finance his purchase of consumers goods. The only source of funds was the English merchant capitalist: and to him the Southern planter was compelled to pay high interest rates, mortgage his land and slaves and turn for the supplying of those necessaries without which his home and plantation could not continue. Constantly weighed down by debt, it was small wonder that the planters of Colonial America ever sought to expand their activities, by extending their tobacco lands and engaging in the more speculative aspects of land dealing; and that they turned to thoughts of inflation as relief from debt oppression was also to be expected.

Because the wild lands of the frontier areas were so important to the maintenance of the stability of the Southern planting economy, Southern capitalists were constantly preoccupied with them. The West was not opened up by the hardy frontiersman; it was opened up by the land speculator who preceded even the Daniel Boones into the wilderness. But the English (and also the Scotch) had also learned to regard with more than a curious interest these wild lands of the West: they saw in them profits from the fur trade and from the speculative exploitation of the region by their own capitalist enterprise. It was at this point that English and Southern merchant capital came into conflict; and when, as a result of the promulgation of the Proclamation Line of 1763 and the Quebec Act of 1774, the Western lands were virtually closed to colonial enterprising, the Southern planting economy began to totter. Without the subsidiary activity of land speculation, planters could not continue solvent; there is no cause for wonder, therefore, that the owners of great plantation properties should be among the first to swell the ranks of the colonial revolutionary host in 1775.

Colonial producers and enterprisers engaged in all those other activities that are associated with a newly-settled region. The trapping and slaying of the wild animals of the forests early attracted pioneers and promoters; and the prevalence of the beaver, otter, mink, bear, racoon and fox in the New England and Middle Colonies and of the deer, racoon, fox and beaver in the Southern Colonies led to the creation of a thriving peltry and hide industry and trade. The Eng-

lish demand for furs and skins was constant, profits were great and quickly capitalism became interested and sought to monopolize the field. This it was not difficult to do, particularly when the lines of the traffic lengthened as the wild lands kept on receding beyond the tidewater settlements. English merchants and the great Southern and Northern landlords financed the individual hunters, trappers and traders, or employed them as their agents, and furnished the truck and firearms which served as the basis for the Indian barter. As the extermination of wild life went on, the keeping open of an ever-extending frontier zone became one of the necessities of the colonial economy: the struggle over the fur trade had involved England and France in the long series of colonial wars in America; and the desire to continue the fur traffic was one of the reasons for colonial interest in the wild lands beyond the crest of the Appalachians—and, hence, collision with the mother country. . . .

There existed no manufacturing, in the commercial or industrial sense, in colonial America: and in this fact we are to find one of the important keys to the outbreak of the American Revolution. Household manufacturing there was: the colonial farming households, particularly of the more modest sort and where the necessaries of indentured servants and Negro slaves were concerned, supplied many of their own needs. . . . Occasionally a surplus of cloth, linen, butter or honey was taken to the local village and sold or exchanged for the salt, iron, paint and tools that were essential to the conduct of the household; for self-sufficiency, of course, was never fully attained.

This was not manufacturing in the

capitalist sense. The conversion of raw materials into finished goods and their sale in large and distant markets, in modern times, has been under the supervision of two different types of organization. Sometimes found side by side but in the broad and abstract sense existing in a sequential relationship, these have been domestic manufacturing, or the putting-out system, and industrial manufacturing, or the factory system. . . .

Neither of this type of manufacturing organization was to be found in colonial America. Why was this? Colonial America did not want for liquid capital: witness the extraordinary extension of capitalist enterprise, the work of both English and American capitalists, in trade, ship-building, land speculation, the financing of the plantation system, and crude iron production. Colonial America had its fair share of wealthy men: as early as 1680, there were said to be at least 30 merchants in Massachusetts alone who were worth between $50,000 and $100,-000. . . . Every colony could boast of its big merchants, who were, in fact, capitalists; indeed, George Washington, the greatest of these, in the 1770's was calling himself not "planter" but "merchant." It did not want for the means of creating a free labor supply: the engrossing, or monopolization, of the lands in the settled areas had compelled small farmers either to become tenants or to move westward where they squatted on the wild lands held by absentee landlords. The frontier had not been made secure against the Indians because of the fur trade, and the necessity for maintaining tidewater land values; but had the owners of the wild lands so desired it, the pacification of the western areas would have driven the landless into domestic manufacturing or workshops. It did not want for a market: by 1770,

concentrated in a relatively small area and excellently served by harbors and rivers, lived a population one-third as great as England's; too, the very rich market for finished goods of the sugar islands easily was capable of exploitation. It did not want for raw materials: for never was a land endowed with richer natural resources. Manufacturing did not appear in colonial America because the very nature of the Mercantilist System prohibited it.

The English Mercantilist System, in its imperial-colonial relations, following the triumph of English merchant capital in the Puritan Revolution, was based on the economic subservience of the colonies. Indeed, every imperial and administrative agency had this end constantly in view: and most significant among these was the Board of Trade. The Board of Trade, in its final form, had been established in 1696, and among its various instruments for control over the colonies, these three were notable: it had the right to deny charters or patents to English-financed companies seeking to engage in enterprises in the colonies which were inimical to the interests of home merchant capitalists; it had the power to review colonial legislation and recommend to the Privy Council the disallowance of such colonial enactments as ran counter to the welfare of the mother country; and it prepared specific instructions for the deportment of the royal governors in the colonies, in particular indicating where the veto power was to be used to prevent colonial encroachments on the privileges and prerogatives of English citizens.

Ever vigilant, the Board of Trade proceeded against the colonies when they threatened to impinge on the interests of Englishmen: it refused to tolerate colonial interference with the mother country's hold on foreign trade and shipping; it checked colonial attempts to control the traffic in convicts and slaves; it prevented colonies from lowering interest rates, easing the judicial burden on debtors and seeking to monopolize the Indian trade. Most significant were the stern checks imposed on attempts by the colonial assemblies to encourage native manufacturing and to relieve the oppression of debts by the increase of the money supply of the colonies.

Following in the footsteps of the English themselves, colonials looked to public authority to aid in the development of native industries. In the best mercantilist tradition, therefore, colonial statute-books came to be filled with legislation which offered bounties to enterprises, extended public credit to them, exempted them from taxation, gave them easy access to raw materials and in their behalf encouraged the location of new towns.

Against such legislation the Board of Trade regularly moved. On important matters, appeal was had to Parliament and general statues were passed, notably the Woolen Act of 1699, which barred colonial wool, woolen yarn and woolen manufactures from intercolonial and foreign commerce; the Hat Act of 1732, which prevented the exportation of hats out of the separate colonies and restricted colonial hatmakers to two apprentices; and the Iron Act of 1750. In addition, the axe of disallowance descended regularly. As early as 1705 a Pennsylvania law for building up the shoemaking industry was disallowed; in 1706, a New York law designed to develop a sail-cloth industry was disallowed; in 1706, 1707 and 1708, laws of Virginia and Maryland, providing for the establishment of new towns, were disallowed on the grounds that such new communities must invariably lead to a desire to found manufacturing industries and that their existence would draw off persons from the countryside where they were engaged in the production of tobacco. Indeed, in 1756, when the Board of Trade recommended disallowance of a Massachusetts law for aiding the production of linen, it could say flatly: "the passing of laws in the plantations for encouraging manufactures, which in any ways interfere with the manufacture of this kingdom, has always been thought improper, and has ever been discouraged."

Also, the royal governors were closely instructed to veto all legislation designed to assist the development of such manufactures as might compete with those of England. This had its effect, so that E. A. Russell, an outstanding American authority upon the subject, has been led to conclude: "Largely as a result of the government's determined attitude in the matter, comparatively few laws for this purpose were enacted in the plantations." In no small measure the general result was heightened by the limitations imposed on English capital seeking investments in the colonies. English balances in the colonies and English new capital were kept away from manufactures; and they might be placed only in land and land operations. The overextension of sugar planting, in the West Indies, and of tobacco planting, in the mainland colonies, undoubtedly was due to this restriction and therefore helped in the shaping of the crisis in the imperial-colonial relations which set in in the 1760's.

Thus, at the very time in England when the domestic system was rapidly being converted into the factory system and great advances were being made in the perfection of machinery exactly because the existence of a growing market was demanding more efficient methods of production, in the colonies methods of production remained at a hopelessly backward level because English and colonial capital could not enter manufacturing. An important outlet for accumulated funds was barred. The colonial capitalist economy, therefore, was narrowly restricted largely to land speculation, the dealing in furs and the carrying trade. When English mercantilism, for the protection of its home merchant capital, began to narrow these spheres then catastrophe threatened. The American Revolution can be understood only in terms of the necessity for colonial merchant capital to escape from the contracting prison walls of the English Mercantilist System.

In an imperial economy the capitalist relationships between mother country and colonies as a rule lead to a colonial unfavorable balance of trade. The colonies buy the goods and services of the mother country and are encouraged to develop those raw materials the home capitalists require. In this they are aided by the investment of the mother country's balances and by new capital. Thus, in the Southern Colonies, tobacco largely was being produced to furnish returns for the English goods and services the plantation lords required; but, because the exchange left England with a favorable balance, by the 1770's its capitalists had more than £4,000,000 invested in Southern planting operations. To meet the charges on this debt, Southern planters were compelled constantly to expand their agricultural operations and to engage in the subsidiary activities of land speculation and the fur trade.

The Northern Colonies were less fortunately placed. The Northern Colonies directly produced little of those staples necessary to the maintenance of the English economy: the grains, provisions and work animals of New England, New York and Pennsylvania could not be permitted to enter England lest they disorganize the home commerical agricultural industry; and the same was true of the New England fishing catches. The Northern Colonies, of course, were a source for lumber, naval stores, furs, whale products and iron, and these England sorely needed to maintain her independence of European supplies. England sought to encourage these industries by bounties and other favored positions; but in vain. Notably unsuccessful was the effort to divert Northern colonial capital from shipbuilding and shipping into the production of naval stores by the Bounty Act of 1706.

The Northern Colonies, therefore, produced little for direct export to England to permit them to pay their balances, that is to say, for the increasing quantities of English drygoods, hardware and house furnishings they were taking. In view of the fact, too, that the Northern Colonies presented slight opportunities for the investment of English capital, it was incumbent upon the merchants of the region to develop returns elsewhere in order to obtain specie and bills of exchange with which to balance payments in England.

Out of this necessity arose the economic significance of the various triangular trading operations (and the subsidiary industries growing out of trade) the Northern merchants organized. Northern merchants and shipowners opened up regular markets in Newfoundland and Nova Scotia for their fishing tackle, salt, provisions and rum; they established an ever-growing commercial intercourse with the wine islands of the

Canaries and Madeira, from which they bought wines direct and to which they sold barrel staves, foodstuffs and live animals; they sold fish to Spain, Portugal and Italy; their ports acted as entrepots for the transshipment of Southern staples to England and Southern Europe.

The trade with the West Indian sugar islands—as well as the traffic in Negro slaves and the manufacture of rum, which grew out of it—became the cornerstone of the Northern colonial capitalist economy. Northern merchants loaded their ships with all those necessaries the sugar planters were unable to produce—work animals for their mills; lumber for houses and outbuildings; staves, heads and hoops for barrels; flour and salted provisions for their tables; and refuse fish for their slaves—and made regular runs to the British islands of Barbadoes, the Leeward Islands and Jamaica, and then increasingly to the French, Spanish, Dutch and Danish islands and settlements dotting the Caribbean. Here they acquired in return specie with which to pay their English balances, indigo, cotton, ginger, allspice and dyewoods for transshipment to England, and, above all, sugar and molasses for conversion into rum in the distilleries of Massachusetts and Rhode Island. It was rum that served as the basis of the intercourse between the Northern Colonies and the African Coast; rum paid for ivory, gums, beeswax and gold dust; and rum paid for Negroes who were carried to the sugar islands on that famous Middle Passage to furnish the labor supply without which the sugar plantation economy could not survive.

Such commercial transactions—in addition, of course, to the profits derived from the fisheries, whaling and shipbuilding—furnished the needed sources of return and their conduct the outlets for Northern merchant capitalist accumulations. But they were not enough with which to pay all the English bills and to absorb all the mounting funds of the Amorys, Faneuils, Hancocks and Boylstons of Boston, the Whartons, Willings and Morrises of Philadelphia, the Livingstons, Lows and Crugers of New York, the Wantons and Lopezes of Newport and the Browns of Providence. In three illegal forms of enterprises—in piracy, smuggling generally, and the illicit sugar and molasses trade with the foreign West Indian islands—Northern merchants found opportunities for the necessary expansion.

Piracy—at least up to the end of the seventeenth century, when England was able to exterminate it—played a significant part in maintaining the merchant capital of the Northern Colonies. English and colonial pirates, fitted out in Northern ports and backed financially by reputable merchants, preyed on the Spanish fleets of the Caribbean and even boldly fared out into the Red Sea and the Indian Ocean to terrorize ships engaged in the East Indies trade; and with their ships heavily laden with plate, drygoods and spices, put back into colonial ports where they sold their loot and divided their profits with the merchants who had financed them.

Smuggling contributed its share to the swelling of merchant fortunes. In the first place, there was the illegal direct intercourse between the colonies and European countries in the expanding list of enumerated articles; and, in the second place, ships on the home-bound voyages from Europe or the West Indies brought large supplies of drygoods, silk, cocoa and brandies into the American Colonies without having declared these articles at English ports and paid the duties. Most important of all was the trade with the foreign West Indian sugar islands which was rendered illegal, after 1733, as a result of the imposition by the Molasses Act of prohibitive duties on the importation into the colonies of foreign sugar, molasses and rum.

In this West Indian trade was to be found the strength and the weakness of colonial merchant capital. The English sugar interest was the darling of the Mercantilist System. Sugar, more so even than tobacco, was the great oversea staple of the eighteenth-century world; and not only to it was bound a ramified English commerical industry made up of carriers, commission men, factors, financiers, processors and distributors: but sugar was converted into molasses and in turn distilled into rum to support the unholy slave traffic and the unsavory Indian trade. The sugar cultivation therefore had the constant solicitude of English imperial officialdom and a sugar bloc, made up of absentee landlords, exerted a powerful influence in Parliament. Indeed, so significant a rôle did sugar play in the imperial economy that in the 1770's the capital worth of West Indian sugar properties stood at £60,-000,000: of which at least one-half was the stake of home English investors. When it is noted that in the whole of the Northern American mainland colonies the English capitalist stake at most was only one-sixth as great, then the reason for the favoring of the sugar colonies as against the Northern commercial colonies, after 1763, is revealed in a single illuminating flash.

The feud had long been smoldering. With the third decade of the eighteenth century, Northern merchants increasingly had taken to buying their sugar and molasses from the foreign sugar islands. Prices were cheaper by from 25% to 40%: due largely to the fact that the English planters were engaged in a single-

crop exploitative agriculture in the interests of an absentee landlordism, while the French, Spanish, Dutch and Danish planters were owners-operators who cultivated directly their small holdings and diversified their crops; too, the foreign sugar was not encumbered by imposts and mercantilist marketing restrictions. In the foreign sugar islands, as well, Northern ship captains and owners found it possible to develop new markets for their flour, provisions, lumber, work animals and fish, thus obtaining another source from which specie and bills of exchange could be derived.

So heavy had this traffic become that the alarmed British sugar interest in Parliament succeeded in having passed the Molasses Act of 1733, which was designed virtually to outlaw the colonial-foreign island trade. But the act did not have the desired effect because it could not be adequately enforced: the British customs machinery in the colonies was weak and venal and the naval patrols that could be allocated to this duty were inadequate because of England's engagement in foreign wars from 1740 almost continuously for twenty years. . . .

It is not to be wondered that British planters, threatened with bankruptcy, kept up a constant clamor for the enforcement of the laws and the total stoppage of the foreign island trade. Beginning with 1760, imperial England began to tighten the screws with the stricter enforcement of the Acts of Trade and Navigation; from thence on, particularly after France had been compelled to sue for peace in 1763, England embarked on a systematic campaign to wipe out the trade between the Northern Colonies and the foreign West Indies. Northern merchant capital, its most important lifeline cut off, was being strangulated; it is not difficult to see why wealthy merchants of Philadelphia, New York, Boston, Newport and Providence should be converted into revolutionists. . . .

Such were the objective economic factors which resulted in making the position of the colonies, within the framework of the imperial-colonial relations, intolerable. The period of 1763–1775 was one of crisis, economically and politically: for in that decade it was demonstrated that English and colonial merchant capital both could not operate within a contracting sphere in which clashes of interest were becoming sharper and sharper. From 1760 on, pushed by those various groups whose wellbeing had been neglected during the years England was engaged in foreign wars, the rulers of the empire labored mightily to repair the rents that had appeared in the Mercantilist System.

The Northern "smuggling interest" was hunted down vigorously. The admiralty courts and their procedure were augmented and strengthened; placemen in the customs service who were living in England were ordered to their colonial posts; in 1763 the navy was converted into a patrol fleet with power of search even on the high seas; informers were encouraged; and suits involving the seizure of cargoes and the payment of revenues were taken out of the hands of the local courts.

Utilizing the tax measures of 1764 and later (presumably designed to raise a revenue for the defense of the colonies) as a screen, Parliament imposed limitation after limitation upon the activities on the merchants. The Act of 1764 and the Stamp Act of 1765 called for the payment of duties and taxes in specie, thus further draining the colonies of currency and contracting the credit base. To divert colonial capital into raw ma-

terials, the first measure increased the bounties paid for the colonial production of hemp and flax, placed high duties on the colonial importation of foreign indigo, and removed the British import duties on colonial whale fins. To cripple the trade with the foreign West Indies a high duty was placed on refined sugar; while the importation of foreign rum was forbidden altogether and lumber was placed on the enumerated list. To give English manufacturers a firmer grip on their raw materials, hides and skins, pig and bar iron, and potash and pearl ashes were also included among the enumerated articles. To maintain the English monopoly of the colonial-finished goods market the entrance into the colonies of certain kinds of French and Oriental drygoods was taxed for the first time.

In 1764, to weaken further colonial merchant activity, high duties were imposed on wine from the wine islands and wine, fruits and oil from Spain and Portugal brought directly to America (in American ships, as a rule), while such articles brought over from England were to pay only nominal duties. And in 1766, in order to extend the market of English merchants in Europe, Parliament ordered that all remaining non-enumerated articles (largely flour, provisions and fish) bound for European ports north of Cape Finisterre be landed first in England.

It is significant to note that the revenue features of these acts were quickly abandoned: the Stamp tax was repealed in 1766; and, in 1770, three years after their passage, the Townshend duties on paper, paint and glass were lifted. Only the slight tax on tea remained: and even this was used as an instrument to bludgeon the aggressive Northern merchant class into helplessness.

In order to save the East India Company from collapse, in 1773 that powerful financial organization was given permission to ship in its own vessels and dispose of, through its own merchandising agencies, a surplus stock of 17,000,000 pounds of tea in America: and, in this way, drive out of business those Americans who carried, imported and sold in retail channels British tea (and, indeed, foreign tea, for the British tea under the new dispensation could be sold cheaper even than the smuggled Holland article). The merchants all over America were not slow to read the correct significance of this measure. As the distinguished historian Arthur M. Schlesinger has put it, pamphleteers set out to show "that the present project of the East India Company was the entering wedge for larger and more ambitious undertakings calculated to undermine the colonial mercantile world. Their opinion was based on the fact that, in addition to the article of tea, the East India Company imported into England vast quantities of silks, calico and other fabrics, spices, drugs and chinaware, all commodities of staple demand; and on their fear that the success of the present venture would result in an extension of the same principle to the sale of the other articles."

The Southern landlords did not escape. The Proclamation Line of 1763, for the purpose of setting up temporary governments in the far western lands wrested from France after the Seven Years' War, in effect shut off the whole area beyond the crest of the Appalachians to colonial fur traders and land dealers. By taking control of the region out of the hands of the colonial governors, putting it in charge of imperial agents and ordering the abandonment of the settlements already planted, the British looked forward to the maintenance of a great Indian reservation in which the fur trade—in the interests of British concessionaires—would continue to flourish. A few years later these rigorous regulations were relaxed somewhat: but the designs of English land speculators on the area, the prohibition of free land grants, the ordering of land sales at auctions only and the imposition of high quit-rents, hardly improved matters. The planters were lost to the English cause. Their situation, already made perilous by the Currency Act of 1764, was now hopeless.

Thus, merchant capitalists—whether land speculators or traders—were converted from contented and loyal subjects into rebellious enemies of the Crown. Tea was destroyed in Boston harbor, turned back unloaded from New York and Philadelphia, and landed but not sold in Charleston. In 1774 the First Continental Congress, to which came delegates from all the colonies, met and wrote the Continental Association, an embargo agreement, which was so successfully enforced that imports from England virtually disappeared in 1775.

The discontents of planters and merchants, in themselves, were not enough to hasten the releasing process. To be successful, assistance was required from the ranks of the more numerous lower middle class small farmers, traders, artisans and mechanics, and the working class seamen, fishermen and laborers. This was not difficult: for the material well-being of the lower classes was tied to the successful enterprising of the upper.

The colonies had enjoyed a period of unprecedented prosperity during the years of the war with France. The expanding market in the West Indies, the great expenditures of the British quartermasters, the illegal and contraband trade with the enemy forces, all had furnished steady employment for workers on the fleets and in the shipyards and ports and lucrative outlets for the produce of small farmers. But with the end of the war and the passage of the restrictive legislation of 1763 and after, depression had set in to last until 1770. Stringency and bankruptcy everywhere confronted the merchants and big farmers; seamen and laborers were thrown out of work, small tradesmen were compelled to close their shops and small farmers were faced by ruin because of their expanded acreage, a diminished market and heavy fixed charges made particularly onerous as a result of currency contraction. Into the bargain, escape into the frontier zones—always the last refuge of the dispossessed—was shut off as a result of the Proclamation of 1763.

In addition, the colonial petty bourgeoisie groaned under specific class political and economic disabilities. Politically, almost universal disfranchisement, unequal legislative representation for the newer areas and the wide absence of local government placed state power in the hands of a small group of big propertied interests closely identified with the Crown. In colonial America only men of sizable properties could vote and hold office; indeed, before the Revolution, the proportion of potential voters varied from one-sixth to one-fiftieth of the male population in the different colonies. In the economic sphere, the constricting hand of monopoly everywhere was to be found. On the land, the legal institutions of entail and primogeniture checked opportunity for younger sons; engrossing landlords and land speculators (whether they were the Crown, the proprietaries,

absentee owners or the New England "common" land proprietors) prevented the settlement and improvement of small properties; in the South, the tidewater lords would not erect warehouses to encourage tobacco cultivation among the farmers of the up-country; and in New York, inadequate boundary surveys furnished the big manor lords with an easy instrument of oppression over their smaller neighbors. Everywhere, the threat of Indian uprisings, in the interests of the fur trade and the maintenance of land values in the settled regions, filled the days and nights of frontiersmen with dread.

In the towns, small tradesmen and mechanics and artisans were compelled to struggle unequally against the great merchant interests. Peddlers were submitted to close regulation and forced to pay high license fees. It was impossible to maintain city markets for long, because small merchants here tended to compete successfully with the big ones. In New England, a small company of candlers had got the whole whaling industry in its grip and not only choked off the competition of the lesser manufacturers but fixed the prices for the basic raw material. In New York, and undoubtedly in the other urban communities as well, opportunities to obtain the freedom of the city—which meant the right to engage in certain occupations, whether as tradesmen or artisans—were very severely restricted.

Men of little property were weighed down by debts and oppressed by an inadequate currency; they were forced to support, in many of the colonies, an established church; and they were at the mercy of arbitrary executive and judicial authority. On many sides, too, they saw looming larger and larger the threat of a slave economy to the free institutions of small properties and independent craftsmen. These were the persons who constituted the left-wing of the colonial revolutionary host.

Such was the concentration of colonial forces that made possible the challenging of the power of Great Britain; and the American Revolution proceeded inexorably through the preliminary stages of discussion and illegal organization into the revolutionary one of armed resistance.

In his major work, *Middle-Class Democracy and the Revolution in Massachusetts, 1691–1780*, ROBERT E. BROWN (b. 1907), who taught at Michigan State University, takes issue with the Progressive historians who hold that the Revolution was an "internal revolution" over who should rule at home. According to Brown, prewar Massachusetts represented a middle-class democracy in action, and the purpose of the Revolution was to preserve the existing social order, not to change it. How does Brown's thesis that there was no "internal revolution" influence his interpretation of the imperial relations between the colonies and mother country?*

Robert E. Brown

The Neo-Conservative Interpretation

For the past fifty years or more a thesis has been current in the teaching and writing of American history, political science, and literature that the society which produced the American Revolution and the federal Constitution was not a democratic society. There are differences of opinion as to just how undemocratic this society was, but in general the point is usually made that even though eighteenth-century America was more democratic than Europe, democracy as we know it did not arrive in this country until the time of Andrew Jackson.

This concept of an undemocratic society is based on two major assumptions: one, that property qualifications for voting eliminated a large portion of the free adult male population from participation in political affairs; the other, that inequitable representation heavily favored the older aristocratic commercial areas along the seacoast at the expense of the more recently settled inland agricultural areas. Hence it followed naturally that colonial political and economic life was dominated by the upper economic classes.

Writers who accept the thesis that colonial society was undemocratic have also generally followed the interpretation that the American Revolution was a "dual" revolution. On one hand, there was the conflict between Great Britain and her American colonies—what might be called the "War for Independence."

*From Robert E. Brown, *Middle-Class Democracy and the Revolution in Massachusetts, 1691–1780* (Ithaca, N.Y., 1955), pp. v–vii, 401–408. Copyright 1955 by the American Historical Association, used with permission of Cornell University Press.

But accompanying this, and of equal or perhaps greater significance, was a struggle within the colonies over which class would dominate economic and political life. According to this theory, the second phase of the conflict, which might well be designated the "American Revolution" to distinguish it from the "War of Independence," was primarily an effort by the unenfranchised and dissatisfied lower classes to gain economic, political, and social equality with their betters.

Both the "War of Independence" and the "American Revolution" succeeded to a greater or lesser extent in their objectives, according to most writers. The first won political independence for the colonies from Great Britain, although economic independence was not achieved until the War of 1812. The second succeeded by the elimination of colonial ruling classes, or a reduction in their power, and by the elevation of the "common man" to a position of importance in society which he had not hitherto enjoyed. This was reflected in the elimination or diminution of such manifestations of aristocratic domination as property qualifications for voting, inequitable representation, established churches, and entail and primogeniture in the distribution of inheritances. Later, aristocratic upper classes staged a "counterrevolution" by putting over a conservative Constitution on the people, and it was not really until the time of Andrew Jackson that democracy came fully into its own.

In the following pages I have raised some questions about this accepted interpretation as it applies to one colony and state, Massachusetts from 1691 to 1780. Did an upper economic class control economic life in the colony? Were property qualifications for voting sufficiently high to exclude an important number of adult men from participation in politics? Is the "American Revolution" interpretation a valid one, and if not, what part did democracy play in the "War for Independence?" And did the Revolution result in social changes in the state of Massachusetts significant enough to justify the concept of an "internal revolt"?

In the process of gathering material for this work, I have also seen sufficient evidence to suggest the need for reconsideration of assumptions with regard to other colonies as well as to Massachusetts. . . .

* * *

In Massachusetts . . . we find one of the unique "revolutions" in world history—a revolution to preserve a social order rather than to change it. It was not, as we have often assumed, a dual revolution in which Americans won their independence from the British on one hand, and in which unenfranchised and underprivileged lower classes wrested democratic rights from a privileged local aristocracy on the other.

To understand what happened, we must first have a clear picture of Massachusetts society. Economically speaking, it was a middle-class society in which property was easily acquired and in which a large portion of the people were property-owning farmers. There was undoubtedly more economic democracy for the common man then than there is now. A large permanent labor class was practically nonexistent; men could either acquire land and become farmers or work for themselves as skilled artisans. If we insist that Americans who came to this country brought their accustomed class or caste lines with them, we must do so in the face of all the evidence to the contrary. If there was anything that observers at the time agreed on, it was that American society was almost the exact opposite of European society. There was nothing approaching the spread between the rich and the poor that Europe had at that time or that we have at present; a much larger proportion of society owned property then than now. Yet today, many people, even including many laborers, look on American society as predominantly middle-class though the opportunity for almost universal ownership of property is far less now than it was before the Revolution.

Economic opportunity, or economic democracy, in turn contributed to political democracy. While it is true that property ownership was a prerequisite for province and town voting, it is also true that the amount of property required for the franchise was very small and that the great majority of men could easily meet the requirements. There were probably a few men who could not qualify for voting, but the number could not have been very large. We cannot condone the practice of excluding even those few, but we should try to place the unenfranchised in their proper perspective. It makes a tremendous difference in our understanding of colonial society whether 95 per cent of the men were disfranchised or only 5 per cent. Furthermore, representation was apportioned in such a way that the farmers, not a merchant aristocracy, had complete control of the legislature.

It is not enough to say that the people of Massachusetts perhaps had more democracy than the people of Europe, but that they still did not have what we call democracy today. Neither is it sufficient to say that the germs of democracy were present, or that democracy, as a growing process if not as a reality, could be found in colonial times. When Hutchinson said that anything that looked like a man was a voter and that policy in general was dictated by the lower classes, he was certainly using the term "democracy" as we mean it now. A Hutchinson might deplore the view that government existed for the benefit of the people and that the people were to decide when government had served its proper functions, but this is the democratic idea. He might also deplore the fact that the people not only elected their representatives but also told them how to vote, yet this, too, is democracy.

In many respects, the people of Massachusetts had a government more responsive to the popular will than we have at the present time. There were far more representatives in proportion to population than we now have, and the representatives were more responsible to their constituents for their actions than are legislators at present. If a man votes against his belief to please his constituents so that he can hold his elected position, we cannot demand much more of democracy.

The number of men who could vote in the colony must not be confused with the number who did vote. These are entirely different problems, for the fact that there was much indifference on election day did not mean that many men could not participate. If we are attempting to explain events in terms of class conflict or internal revolution, it is especially important that we do not confuse the unfranchised and the disinterested. It is one thing if a man wants the vote but cannot meet the property requirements; it is another if he has the vote but fails to use it. Neither should we confuse the issue by giving percentages of voters in terms of the entire population, for probably less than 20 per cent of the people in colonial times were adult men.

In addition to economics and politics, there were also other manifestations of democracy in colonial Massachusetts.

The system of education was, for its day, undoubtedly the best provided for the common people anywhere, and the correct comparison is with other educational systems at the time, not with our own. Many democratic practices were used in the operation of the Congregational church, and again we should remember that some 98 per cent of the people were Congregationalists. Furthermore, the Congregational church was not established as it was in England. Men who belonged to other churches did not pay taxes to the Congregational church; education and political office were open to those who were not Congregationalists. Perhaps there was not the complete religious freedom—or religious indifference—that we now associate with a liberal society, but there was also little dissatisfaction with religion to contribute to internal conflict. Even the colonial militia was democratic in its organization and in the influence which it exerted on politics.

In brief, Massachusetts did not have a social order before the American Revolution which would breed sharp internal class conflicts. The evidence does not justify an interpretation of the Revolution in Massachusetts as an internal class conflict designed to achieve additional political, economic, and social democracy. Although democracy was important as a factor in the conflict, it was a democracy which had already arrived in the colony long before 1776.

If we turn to British-American relations, however, we do not need to search long to find areas of conflict. The British for many years had developed a mercantilist-imperialist colonial system that had not functioned as expected. The aim of the system, as men at the time frankly admitted, was the ultimate benefit of the mother country. They believed that colonies should be regulated, both economically and politically, to further the well-being of the parent state. British officials were fully aware of the shortcomings in colonial administration, but, until 1760, Britain was not in a favorable position to remedy these defects. British officials were also fully aware of the fact that colonial democracy was one of the chief obstacles to effective enforcement of British colonial policy.

These two ingredients—an effective middle-class democracy and British imperial policies which had been thwarted by this democracy—explain what happened in Massachusetts from 1760 to 1776. In order to make their colonial system effective, the British believed that they had to recover authority over colonial officials. This, in turn, called for a colonial revenue which would be administered by Parliament, especially to pay the salaries of colonial officials and thus remove them from under the dominating influence of colonial assemblies. But of course the assembly of Massachusetts was fully aware of the power which control of the purse conferred and was equally determined to retain this power over British officials.

Throughout the story runs another thread—the threat, or at least what the British considered the threat, of colonial independence. This gave an air of urgency to British measures. There was the frequently expressed fear that time was on the side of the colonists. A rapidly growing population, bolstered by a phenomenal birthrate due to economic opportunity and by immigrants attracted by economic and political democracy, posed the problem to the British of recovering authority before the colonies became too large. When the showdown came with the Tea Act and the Coercive Acts, there was no doubt whatever that the British intended to curtail colonial democracy as a necessary step toward recovery of British authority and the prevention of colonial independence. The result was the very thing the British had tried to prevent—American independence.

Obviously democracy played an important part in the events before 1776, not as a condition to be achieved but as a reality which interfered with British policies. If the British had been successful, there would undoubtedly have been much less democracy in Massachusetts —hence the interpretation that the Revolution was designed to *preserve* a social order rather than to change it. We search in vain for evidence of class conflict that was serious enough to justify revolution; we do not have to look far for copious quantities of proof that colonial society was democratic and that the colonists were attempting to prevent British innovations.

Furthermore, the results of the Revolution more than confirm the interpretation presented here. There is a logic to what happened after the Revolution —or perhaps it would be more accurate to say what did not happen—if we accept the fact that the people of Massachusetts were not conducting an internal revolution. We are not confronted with the contradiction, which most writers fail to resolve, of a social revolution which was presumably successful but which failed to achieve social change. Why would a people, who were supposedly demanding a more democratic government, adopt a constitution which restricted democracy even more than it had been restricted in colonial days? On the other hand, the Massachusetts Constitution of 1780 was a logical consequence of a middle-class society which believed in the protection of property

because most men were property owners. The almost complete absence of social revolution in Massachusetts should stand as convincing evidence that internal social revolution was not one of the chief aims of the American Revolution as far as the people of Massachusetts were concerned.

It is not necessary to explain whatever conservatism existed in colonial times in terms of a limited electorate. There is implied in this approach an assumption that universal suffrage will result in increased liberalism, but this is not necessarily so. The elections of 1920, 1924, 1928, and even 1952, when women as well as men had the vote, should convince us that "the people" can and do vote for conservatism. If the people of Massachusetts believed that a man should own property to be a voter or that an official should be a Protestant to be elected to office, they might well vote for both propositions and not be out of character. And since most men in Massachusetts were Protestants and property owners, the fact that both property and religious qualifications found their way into the Constitution of 1780 should not be surprising.

We do not need a "conservative counterrevolution" or a thermidorean reaction to explain either the Massachusetts Constitution of 1780 or the adoption of the federal Constitution in 1788. If there was no "social revolution," there could hardly be a "conservative counterrevolution." Both constitutions must be explained in terms of a middle-class society in which most men could vote.

In recent years it has been frequently said that the British did not intend to tyrannize the colonies by the policies which they adopted. Colonists thought otherwise, however, and judging by the material presented in these chapters, one might suspect that many British policies looked like tyranny to them. Perhaps we of today would also consider as tyranny trials without juries, instructions by the king which were supposed to be law, taxation by a people who were considered foreigners, a declaration by the Parliament of these same "foreign people" that it had the power to legislate in all cases whatsoever, appointed governors who could dissolve assemblies or determine town meetings, and navigation acts regulating colonial trade in British interests. It would be interesting to speculate on the reaction of a modern oleomargarine manufacturer whose suit against the butter interests was to be tried in Wisconsin by a jury of Wisconsin dairy farmers presided over by a judge appointed by the governor of Wisconsin. This hypothetical case might seem exaggerated, but it is not too far removed from the attitude expressed by colonists toward their relations with the British. The fact is that colonists looked on British measures as tyrannical, and if we are going to explain colonial actions, we must consider the colonial point of view.

How should we rate in importance the various factors that entered into this British-American war? That, of course, is difficult to answer, but it is not so difficult to say that many items contributed and that some were probably more important to some individuals than to others.

There is no doubt that economic motives were fundamental. That Americans would oppose a mercantilist system which they considered inimical to their interests should not be surprising. After all, they looked on many British regulations as simply devices by which some segments of the Empire were favored at the expense of other segments. The tax program also had its economic side, for as

many men said, a mother country which could collect a stamp tax could also tax a man's land, his cattle, or his home. Undoubtedly, too, the threat of monopoly contained in the Tea Act had its economic influence. In fact, a middle-class society would almost inevitably place great emphasis on property and its economic interests, a fact which is only too apparent in the sources. The importance of economic factors, however, did not lie in their contribution to class conflict as a cause of the American Revolution.

But economic elements were not the only forces making for revolution. Equally significant was the fact that Massachusetts had long been accustomed to democratic government and intended to maintain its accustomed system. Politics inevitably include economics, since economic subjects are some of the most important items in politics, but not all politics is economic. The very fact that people govern their own destinies is important in itself. As one old soldier of the Revolution put it, the British intended to govern the Americans and the Americans did not intend that they should. To a people accustomed to the democracy both of province and town affairs, the danger inherent in British imperial controls was far more than a mere threat. When the common people talked of dying for their liberties or pledging their lives and property for the defense of their liberties, they were not dealing in abstractions; and they would not have talked in this way if their society had been dominated by a merchant aristocracy.

Neither can religious democracy be ignored as a factor in the Revolution. We must remember that the people of Massachusetts were accustomed to a church organization which lived by democratic procedures and opposition to the

Church of England. We must not forget, either, that many people at the time considered religion more important than politics. The threat that the British might impose the Church of England on them and enforce conformity was not a threat to be taken lightly. As many of them often said, religious and political freedom were inextricably connected and would rise or fall together. Little wonder, then, that the Congregational clergy supported the Revolution almost to a man.

This study of Massachusetts raises some rather serious questions about our interpretation of colonial society and the Revolution in other colonies. Were the other colonies as undemocratic as we have supposed them to be? Was their economic and social life dominated by a coastal aristocracy of planters in the South and merchants in the North? How was property distributed? Exactly how many men could meet the voting qualifi-

cations? Was representation restricted in such a way that conservative areas could dominate the legislature? These are questions for which we need well-documented answers before we interpret the colonial and revolutionary periods with any assurance of accuracy.

Evidence which has turned up in the course of this study suggests that Massachusetts was not fundamentally different from the other colonies and states. If so —and the idea is certainly worth extensive investigation—we might be forced to make some drastic revisions in our interpretation of American history before 1830. Perhaps we will find in America as a whole, as in Massachusetts, that American democracy as we know it goes far deeper than the election of 1828 and that the "common man" in this country had come into his own long before the era of Jacksonian Democracy.

BERNARD BAILYN (b. 1922) of Harvard University is generally regarded as the outstanding scholar representing the view of the Revolution as an ideological movement. His book, *The Ideological Origins of the American Revolution*, from which this selection is drawn, has been the single most influential work in recent years to relate the role of ideas to the coming, conduct, and outcome of the Revolution. Bailyn believes that the Revolution was radical in nature, but what does he mean by his statement: "The radicalism the Americans conveyed to the world in 1776 was a transformed as well as a transforming force"?*

Bernard Bailyn

Ideological Origins of the Revolution

The full bibliography of pamphlets relating to the Anglo-American struggle published in the colonies through the year 1776 contains not a dozen or so items but over four hundred. . . . The pamphlets include all sorts of writings— treatises on political theory, essays on history, political arguments, sermons, correspondence, poems—and they display all sorts of literary devices. But for all their variety they have in common one distinctive characteristic: they are, to an unusual degree, *explanatory*. They reveal not merely positions taken but the reasons why positions were taken; they reveal motive and understanding: the assumptions, beliefs, and ideas—the articulated world view—that lay behind the manifest events of the time. As a result I found myself . . . studying not simply a particular medium of publication but, through these documents, nothing less than the ideological origins of the American Revolution. And I found myself viewing these origins with surprise, for the "interior" view, from the vantage point of the pamphlets, was different from what I had expected. The task, consequently, took on an increasing excitement, for much of the history of the American Revolution has fallen into the condition that overtakes so many of the great events of the past; it is, as Professor Trevor-Roper has written in another connection, taken for granted: "By our explanations, interpretations, assumptions we gradually make it seem automatic, natural, inevitable; we remove from it the sense of wonder, the unpredictability, and therefore the freshness it ought to have." Study of the pamphlets appeared to lead back into the unpredictable reality of the Revolution, and posed a variety of new problems of interpretation. . . .

Study of the pamphlets confirmed my rather old-fashioned view that the American Revolution was above all else an ideological, constitutional, political struggle and not primarily a controversy between social groups undertaken to force changes in the organization of the society or the economy. It confirmed too my belief that intellectual developments in the decade before Independence led to a radical idealization and conceptualization of the previous century and a half of American experience, and that it was this intimate relationship between Revolutionary thought and the circumstances of life in eighteenth-century America that endowed the Revolution with its peculiar force and made it so profoundly a transforming event. But if the pamphlets confirmed this belief, they filled it with unexpected details and gave it new meaning. They shed new light on the question of the sources and character of Revolutionary thought. Most commonly the thought of the Revolution has been seen simply as an expression of the natural rights philosophy: the ideas of the social contract, inalienable rights, natural law, and the contractual basis of government. But some have denounced this interpretation as "obtuse secularism," and, reading the sermons of the time with acute sensitivity, argue that it was only a respect for world opinion that led the Founders to put their case "in

the restricted language of the rational century," and that the success of the Revolutionary movement is comprehensible only in terms of the continuing belief in original sin and the need for grace. Yet others have described the sermons of the time as a form of deliberate propaganda by which revolutionary ideas were fobbed off on an unsuspecting populace by a "black regiment" of clergy committed, for reasons unexplained, to the idea of rebellion. And still others deny the influence of both Enlightenment theory and theology, and view the Revolution as no revolution at all, but rather as a conservative movement wrought by practitioners of the common law and devoted to preserving it, and the ancient liberties embedded in it, intact.

The pamphlets do reveal the influence of Enlightenment thought, and they do show the effective force of certain religious ideas, of the common law, and also of classical literature; but they reveal most significantly the close integration of these elements in a pattern of, to me at least, surprising design—surprising because of the prominence in it of still another tradition, interwoven with, yet still distinct from, these more familiar strands of thought. This distinctive influence had been transmitted most directly to the colonists by a group of early eighteenth-century radical publicists and opposition politicians in England who carried forward into the eighteenth century and applied to the politics of the age of Walpole the peculiar strain of anti-authoritarianism bred in the upheaval of the English Civil War. . . .

It was in the context of the sources and patterns of ideas . . . that I began to see a new meaning in phrases that I, like most historians, had readily dismissed as mere rhetoric and propaganda: "slavery," "corruption," "conspiracy." These inflammatory words were used so forcefully by writers of so great a variety of social statuses, political positions, and religious persuasions; they fitted so logically into the pattern of radical and opposition thought; and they reflected so clearly the realities of life in an age in which monarchical autocracy flourished, in which the stability and freedom of England's "mixed" constitution was a recent and remarkable achievement, and in which the fear of conspiracy against constituted authority was built into the very structure of politics, that I began to suspect that they meant something very real to both the writers and their readers: that there were real fears, real anxieties, a sense of real danger behind these phrases, and not merely the desire to influence by rhetoric and propaganda the inert minds of an otherwise passive populace. The more I read, the less useful, it seemed to me, was the whole idea of propaganda in its modern meaning when applied to the writings of the American Revolution—a view that I hope to develop at length on another occasion. In the end I was convinced that the fear of a comprehensive conspiracy against liberty throughout the English-speaking world— a conspiracy believed to have been nourished in corruption, and of which, it was felt, oppression in America was only the most immediately visible part— lay at the heart of the Revolutionary movement. . . .

Beyond all of this, however, I found in the pamphlets evidence of a transformation that overtook the inheritance of political and social thought as it had been received in the colonies by the early 1760's. Indeliberately, half-knowingly, as responses not to desire but to the logic of the situation, the leaders of colonial thought in the years before Independence forced forward alterations in, or challenged, major concepts and assumptions of eighteenth-century political theory. They reached—then, before 1776, in the debate on the problem of imperial relations—new territories of thought upon which would be built the commanding structures of the first state constitutions and of the Federal Constitution. . . . Finally there was evidence that this transformation of thought, which led to conclusions so remarkably congruent with the realities of American life, was powerfully contagious. It affected areas not directly involved in the Anglo-American controversy, areas as gross as the institution of chattel slavery and as subtle as the assumptions of human relations. . . .

At no point did I attempt to describe all shades of opinion on any of the problems discussed. I decided at the start to present what I took to be the dominant or leading ideas of those who made the Revolution. There were of course articulate and outspoken opponents of the Revolution, and at times I referred to their ideas; but the future lay not with them but with the leaders of the Revolutionary movement, and it is their thought at each stage of the developing rebellion that I attempted to present, using often the shorthand phrase "the colonists" to refer to them and their ideas. . . .

My own subsequent work on early eighteenth-century politics and political thought[1] led me to uncover a deeper and broader documentation of the story; . . . it led me, too, to see deeper implications in the story than those I had been able to see before. In this subsequent and separate study of early eighteenth-century politics and political theory I discovered that the configuration of ideas and attitudes I

---

[1] For Bailyn's subsequent study, see *Origins of American Politics* (New York, 1968).—Ed.

had described ... as the Revolutionary ideology could be found intact—completely formed—as far back as the 1730's; in partial form it could be found even farther back, at the turn of the seventeenth century. The transmission from England to America of the literature of political opposition that furnished the substance of the ideology of the Revolution had been so swift in the early years of the eighteenth century as to seem almost instantaneous; and, for reasons that reach into the heart of early American politics, these ideas acquired in the colonies an importance, a relevance in politics, they did not then have—and never would have—in England itself. There was no sharp break between a placid pre-Revolutionary era and the turmoil of the 1760's and 1770's. The argument, the claims and counter-claims, the fears and apprehensions that fill the pamphlets, letters, newspapers, and state papers of the Revolutionary years had in fact been heard throughout the century. The problem no longer appeared to me to be simply why there was a Revolution but how such an explosive amalgam of politics and ideology first came to be compounded, why it remained so potent through years of surface tranquillity, and why, finally, it was detonated when it was. ...

It was an elevating, transforming vision: a new, fresh, vigorous, and above all morally regenerate people rising from obscurity to defend the battlements of liberty and then in triumph standing forth, heartening and sustaining the cause of freedom everywhere. In the light of such a conception everything about the colonies and their controversy with the mother country took on a new appearance. Provincialism was gone: Americans stood side by side with the heroes of historic battles for freedom and with the few remaining champions of liberty in the present. What were once felt to be defects—isolation, institutional simplicity, primitiveness of manners, multiplicity of religions, weakness in the authority of the state—could now be seen as virtues, not only by Americans themselves but by enlightened spokesmen of reform, renewal, and hope wherever they might be—in London coffeehouses, in Parisian *salons,* in the courts of German princes. The mere existence of the colonists suddenly became philosophy teaching by example. Their manners, their morals, their way of life, their physical, social, and political condition were seen to vindicate eternal truths and to demonstrate, as ideas and words never could, the virtues of the heavenly city of the eighteenth-century philosophers.

But the colonists' ideas and words counted too, and not merely because they repeated as ideology the familiar utopian phrases of the Enlightenment and of English libertarianism. What they were saying by 1776 was familiar in a general way to reformers and illuminati everywhere in the Western world; yet it was different. Words and concepts had been reshaped in the colonists' minds in the course of a decade of pounding controversy—strangely reshaped, turned in unfamiliar directions, toward conclusions they could not themselves clearly perceive. They found a new world of political thought as they struggled to work out the implications of their beliefs in the years before Independence. It was a world not easily possessed; often they withdrew in some confusion to more familiar ground. But they touched its boundaries, and, at certain points, probed its interior. Others, later—writing and revising the first state constitutions, drafting and ratifying the federal constitution, and debating in detail, exhaustively, the merits of these efforts —would resume the search for resolutions of the problems the colonists had broached before 1776.

This critical probing of traditional concepts—part of the colonists' effort to express reality as they knew it and to shape it to ideal ends—became the basis for all further discussions of enlightened reform, in Europe as well as in America. The radicalism the Americans conveyed to the world in 1776 was a transformed as well as a transforming force. . . .

In no obvious sense was the American Revolution undertaken as a social revolution. No one, that is, deliberately worked for the destruction or even the substantial alteration of the order of society as it had been known. Yet it was transformed as a result of the Revolution, and not merely because Loyalist property was confiscated and redistributed, or because the resulting war destroyed the economic bases of some people's lives and created opportunities for others that would not otherwise have existed. Seizure of Loyalist property and displacements in the economy did in fact take place, and the latter if not the former does account for a spurt in social mobility that led earlier arrivés to remark, "When the pot boils, the scum will rise." Yet these were superficial changes; they affected a small part of the population only, and they did not alter the organization of society.

What did now affect the essentials of social organization—what in time would help permanently to transform them— were changes in the realm of belief and attitude. The views men held toward the relationships that bound them to each other—the discipline and pattern of society—moved in a new direction in the decade before Independence.

Americans of 1760 continued to assume, as had their predecessors for generations before, that a healthy society was a hierarchical society, in which it was natural for some to be rich and some poor, some honored and some obscure, some powerful and some weak. And it was believed that superiority was unitary, that the attributes of the favored—wealth, wisdom, power—had a natural affinity to each other, and hence that political leadership would naturallly rest in the hands of the social leaders. Movement, of course, there would be: some would fall and some would rise; but manifest, external differences among men, reflecting the principle of hierarchical order, were necessary and proper, and would remain; they were intrinsic to the nature of things.

Circumstances had pressed harshly against such assumptions. The wilderness environment from the beginning had threatened the maintenance of elaborate social distinctions; many of them in the passage of time had in fact been worn away. Puritanism, in addition, and the epidemic evangelicalism of the mid-eighteenth century, had created challenges to the traditional notions of social stratification by generating the conviction that the ultimate quality of men was to be found elsewhere than in their external condition, and that a cosmic achievement lay within each man's grasp. And the peculiar configuration of colonial politics—a constant broil of petty factions struggling almost formlessly, with little discipline or control, for the benefits of public authority—had tended to erode the respect traditionally accorded the institutions and officers of the state.

Yet nowhere, at any time in the colonial years, were the implications of these circumstances articulated or justified. The assumption remained that society, in its maturity if not in its confused infancy, would conform to the pattern of the past;

that authority would continue to exist without challenge, and that those in superior positions would be responsible and wise, and those beneath them respectful and content. These premises and expectations were deeply lodged; they were not easily or quickly displaced. But the Revolution brought with it arguments and attitudes bred of arguments endlessly repeated, that undermined these premises of the *ancien régime*.

For a decade or more defiance to the highest constituted powers poured from the colonial presses and was hurled from half the pulpits of the land. The right, the need, the absolute obligation to disobey legally constituted authority had become the universal cry. Cautions and qualifications became ritualistic: formal exercises in ancient pieties. One might preface one's charge to disobedience with homilies on the inevitable imperfections of all governments and the necessity to bear "some injuries" patiently and peaceably. But what needed and received demonstration and defense was not the caution, but the injunction: the argument that when injuries touched on "fundamental rights" (and who could say when they did not?) then nothing less than "duty to God and religion, to themselves, to the community, and to unborn posterity require such to assert and defend their rights by all lawful, most prudent, and effectual means in their power." Obedience as a principle was only too well known; disobedience as a doctrine was not. It was therefore asserted again and again that resistance to constituted authority was "a doctrine according to godliness—the doctrine of the English nation . . . by which our rights and constitution have often been defended and repeatedly rescued out of the hands of encroaching tyranny . . . This is the doctrine and grand pillar of the ever memorable and glorious Rev-

olution, and upon which our gracious sovereign George III holds the crown of the British empire." What better credentials could there be? How lame to add that obedience too "is an eminent part of Christian duty without which government must disband and dreadful anarchy and confusion (with all its horrors) take place and reign without control"—how lame, especially in view of the fact that one could easily mistake this "Christian obedience" for that "blind, enslaving obedience which is no part of the Christian institution but is highly injurious to religion, to every free government, and to the good of mankind, and is the stirrup of tyranny, and grand engine of slavery."

Defiance to constituted authority leaped like a spark from one flammable area to another, growing in heat as it went. Its greatest intensification took place in the explosive atmosphere of local religious dissent. Isaac Backus spoke only for certain of the Baptists and Congregational Separates and against the presumptive authority of ministers, when, in the course of an attack on the religious establishment in Massachusetts, he warned that

we are not to obey and follow [ministers] in an implicit or customary way, but each one must consider and follow others no further than they see that the end of their conversation is Jesus Christ the same yesterday, and today, and forever more . . . People are so far from being under obligation to follow teachers who don't lead in this way they incur guilt by such a following of them.

It took little imagination on the part of Backus' readers and listeners to find in this a general injunction against uncritical obedience to authority in any form. Others were even more explicit. The Baptist preacher who questioned not merely the authority of the local orthodox church but the very "etymology of the word [orthodoxy]" assured the world that the colonists

have as just a right, before GOD and man, to oppose King, ministry, Lords, and Commons of England when they violate their rights as Americans as they have to oppose any foreign enemy; and that this is no more, according to the law of nature, to be deemed rebellion than it would be to oppose the King of France, supposing him now present invading the land.

But what to the Baptists was the establishment, to Anglicans was dissent. From the establishment in New England, ever fearful of ecclesiastical impositions from without, came as strong a current of anti-authoritarianism as from the farthest left-wing sect. It was a pillar of the temple, a scion of the church, and an apologist for New England's standing order who sweepingly disclaimed "all human authority in matters of faith and worship. We regard neither pope nor prince as head of the church, nor acknowledge that any Parliaments have power to enact articles of doctrine or forms of discipline or modes of worship or terms of church communion," and, declaring that "we are accountable to none but *Christ*"—words that had struck at the heart of every establishment, civil and religious, since the fall of Rome—concluded with the apparent paradox that *"liberty* is the *fundamental* principle of our establishment."

In such declarations a political argument became a moral imperative. The principle of justifiable disobedience and the instinct to question public authority before accepting it acquired a new sanction and a new vigor. Originally, of course, the doctrine of resistance was applied to Parliament, a nonrepresentative assembly 3,000 miles away. But the composition and location of the institution had not been as crucial in creating opposition as has the character of the actions

Parliament had taken. Were provincial assemblies, simply because they were local and representative, exempt from scrutiny and resistance? Were they any less susceptible than Parliament to the rule that when their authority is extended beyond "the bounds of the law of God and the free constitution . . . 'their acts are, *ipso facto*, void, and cannot oblige any to obedience'"? There could be no doubt of the answer. Any legislature, wherever located or however composed, deserved only the obedience it could command by the justice and wisdom of its proceedings. Representative or not, local or not, any agency of the state could be defied. The freeholders of Augusta, Virginia, could not have been more explicit in applying to local government in 1776 the defiance learned in the struggle with Parliament. They wrote their delegates to Virginia's Provincial Congress that

should the future conduct of our legislative body prove to you that our opinion of their wisdom and justice is ill-grounded, then tell them that your constituents are neither guided nor will ever be influenced by that slavish maxim in politics, "that whatever is enacted by that body of men in whom the supreme power of the state is vested must in all cases be obeyed," and that they firmly believe attempts to repeal an unjust law can be vindicated beyond a simple remonstrance addressed to the legislators.

But such threats as these were only the most obvious ways in which traditional notions of authority came into question. Others were more subtly subversive, silently sapping the traditional foundations of social orders and discipline.

"Rights" obviously lay at the heart of the Anglo-American controversy: the rights of Englishmen, the rights of mankind, chartered rights. But *"rights,"* wrote Richard Bland—that least egalitarian of

Revolutionary leaders—"imply *equality* in the instances to which they belong and must be treated without respect to the dignity of the persons concerned in them." This was by no means simply a worn cliché, for while "equality before the law" was a commonplace of the time, "equality without respect to the dignity of the persons concerned" was not; its emphasis on social equivalence was significant, and though in its immediate context the remark was directed to the invidious distinctions believed to have been drawn between Englishmen and Americans its broader applicability was apparent. Others seized upon it, and developed it, especially in the fluid years of transition when new forms of government were being sought to replace those believed to have proved fatal to liberty. "An affectation of rank" and "the assumed distinction of 'men of consequence'" had been the blight of the Proprietary party, a Pennsylvania pamphleteer wrote in 1776. Riches in a new country like America signified nothing more than the accident of prior settlement. The accumulation of wealth had been "unavoidable to the descendants of the early settlers" since the land, originally cheap, had appreciated naturally with the growth of settlement.

Perhaps it is owing to this accidental manner of becoming rich that wealth does not obtain the same degree of influence here which it does in old countries. Rank, at present, in America is derived more from qualification than property; a sound moral character, amiable manners, and firmness in principle constitute the first class, and will continue to do so till the origin of families be forgotten, and the proud follies of the old world overrun the simplicity of the new.

Therefore, under the new dispensation, "no reflection ought to be made on any man on account of birth, provided that his manners rises decently with his circumstances, and that he affects not to forget the level he came from."

The idea was, in its very nature, corrosive to the traditional authority of magistrates and of established institutions. And it activated other, similar thoughts whose potential threat to stability lay till then inert. There was no more familiar notion in eighteenth-century political thought—it was propounded in every tract on government and every ministerial exhortation to the civil magistracy—than that those who wield power were "servants of society" as well as "ministers of God," and as such had to be specially qualified: they must be acquainted with the affairs of men; they must have wisdom, knowledge, prudence; and they must be men of virtue and true religion. But how far should one go with this idea? The doctrine that the qualifications for magistracy were moral, spiritual, and intellectual could lead to conflict with the expectation that public leaders would be people of external dignity and social superiority; it could be dangerous to the establishment in any settled society. For the ancient notion that leadership must devolve on men whose "personal authority and greatness," whose "eminence or nobility," were such that "every man subordinate is ready to yield a willing submission without contempt or repining"—ordinary people not easily conceding to an authority "conferred upon a mean man . . . no better than selected out of their own rank"—this traditional notion had never been repudiated, was still honored and repeated. But now, in the heated atmosphere of incipient rebellion, the idea of leaders as servants of the people was pushed to its logical extreme, and its subversive potentialities revealed. By 1774 it followed from the belief that "lawful rulers are the servants of the people" that they were "exalted above their brethren not for their own sakes, but for the benefit of the people; and submission is yielded, not on account of their persons considered exclusively on the authority they are clothed with, but of those laws which in the exercise of this authority are made by them conformably to the laws of nature and equity." In the distribution of offices, it was said in 1770, "merit only in the candidate" should count—not birth, or wealth, or loyalty to the great; but merit only. Even a deliberately judicious statement of this theme rang with defiance to traditional forms of authority: "It is not wealth—it is not family—it is not either of these alone, nor both of them together, though I readily allow neither is to be disregarded, that will qualify men for important seats in government, unless they are rich and honorable in other and more important respects." Indeed, one could make a complete inversion and claim that, properly, the external affluence of magistrates should be the consequence of, not the prior qualification for, the judicious exercise of public authority over others.

Where would it end? Two generations earlier, in the fertile seedtime of what would become the Revolutionary ideology, the ultimate subversiveness of the arguments advanced by "the men of the rights" had already been glimpsed. "The sum of the matter betwixt Mr. Hoadly and me," the Jacobite, High Church polemicist Charles Leslie had written in 1711, is this:

I think it most natural that *authority* should *descend*, that is, be *derived* from a *superior* to an *inferior*, from *God* to *fathers* and *kings*, and from *kings* and *fathers* to *sons* and *servants*. But Mr. Hoadly would have it *ascend* from *sons* to *fathers* and from *subjects* to *sovereigns*, nay to *God* himself, whose *kingship* the men of the *rights* say is *derived* to *Him*

from the *people!* And the *argument* does naturally carry it all that *way*. For if *authority* does *ascend*, it must *ascend* to the *height*.

By 1774 it seemed undeniable to many, uninvolved in or hostile to the Revolutionary effort, that declarations "before GOD . . . that it is no rebellion to oppose any king, ministry, or governor [who] destroys by any violence or authority whatever the rights of the people" threatened the most elemental principles of order and discipline in society. A group of writers, opposed not merely to the politics of resistance but to the effect it would have on the primary linkages of society— on that patterning of human relations that distinguishes a civilized community from a primitive mob—attempted to recall to the colonists the lessons of the past, the wisdom, as they thought of it, of the ages. Citing adages and principles that once had guided men's thoughts on the structure of society; equating all communities, and England's empire in particular, with families; quoting generously from Filmer if not from Leslie; and explaining that anarchy results when social inferiors claim political authority, they argued, with increasing anxiety, that the essence of social stability was being threatened by the political agitation of the time. Their warnings, full of nostalgia for ancient certainties, were largely ignored. But in the very extremism of their reaction to the events of the time there lies a measure of the distance Revolutionary thought had moved from an old to a very new world.

One of the earliest such warnings was written by a young Barbadian, Isaac Hunt, only recently graduated from the College of Philadelphia but already an expert in scurrilous pamphleteering. Opening his *Political Family*, an essay published in 1775 though written for a prize competition in 1766, with a discourse on the necessary reciprocity of parts in the body politic he developed as his central point the idea that "in the *body politic* all inferior jurisdictions should flow from *one superior fountain* . . . a due subordination of the less parts to the greater is . . . necessary to the *existence* of BOTH." Colonies were the children and inferiors of the mother country; let them show the gratitude and obedience due to parents, and so let the principle of order through subordination prevail in the greater as in the lesser spheres of life.

This, in the context of the widespread belief in equal rights and the compact theory of government, was anachronistic. But it expressed the fears of many as political opposition turned into revolutionary fervor. Arguments such as Hunt's were enlarged and progressively dramatized, gaining in vituperation with successive publications until by 1774 they were bitter, shrill, and full of despair. Three Anglican clergymen wrote wrathful epitaphs to this ancient, honorable, and moribund philosophy.

Samuel Seabury—Hamilton's anonymous opponent in the pamphlet wars and the future first bishop of the Episcopal Church in America—wrote desperately of the larger, permanent dangers of civil disobedience. The legal, established authorities in New York—the courts of justice, above all—have been overthrown, he wrote, and in their places there were now "delegates, congresses, committees, riots, mobs, insurrections, associations." Who comprised the self-constituted Committee of Safety of New York that had the power to brand innocent people outlaws and deliver them over "to the vengeance of a lawless, outrageous mob, to be *tarred, feathered, hanged, drawn, quartered, and burnt*"? A parcel of upstarts "chosen by the weak, foolish, turbulent part of the country people"— "half a dozen fools in your neighborhood." Was the slavery imposed by their riotous wills to be preferred to the tyranny of a king? No: "If I must be devoured, let me be devoured by the jaws of a lion, and not *gnawed* to death by rats and vermin." If the upstart, pretentious committeemen triumph, order and peace will be at an end, and anarchy will result. . . .

His colleague, the elegant, scholarly Thomas Bradbury Chandler, was at once cleverer, more thoughtful, and, for those who heeded arguments, more likely to have been convincing. Two of his pamphlets published in 1774 stated with peculiar force the traditional case for authority in the state, in society, and in the ultimate source and ancient archetype of all authority, the family. His *American Querist,* that extraordinary list of one hundred rhetorical questions, put the point obliquely. It asked:

Whether some degree of respect be not always due from inferiors to superiors, and especially from children to parents; and whether the refusal of this on any occasion be not a violation of the general laws of society, to say nothing here of the obligations of religion and morality?

And is not Great Britain in the same relation to the colonies as a parent to children? If so, how can such "disrespectful and abusive treatment from children" be tolerated? God has given no dispensation to people under any government "to refuse *honor* or *custom* or *tribute* to whom they are *due;* to contract habits of thinking and *speaking evil of dignities,* and to weaken the natural principle of respect for those in authority." God's command is clear: his will is that we *"submit to every ordinance of man for the Lord's sake; and* require[s] us on pain of *damnation* to be duly *subject to the higher powers,* and *not to resist* their lawful authority."

Chandler's *Friendly Address to All Reasonable Americans* was more direct. It touched the central theme of authority at the start, and immediately spelled out the implications of resistance. The effort "to disturb or threaten an established government by popular insurrections and tumults has always been considered and treated, in every age and nation of the world, as an unpardonable crime." Did not an Apostle, "who had a due regard for the rights and liberties of mankind," order submission even to that cruelest of all despots, Nero? And properly so: "The bands of society would be dissolved, the harmony of the world confounded, and the order of nature subverted, if reverence, respect, and obedience might be refused to those whom the constitution has vested with the highest authority."

The insistence, the violence of language, increased in the heightening crisis. "Rebellion," Daniel Leonard wrote flatly in 1775, "is the most atrocious offense that can be perpetrated by man," except those committed directly against God. "It dissolves the social band, annihilates the security resulting from law and government; introduces fraud, violence, rapine, murder, sacrilege, and the long train of evils that riot uncontrolled in a state of nature." But the end was near. By the spring of 1775 such sentiments, fulminous and despairing, were being driven underground.

Jonathan Boucher's sermon "On Civil Liberty, Passive Obedience, and Non-resistance" had been written in 1775 "with a view to publication," and though it had been delivered publicly enough in Queen Anne's Parish, Maryland, it was promptly thereafter suppressed; "the press," Boucher later wrote, "was shut to every publication of the kind." Its publication twenty-two years afterward in a volume of Boucher's sermons entitled *A View of the Causes and Consequences of the American Revolution* was the result of the French Revolution's reawakening in the author, long since safely established in England, the fears of incipient anarchy and social incoherence that had agitated him two decades before. It was a fortunate result, for the sermon is a classic of its kind. It sums up, as no other essay of the period, the threat to the traditional ordering of human relations implicit in Revolutionary thought.

Boucher sought, first and foremost, to establish the divine origins of the doctrine of obedience to constituted authority—a necessity, he felt, not merely in view of the arguments of the Reverend Jacob Duché whom he was ostensibly refuting, but, more important, in view of the gross misinterpretation rebellious Americans had for years been making of that suggestive verse of Galatians v,1: "Stand fast, therefore, in the liberty wherewith Christ hath made us free." What had been meant by "liberty" in that passage, he said, was simply and unambiguously freedom from sin, for "every sinner is, literally, a slave . . . the only true liberty is the liberty of being the servants of God." Yet the Gospel does speak to the question of public obligations, and its command could hardly be more unmistakable: it orders, always, "obedience to the laws of every country, in every kind or form of government." The rumor promoted in the infancy of Christianity "that the Gospel was designed to undermine kingdoms and commonwealths" had probably been the work of Judas, and patently mixed up the purpose of the First Coming with that of the Second. Submission to the higher powers is what the Gospel intends for man: "obedience to government is every man's duty because it is every man's interest; but it is particularly incumbent on Christians, because . . . it is enjoined by the positive commands of God."

So much was scriptural, and could be buttressed by such authorities as Edmund Burke, Bishop Butler, "the learned Mr. Selden," and Lancelot Andrewes, whose Biblical exegesis of 1650 was quoted to the effect that "princes receive their power only from God, and are by him constituted and entrusted with government of others chiefly for his own glory and honor, as his deputies and viceregents upon earth." More complicated was the application of this central thesis to the associated questions of the origins and aims of government and of the equality of men. As for the former, the idea that the aim of government is "the common good of mankind" is in itself questionable; but even if it were correct, it would not follow that government should rest on consent, for common consent can only mean common feeling, and this a "vague and loose" thing not susceptible to proof. Mankind has never yet agreed on what the common good is, and so, there being no "common feeling" that can clearly designate the "common good," one can scarcely argue that government is, or should be, instituted by "common consent."

Similarly popular, dangerous, and fallacious to Boucher was the notion "that the whole human race is born equal; and that no man is naturally inferior, or in any respect subjected to another, and that he can be made subject to another only by his own consent." This argument, he wrote, is "ill-founded and false both in its premises and conclusions." It is hard to see how it could conceivably be true in any sense. "Man differs from man in everything that can be supposed to lead to supremacy and subjection, *as one star differs from another star in glory.*" God intended man to be a social animal; but

society requires government, and "without some relative inferiority and superiority" there can be no government.

A musical instrument composed of chords, keys, or pipes all perfectly equal in size and power might as well be expected to produce harmony as a society composed of members all perfectly equal to be productive of order and peace . . . On the principle of equality, neither his parents nor even the vote of a majority of the society . . . can have . . . authority over any man . . . Even an implicit consent can bind a man no longer than he chooses to be bound. The same principle of equality . . . clearly entitles him to recall and resume that consent whenever he sees fit, and he alone has a right to judge when and for what reasons it may be resumed.

A social and political system based on the principles of consent and equality would be "fantastic"; it would result in "the whole business of social life" being reduced to confusion and futility. People would first express and then withdraw their consent to an endless succession of schemes of government. "Governments, though always forming, would never be completely formed, for the majority today might be the minority tomorrow, and, of course, that which is now fixed might and would be soon unfixed."

Consent, equality—these were "particularly loose and dangerous" ideas, Boucher wrote; illogical, unrealistic, and lacking in scriptural sanction. There need be no mystery about the origins of government. Government was created by God. "As soon as there were some to be governed, there were also some to govern; and the first man, by virtue of that paternal claim on which all subsequent governments have been founded, was first invested with the power of government . . . The first father was the first king: and . . . it was thus that all government originated; and monarchy is its most ancient form." From this origin it follows directly that resistance to constituted authority is a sin, and that mankind is "commanded to *be subject to the higher powers.*" True, "kings and princes . . . were doubtless created and appointed not so much for their own sakes as for the sake of the people committed to their charge: yet they are not, therefore, the creatures of the people. So far from deriving their authority from any supposed consent or suffrage of men, they receive their commission from Heaven; they receive it from God, the source and original of all power." The judgment of Jesus Christ is evident: the most essential duty of subjects with respect to government is simply "(in the phraseology of a prophet) *to be quiet, and to sit still.*"

How simple but yet how demanding an injunction, for men are ever "*prone* to be presumptuous and self-willed, always disposed and ready to despise *dominion,* and *to speak evil of dignities.*" And how necessary to be obeyed in the present circumstance. Sedition has already penetrated deeply; it tears at the vitals of social order. It threatens far more than "the persons invested with the supreme power either legislative or executive"; "the resistance which your political counselors urge you to practice [is exerted] clearly and literally against *authority* . . . you are encouraged to resist not only all authority over us as it now exists, but any and all that it is possible to constitute."

This was the ultimate concern. What Boucher, Leonard, Chandler, and other articulate defenders of the *status quo* saw as the final threat was not so much the replacement of one set of rulers by another as the triumph of ideas and attitudes incompatible with the stability of any standing order, any establishment—incompatible with society itself, as it had been traditionally known. Their fears were in a sense justified, for in the context of eighteenth-century social thought it

was difficult to see how any harmonious, stable social order could be constructed from such materials. To argue that all men were equal would not make them so; it would only help justify and perpetuate that spirit of defiance, that refusal to concede to authority whose ultimate resolution could only be anarchy, demagoguery, and tyranny. If such ideas prevailed year after year, generation after generation, the "latent spark" in the breasts of even the most humble of men would be kindled again and again by entrepreneurs of discontent who would remind the people "of the elevated rank they hold in the universe, as men; that all men by nature are equal; that kings are but the ministers of the people; that their authority is delegated to them by the people for their good, and they have a right to resume it, and place it in other hands, or keep it themselves, whenever it is made use of to oppress them." Seeds of sedition would thus constantly be sown, and harvests of licentiousness reaped.

How else could it end? What reasonable social and political order could conceivably be built and maintained where authority was questioned before it was obeyed, where social differences were considered to be incidental rather than essential to community order, and where superiority, suspect in principle, was not allowed to concentrate in the hands of a few but was scattered broadly through the populace? No one could clearly say. But some, caught up in a vision of the future in which the peculiarities of American life became the marks of a chosen people, found in the defiance of traditional order the firmest of all grounds for their hope for a freer life. The details of this new world were not as yet clearly depicted; but faith ran high that a better world than any that had ever been known could be built where authority was distrusted and held in constant scrutiny;

where the status of men flowed from their achievements and from their personal qualities, not from distinctions ascribed to them at birth; and where the use of power over the lives of men was jealously guarded and severely restricted. It was only where there was this defiance, this refusal to truckle, this distrust of all authority, political or social, that institutions would express human aspirations, not crush them.

GORDON S. WOOD (b. 1933), who teaches at Brown University is best known for his prize-winning book, *The Creation of the American Republic, 1776–1787*. In writing about the Revolution, Wood had to come to grips with the problem of historical methodology. In this article he presents some of the historiographical issues with which scholars must grapple. What are the limitations of the "idealist" interpretation of the Revolution which stresses the ideas and rhetoric of the American revolutionaries? What are the limitations of the Progressive historians who de-emphasized the importance of ideas and placed greater weight on economic and social factors?*

Gordon S. Wood

A Critique of the Ideological Interpretation

If any catch phrase is to characterize the work being done on the American Revolution by this generation of historians, it will probably be "the American Revolution considered as an intellectual movement." For we now seem to be fully involved in a phase of writing about the Revolution in which the thought of the Revolutionaries, rather than their social and economic interests, has become the major focus of research and analysis. This recent emphasis on ideas is not of course new, and indeed right from the beginning it has characterized almost all our attempts to understand the Revolution. The ideas of a period which Samuel Eliot Morison and Harold Laski once described as, next to the English revolutionary decades of the seventeenth century, the most fruitful era in the history of Western political thought could never be completely ignored in any phase of our history writing.

It has not been simply the inherent importance of the Revolutionary ideas, those "great principles of freedom," that has continually attracted the attention of historians. It has been rather the unusual nature of the Revolution and the constant need to explain what on the face of it seems inexplicable that has compelled almost all interpreters of the Revolution, including the participants themselves, to stress its predominantly intellectual character and hence its uniqueness among

*Gordon S. Wood, "Rhetoric and Reality in the American Revolution," *William and Mary Quarterly,* Third Series, Vol. XXIII, No. 1 (Jan., 1966) pp. 3–32. Printed without footnotes by permission of the author.

Western revolutions. Within the context of Revolutionary historiography the one great effort to disparage the significance of ideas in the Revolution—an effort which dominated our history writing in the first half of the twentieth century—becomes something of an anomaly, a temporary aberration into a deterministic social and economic explanation from which we have been retreating for the past two decades. Since roughly the end of World War II we have witnessed a resumed and increasingly heightened insistence on the primary significance of conscious beliefs, and particularly of constitutional principles, in explaining what once again has become the unique character of the American Revolution. In the hands of idealist-minded historians the thought and principles of the Americans have consequently come to repossess that explanative force which the previous generation of materialist-minded historians had tried to locate in the social structure.

Indeed, our renewed insistence on the importance of ideas in explaining the Revolution has now attained a level of fullness and sophistication never before achieved, with the consequence that the economic and social approach of the previous generation of behaviorist historians has never semed more anomalous and irrelevant than it does at present. Yet paradoxically it may be that this preoccupation with the explanatory power of the Revolutionary ideas has become so intensive and so refined, assumed such a character that the apparently discredited social and economic approach of an earlier generation has at the same time never seemed more attractive and relevant. In other words, we may be approaching a crucial juncture in our writing about the Revolution where idealism and behaviorism meet.

It was the Revolutionaries themselves who first described the peculiar character of what they had been involved in. The Revolution, as those who took stock at the end of three decades of revolutionary activity noted, was not "one of those events which strikes the public eye in the subversions of laws which have usually attended the revolutions of governments." Because it did not seem to have been a typical revolution, the sources of its force and its momentum appeared strangely unaccountable. "In other revolutions, the sword has been drawn by the arm of offended freedom, under an oppression that threatened the vital powers of society." But this seemed hardly true of the American Revolution. There was none of the legendary tyranny that had so often driven desperate peoples into revolution. The Americans were not an oppressed people; they had no crushing imperial shackles to throw off. In fact, the Americans knew they were probably freer and less burdened with cumbersome feudal and monarchical restraints than any part of mankind in the eighteenth century. To its victims, the Tories, the Revolution was truly incomprehensible. Never in history, said Daniel Leonard, had there been so much rebellion with so "little real cause." It was, wrote Peter Oliver, "the most wanton and unnatural rebellion that ever existed." The Americans' response was out of all proportion to the stimuli. The objective social reality scarcely seemed capable of explaining a revolution.

Yet no American doubted that there had been a revolution. How then was it to be justified and explained? If the American Revolution, lacking "those mad, tumultuous actions which disgraced many of the great revolutions of antiquity," was not a typical revolution, what kind of revolution was it? If the origin of the American Revolution lay not in the usual passions and interests of men, wherein did it lay? Those Americans who look back at what they had been through could only marvel at the rationality and moderation, "supported by the energies of well weighed choice," involved in their separation from Britain, a revolution remarkably "without violence or convulsion." It seemed to be peculiarly an affair of the mind. Even two such dissimilar sorts of Whigs as Thomas Paine and John Adams both came to see the Revolution they had done so much to bring about as especially involved with ideas, resulting from "a mental examination," a change in "the minds and hearts of the people." The Americans were fortunate in being born at a time when the principles of government and freedom were better known than at any time in history. The Americans had learned "how to define the rights of nature,— how to search into, to distinguish, and to comprehend, the principles of physical, moral, religious, and civil liberty," how, in short, to discover and resist the forces of tyranny before they could be applied. Never before in history had a people achieved "a revolution by reasoning" alone.

The Americans, "born the heirs of freedom," revolted not to create but to maintain their freedom. American society had developed differently from that of the Old World. From the time of the first settlements in the seventeenth century, wrote Samuel Williams in 1794, "every thing tended to produce, and to establish the spirit of freedom." While the speculative philosophers of Europe were laboriously searching their minds in an effort to decide the first principles of liberty, the Americans had come to experience vividly that liberty in their everyday lives. The American Revolution, said Williams, joined together these enlightened ideas with America's experience. The Revolution was thus essentially intellectual and declaratory: it "explained the business to the world, and served to confirm what nature and society had before produced." "All was the result of reason. . . ." The Revolution had taken place not in a succession of eruptions that had crumbled the existing social structure, but in a succession of new thoughts and new ideas that had vindicated that social structure.

The same logic that drove the participants to view the Revolution as peculiarly intellectual also compelled Moses Coit Tyler, writing at the end of the nineteenth century, to describe the American Revolution as "preeminently a revolution caused by ideas, and pivoted on ideas." That ideas played a part in all revolutions Tyler readily admitted. But in most revolutions, like that of the French, ideas had been perceived and acted upon only when the social reality had caught up with them, only when the ideas had been given meaning and force by long-experienced "real evils." The American Revolution, said Tyler, had been different: it was directed "not against tyranny inflicted, but only against tyranny anticipated." The Americans revolted not out of actual suffering but out of reasoned principle. "Hence, more than with most other epochs of revolutionary strife, our epoch of revolutionary strife was a strife of ideas: a long warfare of political logic; a succession of annual campaigns in which the marshalling of arguments not only preceded the marshalling of armies, but often exceeded them in impression upon the final result."

It is in this historiographical context developed by the end of the nineteenth century, this constant and at times extravagant emphasis on the idealism of the Revolution, that the true radical quality of the Progressive generation's interpretation of the Revolution becomes so vividly apparent. For the work of these Progressive historians was grounded in a social and economic explanation of the Revolutionary era that explicitly rejected the causal importance of ideas. These historians could scarcely have avoided the general intellectual climate of the first part of the twentieth cenutry which regarded ideas as suspect. By absorbing the diffused thinking of Marx and Freud and the assumptions of behaviorist psychology, men had come to conceive of ideas as ideologies or rationalizations, as masks obscuring the underlying interests and drives that actually determined social behavior. For too long, it seemed, philosophers had reified thought, detaching ideas from the material conditions that produced them and investing them with an independent will that was somehow alone responsible for the determination of events. As Charles Beard pointed out in his introduction to the 1935 edition of *An Economic Interpretation of the Constitution*, previous historians of the Constitution had assumed that ideas were "entities, particularities, or forces, apparently independent of all earthly considerations coming under the head of 'economic.'" It was Beard's aim, as it was the aim of many of his contemporaries, to bring into historical consideration "those realistic features of economic conflict, stress, and strain" which previous interpreters of the Revolution had largely ignored. The product of this aim was a generation or more of historical writing about the Revolutionary period (of which Beard's was but the most famous expression) that sought to explain the Revolution and

the formation of the Constitution in terms of socio-economic relationships and interests rather than in terms of ideas.

Curiously, the consequence of this reversal of historical approaches was not the destruction of the old-fashioned conception of the nature of ideas. As Marx had said, he intended only to put Hegel's head in its rightful place; he had no desire to cut it off. Ideas as rationalization, as ideology, remained—still distinct entities set in opposition to interests, now however lacking any deep causal significance, becoming merely a covering superstructure for the underlying and determinative social reality. Ideas therefore could still be the subject of historical investigation, as long as one kept them in their proper place, interesting no doubt in their own right but not actually counting for much in the movement of events.

Even someone as interested in ideas as Carl Becker never seriously considered them to be in any way determinants of what happened. Ideas fascinated Becker, but it was as superstructure that he enjoyed examining them, their consistency, their logic, their clarity, the way men formed and played with them. In his *Declaration of Independence: A Study in the History of Political Ideas* the political theory of the Americans takes on an unreal and even fatuous quality. It was as if ideas were merely refined tools to be used by the colonists in the most adroit manner possible. The entire Declaration of Independence, said Becker, was calculated for effect, designed primarily "to convince a candid world that the colonies had a moral and legal right to separate from Great Britain." The severe indictment of the King did not spring from unfathomable passions but was contrived conjured up, to justify a rebellion whose sources lay elsewhere. Men to Becker were never the victims of their thought, always the masters of it. Ideas were a kind of legal brief. "Thus step by step, from 1764 to 1776, the colonists modified their theory to suit their needs." The assumptions behind Becker's 1909 behaviorist work on New York politics in the Revolution and his 1922 study of the political ideas in the Declaration of Independence were more alike than they at first might appear.

Bringing to their studies of the Revolution similar assumptions about the nature of ideas, some of Becker's contemporaries went on to expose starkly the implications of those assumptions. When the entire body of Revolutionary thinking was examined, these historians could not avoid being struck by its generally bombastic and overwrought quality. The ideas expressed seemed so inflated, such obvious exaggerations of reality, that they could scarcely be taken seriously. The Tories were all "wretched hirelings, and execrable parricides"; George III, the "tyrant of the earth," a "monster in human form"; the British soldiers, "a mercenary, licentious rabble of banditti," intending to "tear the bowels and vitals of their brave but peaceable fellow subjects, and *to wash the ground with a profusion of innocent blood.*" Such extravagant language, it seemed, could be nothing but calculated deception, at best an obvious distortion of fact, designed to incite and mold a revolutionary fervor. "The stigmatizing of British policy as 'tyranny,' 'oppression' and 'slavery,'" wrote Arthur M. Schlesinger, the dean of the Progressive historians, "had little or no objective reality, at least prior to the Intolerable Acts, but ceaseless repetition of the charge kept emotions at fever pitch."

Indeed, so grandiose, so overdrawn, it seemed, were the ideas that the historians were necessarily led to ask not whether such ideas were valid but why men should have expressed them. It was not the content of such ideas but the function that was really interesting. The Revolutionary rhetoric, the profusion of sermons, pamphlets, and articles in the patriotic cause, could best be examined as propaganda, that is, as a concerted and self-conscious effort by agitators to manipulate and shape public opinion. Because of the Progressive historians' view of the Revolution as the movement of class minorities bent on promoting particular social and economic interests, the conception of propaganda was crucial to their explanation of what seemed to be a revolutionary consensus. Through the use of ideas in provoking hatred and influencing opinion and creating at least "an appearance of unity," the influence of a minority of agitators was out of all proportion to their number. The Revolution thus became a display of extraordinary skillfulness in the manipulation of public opinion. In fact, wrote Schlesinger, "no disaffected element in history has ever risen more splendidly to the occasion."

Ideas thus became, as it were, parcels of thought to be distributed and used where they would do the most good. This propaganda was not of course necessarily false, but it was always capable of manipulation. "Whether the suggestions are to be true or false, whether the activities are to be open or concealed," wrote Philip Davidson, "are matters for the propagandist to decide." Apparently ideas could be turned on or off at will, and men controlled their rhetoric in a way they could not control their interests. Whatever the importance of propaganda, its connection with social reality was tenuous. Since ideas were so self-consciously manageable, the Whigs were not actually expressing anything meaningful about themselves but were rather feigning and exaggerating for effect. What the Americans said could not be taken at face value but must be considered as a rhetorical disguise for some hidden interest. The expression of even the classic and well-defined natural rights philosophy became, in Davidson's view, but "the propagandist's rationalization of his desire to protect his vested interests."

With this conception of ideas as weapons shrewdly used by designing propagandists, it was inevitable that the thought of the Revolutionaries should have been denigrated. The Revolutionaries became by implication hypocritical demagogues, "adroitly tailoring their arguments to changing conditions." Their political thinking appeared to possess neither consistency nor significance. "At best," said Schlesinger in an early summary of his interpretation, "an exposition of the political theories of the anti-parliamentary party is an account of their retreat from one strategic position to another." So the Whigs moved, it was strongly suggested, easily if not frivolously from a defense of charter rights, to the rights of Englishmen, and finally to the rights of man, as each position was exposed and became untenable. In short, concluded Schlesinger, the Revolution could never be understood if it were regarded "as a great forensic controversy over abstract governmental rights."

It is essentially on this point of intellectual consistency that Edmund S. Morgan has fastened for the past decade and a half in an attempt to bring down the entire interpretive framework of the socio-economic argument. If it could be shown that the thinking of the Revolutionaries was not inconsistent after all, that the Whigs did not actually skip from one constitutional notion to the next, then the imputation of Whig frivolity and hypocrisy would lose its force. This was a central intention of Morgan's study of the political thought surrounding the Stamp Act. As Morgan himself has noted and others have repeated, "In the last analysis the significance of the Stamp Act crisis lies in the emergence, not of leaders and methods and organizations, but of well-defined constitutional principles." As early as 1765 the Whigs "laid down the line on which Americans stood until they cut their connections with England. Consistently from 1765 to 1776 they denied the authority of Parliament to tax them externally or internally; consistently they affirmed their willingness to submit to whatever legislation Parliament should enact for the supervision of the empire as a whole." This consistency thus becomes, as one scholar's survey of the current interpretation puts it, "an indication of American devotion to principle."

It seemed clear once again after Morgan's study that the Americans were more sincerely attached to constitutional principles than the behaviorist historians had supposed, and that their ideas could not be viewed as simply manipulated propaganda. Consequently the cogency of the Progressive historians' interpretation was weakened if not unhinged. And as the evidence against viewing the Revolution as rooted in internal class-conflict continued to mount from various directions, it appeared more and more comprehensible to accept the old-fashioned notion that the Revolution was after all the consequence of "a great forensic controversy over abstract governmental rights." There were, it seemed, no deprived and depressed populace yearning for a participation in politics that had long been denied; no coherent merchant class victimizing a mass of insolvent debtors; no seething discontent with the British mercantile system; no privileged aristocracy, protected by law, anxiously and insecurely holding power against a clamoring democracy. There was, in short, no internal class upheaval in the Revolution.

If the Revolution was not to become virtually incomprehensible, it must have been the result of what the American Whigs always contended it was—a dispute between Mother Country and colonies over constitutional liberties. By concentrating on the immediate events of the decade leading up to independence, the historians of the 1950's have necessarily fled from the economic and· social determinism of the Progressive historians. And by emphasizing the consistency and devotion with which Americans held their constitutional beliefs they have once again focused on what seems to be the extraordinary intellectuality of the American Revolution and hence its uniqueness among Western revolutions. This interpretation, which, as Jack P. Greene notes, "may appropriately be styled neo-whig," has turned the Revolution into a rationally conservative movement, involving mainly a constitutional defense of existing political liberties against the abrupt and unexpected provocations of the British government after 1760. "The issue then, according to the neo-whigs, was no more and no less than separation from Britain and the preservation of American liberty." The Revolution has therefore become "more political, legalistic, and constitutional than social or economic." Indeed, some of the neo-Whig historians have implied not just that social and economic conditions were less important in bringing on the Revolution as we once thought, but

rather that the social situation in the colonies had little or nothing to do with causing the Revolution. The Whig statements of principle iterated in numerous declarations appear to be the only causal residue after all the supposedly deeper social and economic causes have been washed away. As one scholar who has recently investigated and carefully dismissed the potential social and economic issues in pre-Revolutionary Virginia has concluded, "What remains as the fundamental issue in the coming of the Revolution, then, is nothing more than the contest over constitutional rights."

In a different way Bernard Bailyn in a recent article has clarified and reinforced this revived idealistic interpretation of the Revolution. The accumulative influence of much of the latest historical writing on the character of eighteenth-century American society has led Bailyn to the same insight expressed by Samuel Williams in 1794. What made the Revolution truly revolutionary was not the wholesale disruption of social groups and political institutions, for compared to other revolutions such disruption was slight; rather it was the fundamental alteration in the Americans' structure of values, the way they looked at themselves and their institutions. Bailyn has seized on this basic intellectual shift as a means of explaining the apparent contradiction between the seriousness with which the Americans took their Revolutionary ideas and the absence of radical social and institutional change. The Revolution, argues Bailyn, was not so much the transformation as the realization of American society.

The Americans had been gradually and unwittingly preparing themselves for such a mental revolution since they first came to the New World in the seventeenth century. The substantive changes in American society had taken place in the course of the previous century, slowly, often imperceptibly, as a series of small piecemeal deviations from what was regarded by most Englishmen as the accepted orthodoxy in society, state, and religion. What the Revolution marked, so to speak, was the point when the Americans suddenly blinked and saw their society, its changes, its differences, in a new perspective. Their deviation from European standards, their lack of an established church and a titled aristocracy, their apparent rusticity and general equality, now became desirable, even necessary, elements in the maintenance of their society and politics. The comprehending and justifying, the endowing with high moral purpose, of these confusing and disturbing social and political divergences, Bailyn concludes, was the American Revolution.

Bailyn's more recent investigation of the rich pamphlet literature of the decades before Independence has filled out and refined his idealist interpretation, confirming him in his "rather old-fashioned view that the American Revolution was above all else an ideological-constitutional struggle and not primarily a controversy between social groups undertaken to force changes in the organization of society." While Bailyn's book-length introduction to the first of a multivolumed edition of Revolutionary pamphlets makes no effort to stress the conservative character of the Revolution and indeed emphasizes (in contrast to the earlier article) its radicalism and the dynamic and transforming rather than the rationalizing and declarative quality of Whig thought, it nevertheless represents the culmination of the idealist approach to the history of the Revolution. For "above all else," argues Bailyn, it was the Americans' world-view, the

peculiar bundle of notions and beliefs they put together during the imperial debate, "that in the end propelled them into Revolution." Through his study of the Whig pamphlets Bailyn became convinced "that the fear of a comprehensive conspiracy against liberty throughout the English-speaking world—a conspiracy believed to have been nourished in corruption, and of which, it was felt, oppression in America was only the most immediately visible part—lay at the heart of the Revolutionary movement." No one of the various acts and measures of the British government after 1763 could by itself have provoked the extreme and violent response of the American Whigs. But when linked together they formed in the minds of the Americans, imbued with a particular historical understanding of what constituted tyranny, an extensive and frightening program designed to enslave the New World. The Revolution becomes comprehensible only when the mental framework, the Whig world-view into which the Americans fitted the events of the 1760's and 1770's, is known. "It is the development of this view to the point of overwhelming persuasiveness to the majority of American leaders and the meaning this view gave to the events of the time, and not simply an accumulation of grievances," writes Bailyn, "that explains the origins of the American Revolution."

It now seems evident from Bailyn's analysis that it was the Americans' peculiar conception of reality more than anything else that convinced them that tyranny was afoot and that they must fight if their liberty was to survive. By an empathic understanding of a wide range of American thinking Bailyn has been able to offer us a most persuasive argument for the importance of ideas in bringing on the Revolution. Not since

Tyler has the intellectual character of the Revolution received such emphasis and never before has it been set out so cogently and completely. It would seem that the idealist explanation of the Revolution has nowhere else to go.

Labeling the recent historical interpretations of the Revolution as "neo-whig" is indeed appropriate, for, as Page Smith has pointed out, "after a century and a half of progress in historical scholarship, in research techniques, in tools and methods, we have found our way to the interpretation held, substantially, by those historians who themselves participated in or lived through the era of, the Revolution." By describing the Revolution as a conservative, principled defense of American freedom against the provocations of the English government, the neo-Whig historians have come full circle to the position of the Revolutionaries themselves and to the interpretation of the first generation of historians. Indeed, as a consequence of this historical atavism, praise for the contemporary or early historians has become increasingly common.

But to say "that the Whig interpretation of the American Revolution may not be as dead as some historians would have us believe" is perhaps less to commend the work of David Ramsay and George Bancroft than to indict the approach of recent historians. However necessary and rewarding the neo-Whig histories have been, they present us with only a partial perspective on the Revolution. The neo-Whig interpretation is intrinsically polemical; however subtly presented, it aims to justify the Revolution. It therefore cannot accommodate a totally different, an opposing, perspective, a Tory view of the Revolution. It is for this reason that the recent publication of Peter Oliver's "Origin and Progress of the American Rebellion" is of major significance, for it offers us—"by attacking the hallowed traditions of the revolution, challenging the motives of the founding fathers, and depicting revolution as passion, plotting, and violence"—an explanation of what happened quite different from what we have been recently accustomed to. Oliver's vivid portrait of the Revolutionaries with his accent on their vicious emotions and interests seriously disturbs the present Whiggish interpretation of the Revolution. It is not that Oliver's description of, say, John Adams as madly ambitious and consumingly resentful is any more correct than Adams's own description of himself as a virtuous and patriotic defender of liberty against tyranny. Both interpretations of Adams are in a sense right, but neither can comprehend the other because each is preoccupied with seemingly contradictory sets of motives. Indeed, it is really these two interpretations that have divided historians of the Revolution ever since.

Any intellectually satisfying explanation of the Revolution must encompass the Tory perspective as well as the Whig, for if we are compelled to take sides and choose between opposing motives—unconscious or avowed, passion or principle, greed or liberty—we will be endlessly caught up in the polemics of the participants themselves. We must, in other words, eventually dissolve the distinction between conscious and unconscious motives, between the Revolutionaries' stated intentions and their supposedly hidden needs and desires, a dissolution that involves somehow relating beliefs and ideas to the social world in which they operate. If we are to understand the causes of the Revolution we must therefore ultimately transcend this problem of motivation. But this we can never do as long as we attempt to explain the Revolution mainly in terms of the intentions of the participants. It is not that men's motives are unimportant; they indeed make events, including revolutions. But the purposes of men, especially in a revolution, are so numerous, so varied, and so contradictory that their complex interaction produces results that no one intended or could even foresee. It is this interaction and these results that recent historians are referring to when they speak so disparagingly of those "underlying determinants" and "impersonal and inexorable forces" bringing on the Revolution. Historical explanation which does not account for these "forces," which, in other words, relies simply on understanding the conscious intentions of the actors, will thus be limited. This preoccupation with men's purposes was what restricted the perspectives of the contemporaneous Whig and Tory interpretations; and it is still the weakness of the neo-Whig histories, and indeed of any interpretation which attempts to explain the events of the Revolution by discovering the calculations from which individuals supposed themselves to have acted.

No explanation of the American Revolution in terms of the intentions and designs of particular individuals could have been more crudely put than that offered by the Revolutionaries themselves. American Whigs like men of the eighteenth century generally, were fascinated with what seemed to the age to be the newly appreciated problem of human motivation and causation in the affairs of the world. In the decade before independence the Americans sought endlessly to discover the supposed calculations and purposes of individuals or groups that lay behind the otherwise

incomprehensible rush of events. More than anything else perhaps, it was this obsession with motives that led to the prevalence in the eighteenth century of beliefs in conspiracies to account for the confusing happenings in which men found themselves caught up. Bailyn has suggested that this common fear of conspiracy was "deeply rooted in the political awareness of eighteenth-century Britons, involved in the very structure of their political life"; it "reflected so clearly the realities of life in an age in which monarchical autocracy flourished, [and] in which the stability and freedom of England's 'mixed' constitution was a recent and remarkable achievement." Yet it might also be argued that the tendency to see conspiracy behind what happened reflected as well the very enlightenment of the age. To attribute events to the designs and purposes of human agents seemed after all to be an enlightened advance over older beliefs in blind chance, providence, or God's interventions. It was rational and scientific, a product of both the popularization of politics and the secularization of knowledge. It was obvious to Americans that the series of events in the years after 1763, those "unheard of intolerable calamities, spring not of the dust, come not causeless." "Ought not the PEOPLE therefore," asked John Dickinson, "to watch? to observe facts? to search into causes? to investigate designs?" And these causes and designs could be traced to individuals in high places, to ministers, to royal governors, and their lackeys. The belief in conspiracy grew naturally out of the enlightened need to find the human purposes behind the multitude of phenomena, to find the causes for what happened in the social world just as the natural scientist was discovering the causes for what happened in the physical world. It was a necessary consequence of the search for connections and patterns in events. The various acts of the British government, the Americans knew, should not be "regarded according to the simple force of each, but as parts of a system of oppression." The Whigs' intense search for the human purposes behind events was in fact an example of the beginnings of modern history.

In attempting to rebut those interpretations disparaging the colonists' cause, the present neo-Whig historians have been drawn into writing as partisans of the Revolutionaries. And they have thus found themselves entangled in the same kind of explanation used by the original antagonists, an explanation, despite obvious refinements, still involved with the discovery of motives and its corollary, the assessing of a personal sort of responsibility for what happened. While most of the neo-Whig historians have not gone so far as to see conspiracy in British actions (although some have come close), they have tended to point up the blundering and stupidity of British officials in contrast to "the breadth of vision" that moved the Americans. If George III was in a position of central responsibility in the British government, as English historians have recently said, then, according to Edmund S. Morgan, "he must bear most of the praise or blame for the series of measures that alienated and lost the colonies, and it is hard to see how there can be much praise." By seeking "to define issues, fix responsibilities," and thereby to shift the "burden of proof" onto those who say the Americans were narrow and selfish and the empire was basically just and beneficent, the neo-Whigs have attempted to redress what they felt was an unfair neo-Tory bias of previous explanations of the Revolution; they have not, however, challenged the terms of the argument. They are still obsessed with why men said they acted and with who was right and who was wrong. Viewing the history of the Revolution in this judiciary manner has therefore restricted the issues over which historians have disagreed to those of motivation and responsibility, the very issues with which the participants themselves were concerned.

The neo-Whig "conviction that the colonists' attachment to principle was genuine" has undoubtedly been refreshing, and indeed necessary, given the Tory slant of earlier twentieth-century interpretations. It now seems clearer that the Progressive historians, with their naive and crude reflex conception of human behavior, had too long treated the ideas of the Revolution superficially if not superciliously. Psychologists and sociologists are now willing to grant a more determining role to beliefs, particularly in revolutionary situations. It is now accepted that men act not simply in response to some kind of objective reality but to the meaning they give to that reality. Since men's beliefs are as much a part of the given stimuli as the objective environment, the beliefs must be understood and taken seriously if men's behavior is to be fully explained. The American Revolutionary ideas were more than cooked up pieces of thought served by an aggressive and interested minority to a gullible and unsuspecting populace. The concept of propaganda permitted the Progressive historians to account for the presence of ideas but it prevented them from recognizing ideas as an important determinant of the Americans' behavior. The weight attributed to ideas and constitutional principles by the neo-Whig historians was thus an essential corrective to the propagandist studies.

Yet in its laudable effort to resurrect the importance of ideas in historical explanation much of the writing of the neo-Whigs has tended to return to the simple nineteenth-century intellectualist assumption that history is the consequence of a rational calculation of ends and means, that what happened was what was consciously desired and planned. By supposing "that individual actions and immediate issues are more important than underlying determinants in explaining particular events," by emphasizing conscious and articulated motives, the neo-Whig historians have selected and presented that evidence which is most directly and clearly expressive of the intentions of the Whigs, that is, the most well-defined, the most constitutional, the most reasonable of the Whig beliefs, those found in their public documents, their several declarations of grievances and causes. It is not surprising that for the neo-Whigs the history of the American Revolution should be more than anything else "the history of the Americans' search for principles." Not only, then, did nothing in the Americans' economic and social structure really determine their behavior, but the colonists in fact acted from the most rational and calculated of motives: they fought, as they said they would, simply to defend their ancient liberties against British provocation.

By implying that certain declared rational purposes are by themselves an adequate explanation for the Americans' revolt, in other words that the Revolution was really nothing more than a contest over constitutional principles, the neo-Whig historians have not only threatened to deny what we have learned of human psychology in the twentieth century, but they have also in fact failed to exploit fully the terms of their own

idealist approach by not taking into account all of what the Americans believed and said. Whatever the deficiencies and misunderstandings of the role of ideas in human behavior present in the propagandist studies of the 1930's, these studies did for the first time attempt to deal with the entirety and complexity of American Revolutionary thought—to explain not only all the well-reasoned notions of law and liberty that were so familiar but, more important, all the irrational and hysterical beliefs that had been so long neglected. Indeed, it was the patent absurdity and implausibility of much of what the Americans said that lent credence and persuasiveness to their mistrustful approach to the ideas. Once this exaggerated and fanatical rhetoric was uncovered by the Progressive historians, it should not have subsequently been ignored—no matter how much it may have impugned the reasonableness of the American response. No widely expressed ideas can be dismissed out of hand by the historian.

In his recent analysis of Revolutionary thinking Bernard Bailyn has avoided the neo-Whig tendency to distort the historical reconstruction of the American mind. By comprehending "the assumptions, beliefs, and ideas that lay behind the manifest events of the time," Bailyn has attempted to get inside the Whigs' mind, and to experience vicariously all of what they thought and felt, both their rational constitutional beliefs and their hysterical and emotional ideas as well. The inflammatory phrases, "slavery," "corruption," "conspiracy," that most historians had either ignored or readily dismissed as propaganda, took on a new significance for Bailyn. He came "to suspect that they meant something very real to both the writers and their readers: that there were real fears, real anxieties, a sense of real danger behind these phrases, and not merely the desire to influence by rhetoric and propaganda the inert minds of an otherwise passive populace." No part of American thinking, Bailyn suggests—not the widespread belief in a ministerial conspiracy, not the hostile and vicious indictments of individuals, not the fear of corruption and the hope for regeneration, not any of the violent seemingly absurd distortions and falsifications of what we now believe to be true, in short, none of the frenzied rhetoric—can be safely ignored by the historian seeking to understand the causes of the Revolution.

Bailyn's study, however, represents something other than a more complete and uncorrupted version of the common idealist interpretations of the Revolution. By viewing from the "interior" the Revolutionary pamphlets, which were "to an unusual degree, *explanatory*," revealing "not merely positions taken but the reasons why positions were taken," Bailyn like any idealist historian has sought to discover the motives the participants themselves gave for their actions, to re-enact their thinking at crucial moments, and thereby to recapture some of the "unpredictable reality" of the Revolution. But for Bailyn the very unpredictability of the reality he has disclosed has undermined the idealist obsession with explaining why, in the participants' own estimation, they acted as they did. Ideas emerge as more than explanatory devices, as more than indicators of motives. They become as well objects for analysis in and for themselves, historical events in their own right to be treated as other historical events are treated. Although Bailyn has examined the Revolutionary ideas subjectively from the inside, he has also analyzed them objectively from the outside.

Thus, in addition to a contemporary Whig perspective, he presents us with a retrospective view of the ideas—their complexity, their development, and their consequences—that the actual participants did not have. In effect his essay represents what has been called "a Namierism of the history of ideas," a structural analysis of thought that suggests a conclusion about the movement of history not very different from Sir Lewis Namier's, where history becomes something "started in ridiculous beginnings, while small men did things both infinitely smaller and infinitely greater than they knew."

In his *England in the Age of the American Revolution* Namier attacked the Whig tendency to overrate "the importance of the conscious will and purpose in individuals." Above all he urged us "to ascertain and recognize the deeper irrelevancies and incoherence of human actions, which are not so much directed by reason, as invested by it *ex post facto* with the appearances of logic and rationality," to discover the unpredictable reality, where men's motives and intentions were lost in the accumulation and momentum of interacting events. The whole force of Namier's approach tended to squeeze the intellectual content out of what men did. Ideas setting forth principles and purposes for action, said Namier, did not count for much in the movement of history.

In his study of the Revolutionary ideas Bailyn has come to an opposite conclusion: ideas counted for a great deal, not only being responsible for the Revolution but also for transforming the character of American society. Yet in his hands ideas lose that static quality they have commonly had for the Whig historians, the simple statements of intention that so exasperated Namier. For

Bailyn the ideas of the Revolutionaries take on an elusive and unmanageable quality, a dynamic self-intensifying character that transcended the intentions and desires of any of the historical participants. By emphasizing how the thought of the colonists was "strangely reshaped, turned in unfamiliar directions," by describing how the Americans "indeliberately, half-knowingly" groped toward "conclusions they could not themselves clearly perceive," by demonstrating how new beliefs and hence new actions were the responses not to desire but to the logic of developing situations, Bailyn has wrest the explanation of the Revolution out of the realm of motivation in which the neo-Whig historians had confined it.

With this kind of approach to ideas, the degree of consistency and devotion to principles become less important, and indeed the major issues of motivation and responsibility over which historians have disagreed become largely irrelevant. Action becomes not the product of rational and conscious calculation but of dimly perceived and rapidly changing thoughts and situations, "where the familiar meaning of ideas and words faded away into confusion, and leaders felt themselves peering into a haze, seeking to bring shifting conceptions somehow into focus." Men become more the victims than the manipulators of their ideas, as their thought unfolds in ways few anticipated, "rapid, irreversible, and irresistible," creating new problems, new considerations, new ideas, which have their own unforeseen implications. In this kind of atmosphere the Revolution, not at first desired by the Americans, takes on something of an inevitable character, moving through a process of escalation into levels few had intended or perceived. It no longer makes sense to assign motives or responsibility to particular individuals for the totality of what happened. Men were involved in a complicated web of phenomena, ideas, and situations, from which in retrospect escape seems impossible.

By seeking to uncover the motives of the Americans expressed in the Revolutionary pamphlets, Bailyn has ended by demonstrating the autonomy of ideas as phenomena, where the ideas operate, as it were, over the heads of the participants, taking them in directions no one could have foreseen. His discussion of Revolutionary thought thus represents a move back to a deterministic approach to the Revolution, a determinism, however, which is different from that which the neo-Whig historians have so recently and self-consciously abandoned. Yet while the suggested determinism is thoroughly idealist—indeed never before has the force of ideas in bringing on the Revolution been so emphatically put—its implications are not. By helping to purge our writing about the Revolution of its concentration on constitutional principles and its stifling judicial-like preoccupation with motivation and responsibility, the study serves to open the way for new questions and new appraisals. In fact, it is out of the very completeness of his idealist interpretation, out of his exposition of the extraordinary nature—the very dynamism and emotionalism—of the Americans' thought that we have the evidence for an entirely different, a behaviorist, perspective on the causes of the American Revolution. Bailyn's book-length introduction to his edition of Revolutionary pamphlets is therefore not only a point of fulfillment for the idealist approach to the Revolution, it is also a point of departure for a new look at the social sources of the Revolution.

It seems clear that historians of eighteenth-century America and the Revolution cannot ignore the force of ideas in history to the extent that Namier and his students have done in their investigations of eighteenth-century English politics. This is not to say, however, that the Namier approach to English politics has been crucially limiting and distorting. Rather it may suggest that the Namier denigration of ideas and principles is inapplicable for American politics because the American social situation in which ideas operated was very different from that of the eighteenth-century England. It may be that ideas are less meaningful to a people in a socially stable situation. Only when ideas have become stereotyped reflexes do evasion and hypocrisy and the Namier mistrust of what men believe become significant. Only in a relatively settled society does ideology become a kind of habit, a bundle of widely shared and instinctive conventions, offering ready-made explanations for men who are not being compelled to ask any serious questions. Conversely, it is perhaps only in a relatively unsettled, disordered society, where the questions come faster than men's answers, that ideas become truly vital and creative.

Paradoxically it may be the very vitality of the Americans' ideas, then, that suggests the need to examine the circumstances in which they flourished. Since ideas and beliefs are ways of perceiving and explaining the world, the nature of the ideas expressed is determined as much by the character of the world being confronted as by the internal development of inherited and borrowed conceptions. Out of the multitude of inherited and transmitted ideas available in the eighteenth century, Americans selected and emphasized those which seemed to make meaningful what was happening to them. In the colonists' use of classical literature, for example, "their detailed knowledge and engaged interest covered only one era and one small group of writers," Plutarch, Livy, Cicero, Sallust, and Tacitus—those who "had hated and feared the trends of their own time, and in their writing had contrasted the present with a better past, which they endowed with qualities absent from their own, corrupt era." There was always, in Max Weber's term, some sort of elective affinity between the Americans' interests and their beliefs, and without that affinity their ideas would not have possessed the peculiar character and persuasiveness they did. Only the most revolutionary social need and circumstances could have sustained such revolutionary ideas.

When the ideas of the Americans are examined comprehensively, when all of the Whig rhetoric, irrational as well as rational, is taken into account, one cannot but be struck by the predominant characteristics of fear and frenzy, the exaggerations and the enthusiasm, the general sense of social corruption and disorder out of which would be born a new world of benevolence and harmony where Americans would become the "eminent examples of every divine and social virtue." As Bailyn and the propaganda studies have amply shown, there is simply too much fanatical and millennial thinking even by the best minds that must be explained before we can characterize the Americans' ideas as peculiarly rational and legalistic and thus view the Revolution as merely a conservative defense of constitutional liberties. To isolate refined and nicely-reasoned arguments from the writing of John Adams and Jefferson is not only to disregard the more inflamed expressions of the rest of the Whigs but also to overlook the enthusiastic extravagance—the paranoiac obsession with a diabolical Crown conspiracy and the dream of a restored Saxon era—in the thinking of Adams and Jefferson themselves.

The ideas of the Americans seem, in fact, to form what can only be called a revolutionary syndrome. If we were to confine ourselves to examining the Revolutionary rhetoric alone, apart from what happened politically or socially, it would be virtually impossible to distinguish the American Revolution from any other revolution in modern Western history. In the kinds of ideas expressed the American Revolution is remarkably similar to the seventeenth-century Puritan Revolution and to the eighteenth-century French Revolution: the same general disgust with a chaotic and corrupt world, the same anxious and angry bombast, the same excited fears of conspiracies by depraved men, the same utopian hopes for the construction of a new and virtuous order. It was not that this syndrome of ideas was simply transmitted from one generation or from one people to another. It was rather perhaps that similar, though hardly identical, social situations called forth, within the limitations of inherited and available conceptions, similar modes of expression. Although we need to know much more about the sociology of revolutions and collective movements, it does seem possible that particular patterns of thought, particular forms of expression, correspond to certain basic social experiences. There may be, in other words, typical modes of expression, typical kinds of beliefs and values, characterizing a revolutionary situation, at least within roughly similar Western societies. Indeed, the types of ideas manifested may be the best way of identifying a collec-

tive movement as a revolution. As one student of revolutions writes, "It is on the basis of a knowledge of men's beliefs that we can distinguish their behaviour from riot, rebellion or insanity."

It is thus the very nature of the Americans' rhetoric—its obsession with corruption and disorder, its hostile and conspiratorial outlook, and its millennial vision of a regenerated society—that reveals as nothing else apparently can the American Revolution as a true revolution with its sources lying deep in the social structure. For this kind of frenzied rhetoric could spring only from the most severe sorts of social strain. The grandiose and feverish language of the Americans was indeed the natural, even the inevitable, expression of a people caught up in a revolutionary situation, deeply alienated from the existing sources of authority and vehemently involved in a basic reconstruction of their political and social order. The hysteria of the Americans' thinking was but a measure of the intensity of their revolutionary passions. Undoubtedly the growing American alienation from British authority contributed greatly to this revolutionary situation. Yet the very weakness of the British imperial system and the accumulating ferocity of American antagonism to it suggests that other sources of social strain were being fed into the revolutionary movement. It may be that the Progressive historians in their preoccupation with internal social problems were more right than we have recently been willing to grant. It would be repeating their mistake, however, to expect this internal social strain necessarily to take the form of coherent class conflict or overt social disruption. The sources of revolutionary social stress may have been much more subtle but no less severe.

Of all of the colonies in the mid-eighteenth century, Virginia seems the most settled, the most lacking in obvious social tensions. Therefore, as it has been recently argued, since conspicuous social issues were nonexistent, the only plausible remaining explanation for the Virginians' energetic and almost unanimous commitment to the Revolution must have been their devotion to constitutional principles. Yet it may be that we have been looking for the wrong kind of social issues, for organized conflicts, for conscious divisions, within the society. It seems clear that Virginia's difficulties were not the consequence of any obvious sectional or class antagonism, Tidewater versus Piedmont, aristocratic planters versus yeomen farmers. There was apparently no discontent with the political system that went deep into the social structure. But there does seem to have been something of a social crisis within the ruling group itself, which intensely aggravated the Virginians' antagonism to the imperial system. Contrary to the impression of confidence and stability that the Virginia planters have historically acquired, they seemed to have been in very uneasy circumstances in the years before the Revolution. The signs of the eventual nineteenth-century decline of the Virginia gentry were, in other words, already felt if not readily apparent.

The planters' ability to command the acquiescence of the people seems extraordinary compared to the unstable politics of the other colonies. But in the years before independence there were signs of increasing anxiety among the gentry over their representative role. The ambiguities in the relationship between the Burgesses and their constituents erupted into open debate in the 1750's. And men began voicing more and more concern over the mounting costs of elections and growing corruption in the soliciting of votes, especially by "those who have neither natural nor acquired parts to recommend them." By the late sixties and early seventies the newspapers were filled with warnings against electoral influence, bribery, and vote seeking. The freeholders were stridently urged to "strike at the Root of this growing Evil; be influenced by Merit alone," and avoid electing "obscure and inferior persons." It was as if ignoble ambition and demagoguery, one bitter pamphlet remarked, were a "Daemon lately come among us to disturb the peace and harmony, which had so long subsisted in this place." In this context Robert Munford's famous play, *The Candidates*, written in 1770, does not so much confirm the planters' confidence as it betrays their uneasiness with electoral developments in the colony, "when coxcombs and jockies can impose themselves upon it for men of learning." Althought disinterested virtue eventually wins out, Munford's satire reveals the kinds of threats the established planters faced from ambitious knaves and blockheads who were turning representatives into slaves of the people.

By the eve of the Revolution the planters were voicing a growing sense of impending ruin, whose sources seemed in the minds of many to be linked more and more with the corrupting British connection and the Scottish factors, but for others frighteningly rooted in "our Pride, our Luxury, and Idleness." The public and private writings of Virginians became obsessed with "corruption," "virtue," and "luxury." The increasing defections from the Church of England, even among ministers and vestrymen, and the remarkable growth of dissent in the years before the Revolution, "so much complained of in many parts of the colony," further suggests some sort of social stress. The strange religious conversions of Robert Carter may represent only the most dramatic example of what was taking place less frenziedly elsewhere among the gentry. By the middle of the eighteenth century it was evident that many of the planters were living on the edge of bankruptcy, seriously overextended and spending beyond their means in an almost frantic effort to fulfill the aristocratic image they had created of themselves. Perhaps the importance of the Robinson affair in the 1760's lies not in any constitutional changes that resulted but in the shattering effect the disclosures had on that virtuous image. Some of the planters expressed openly their fears for the future, seeing the products of their lives being destroyed in the reckless gambling and drinking of their heirs, who, as Landon Carter put it, "play away and play it all away."

The Revolution in Virginia, "produced by the wantonness of the Gentleman," as one planter suggested, undoubtedly gained much of its force from this social crisis within the gentry. Certainly more was expected from the Revolution than simply a break from British imperialism, and it was not any crude avoidance of British debts. The Revolutionary reforms, like the abolition of entail and primogeniture, may have signified something other than mere symbolic legal adjustments to an existing reality. In addition to being an attempt to make the older Tidewater plantations more economically competitive with lands farther west, the reforms may have represented a real effort to redirect what was believed to be a dangerous tendency in social and family development within the ruling gentry. The Virginians were not after all aristocrats who could afford having their entailed families' estates in

the hands of weak or ineffectual eldest sons. Entail, as the preamble to the 1776 act abolishing it stated, had often done "injury to the morals of youth by rendering them independent of, and disobedient to, their parents." There was too much likelihood, as the Nelson family sadly demonstrated, that a single wayward generation would virtually wipe out what had been so painstakingly built. George Mason bespoke the anxieties of many Virginians when he warned the Philadelphia Convention in 1787 that "our own Children will in a short time be among the general mass."

Precisely how the strains within Virginia society contributed to the creation of a revolutionary situation and in what way the planters expected independence and republicanism to alleviate their problems, of course, need to be fully explored. It seems clear, however, from the very nature of the ideas expressed that the sources of the Revolution in Virginia were much more subtle and complicated than a simple antagonism to the British government. Constitutional principles alone do not explain the Virginians' almost unanimous determination to revolt. And if the Revolution in the seemingly stable colony of Virginia possessed internal social roots, it is to be expected that the other colonies were experiencing their own forms of social strain that in a like manner sought mitigation through revolution and republicanism.

It is through the Whigs' ideas, then, that we may be led back to take up where the Progressive historians left off in their investigation of the internal social sources of the Revolution. By working through the ideas—by reading them imaginatively and relating them to the objective social world they both reflected and confronted—we may be able to eliminate the unrewarding distinction between conscious and unconscious motives, and eventually thereby to combine a Whig with a Tory, an idealist with a behaviorist, interpretation. For the ideas, the rhetoric, of the Americans was never obscuring but remarkably revealing of their deepest interests and passions. What they expressed may not have been for the most part factually true, but it was always psychologically true. In this sense their rhetoric was never detached from the social and political reality; and indeed it becomes the best entry into an understanding of that reality. Their repeated overstatements of reality, their incessant talk of "tyranny" when there seems to have been no real oppression, their obsession with "virtue," "luxury," and "corruption," their devotion to "liberty" and "equality"—all these notions were neither manipulated propaganda nor borrowed empty abstractions, but ideas with real personal and social significance for those who used them. Propaganda could never move men to revolution. No popular leader, as John Adams put it, has ever been able "to persuade a large people, for any length of time together, to think themselves wronged, injured, and oppressed, unless they really were, and saw and felt it to be so." The ideas had relevance; the sense of oppression and injury, although often displaced onto the imperial system, was nonetheless real. It was indeed the meaningfulness of the connection between what the Americans said and what they felt that gave the ideas their propulsive force and their overwhelming persuasiveness.

It is precisely the remarkable revolutionary character of the Americans' ideas now being revealed by historians that best indicates that something profoundly unsettling was going on in the society, that raises the question, as it did for the Progressive historians, why the Americans should have expressed such thoughts. With their crude conception of propaganda the Progressive historians at least attempted to grapple with the problem. Since we cannot regard the ideas of the Revolutionaries as simply propaganda, the question still remains to be answered. "When 'ideas' in full cry drive past," wrote Arthur F. Bentley in his classic behavioral study, *The Process of Government*, "the thing to do with them is to accept them as an indication that something is happening; and then search carefully to find out what it really is they stand for, what the factors of the social life are that are expressing themselves through the ideas." Precisely because they sought to understand both the Revolutionary ideas and American society, the behaviorist historians of the Progressive generation, for all of their crude conceptualizations, their obsession with "class" and hidden economic interests, and their treatment of ideas as propaganda, have still offered us an explanation of the Revolutionary era so powerful and so comprehensive that no purely intellectual interpretation will ever replace it.

JESSE LEMISCH (b. 1936), who teaches at S.U.N.Y.-Buffalo, suggests that historians in the past may have been looking at the Revolution from the wrong perspective. Instead of viewing the event "through the eyes of a few at the top"—the Washingtons, Jeffersons, and Adamses—Lemisch proposes that scholars examine the Revolution "from the bottom up"—from the perspective of the inarticulate masses. Employing this approach, how does Lemisch's treatment of the events in the decade 1765–1775 differ from the traditional accounts of these episodes?*

Jesse Lemisch

A New Left Explanation

Despite our pretensions to social science, we would seem to be hardly more genuinely scientific than we were fifty years ago. Many social scientists continue to draw conclusions about entire societies on the basis of examinations of the minority at the top. This approach has distorted our view and, sometimes, cut us off from past reality. Our earliest history has been seen as a period of consensus and classlessness, in part because our historians have chosen to see it that way. One of them, describing colonial Massachusetts as a "middle-class democracy," has tried to show that urban workers could qualify for the vote by offering evidence which sometimes proves only that their *employers* could do so, much as one might demonstrate that slaves had it easy by describing the life of the antebellum Southern belle. Another has diluted a useful study of Loyalism and blocked our understanding of any possible class aspects of this phenomenon by presenting his data in a form which does not distinguish between employers and employees. In a valuable study of legislatures before and after the Revolution, another tells us that "colonials . . . did not yet conceive that the *demos* should actually govern." *Which* colonials? Earlier in the same article he had noted that "the majority . . . were not asked, and as they were unable to

*Jesse Lemisch, "The American Revolution Seen from the Bottom Up," pp. 4–29. Condensed from *Towards a New Past*, edited by Barton J. Bernstein, by permission of Pantheon Books, a division of Random House, Inc. Copyright © 1967, 1968 by Random House, Inc. Reprinted by permission of Pantheon Books and Chatto and Windus, Ltd., London. Footnotes omitted.

speak or write on the subject, their opinions were uncertain." Thus the conclusion about "colonials" indicates either that the historian has allowed the opinions of an elite to stand for those of a majority or that he has forgotten that he really does not know what the majority thought. This dilemma suggests two very different ways of writing history.

The first way, the one criticized so far, assumes the absence of conflict without demonstrating it. After consensus has been assumed, the very categories of analysis foreclose the possibility that the researcher will find evidence of conflict. . . . And in our history we can no longer allow the powerful to speak for the powerless.

Those who rule may have, as Barrington Moore has put it, "the most to hide about the way society works." And these are the very people who are most favored by history and historical sources. Thus "sympathy with the victims of historical processes and skepticism about the victors' claims provide essential safeguards against being taken in by the dominant mythology." . . . This sympathy for the powerless brings us closer to objectivity; in practice, it leads the historian to describe past societies as they appeared from the bottom rather than the top, more from the point of view of the inarticulate than of the articulate. Such an approach will have two components. It will continue to examine the elite, but instead of using them as surrogates for the society beneath them, it will ask how their beliefs and conduct impinged on that society. Having determined the place of those who were ruled in the ideology of those who rule, it will study the conduct and ideology of the people on the bottom: this is nothing less than an attempt to make the inarticulate speak. This second task is perhaps more difficult than the first. But both can and indeed must be done if our generalizations about past societies are to have more than limited validity. . . . It is the purpose of this essay to suggest how we might approach the history of the inarticulate in the period of the American Revolution and to outline what such a history might look like. We begin with a critical examination of the place of the inarticulate in the political thought and practice of the colonial elite and proceed to an examination of the thought and conduct of the inarticulate themselves.

In 1955 Robert E. Brown joined the throng of social scientists who have been telling us that America is a classless society, a land of unblocked opportunity. Brown said it had always been so, or at least as far back as seventeenth-century Massachusetts, which he labeled a "middle-class democracy"; the "common man" in America "had come into his own long before the era of Jacksonian Democracy." Brown argued persuasively against the idea that colonial America was "undemocratic" and especially against the idea that "property qualifications for voting eliminated a large portion of the free adult male population from participation in political affairs." He showed that qualifications were often waived in practice: election officials often winked at voting by the underage or financially unqualified. At any rate, the qualifications were low enough and economic opportunity high enough so that, Brown's sampling technique indicated, most men could meet them. Of course there were a few exceptions: men whose work carried them to sea, some tenant farmers, a few town dwellers; but even these could expect, some day, to make it. Surrounded with all these blessings, Americans went to war to hold on to a good thing: the "revolution," said Brown (his quotation marks questioning the very relevance of such a term), aimed "to preserve a social order rather than to change it."

Brown's methods have come under heavy fire, with Lee Benson suggesting that there may be "no basis in fact" for the Brown thesis. Using statistical techniques similar to Brown's, John Cary has been able to demonstrate that 100 percent of the farmers and artisans of Massachusetts were disfranchised by the property requirements. Cary attaches no particular significance to his results: for a sample to mean anything, we must have some definition of the criteria used in selecting it. Brown's reply has been a partial backdown, but he has stuck to his guns in saying that the materials which he took from deeds and wills "could be called samples only in the sense of being examples, but they were *typical examples.*" . . . So let us examine more closely the contention that colonial America was democratic.

In a recent study . . . optimistic . . . about mobility in revolutionary America . . . , Jackson Turner Main nonetheless uncovered a "proletariat" comprising "nearly 40 percent" of the population. Geographical mobility was extremely high among the poor. Did this translate into vertical mobility: was mobility out the same as mobility up? Main tells us that mobility is "almost impossible to study in detail," but he proceeds to equate the frontier with upward mobility. Thus, although there was a "permanent proletariat" *within* the proletariat, it was very small. How small? "Habitual drifters" made up between 5 and 15 percent of the population, he estimates. He offers figures which bring the total up to between 26.9 and 30.7 percent and indicates that

in the pre-Revolutionary years 80 percent of indentured servants "died, became landless workers, or returned to England."

Main concludes that "the long-term tendency seems to have been toward greater inequality" and a "growing number of poor." Elsewhere, J. R. Pole has noted the potential for increasing disfranchisement if suffrage is attached to property in an area undergoing the kind of economic changes which were taking place in eighteenth-century America. That potentiality was fast becoming actuality on Brown's ground—Boston—where James Henretta's statistical work reveals the existence of a propertyless proletariat comprising 14 percent of the adult males in 1687 and 29 percent in 1771. With the population doubled, "for every man who slept in the back of a shop, in a tavern, or in a rented room in 1687, there were four" in 1771. Increasingly, colonial Boston was less a place of equality and opportunity, more a place of social stratification. Throughout America property qualifications excluded more and more people from voting until a "Jacksonian Revolution" was necessary to overthrow what had become a very limited middle-class "democracy" indeed.

What if Brown *were* right? What if every single person could vote in the colonies? Would that prove that the common man had come into his own? The common man rarely ran for office: the obstacles in the way of attaining office were far greater than those in the way of voting. Throughout America, custom and law dictated the perpetuation in power of a ruling oligarchy similar in profile to the exclusive club which ruled England. "Birth into one of the ruling families was almost essential to the making of a political career in 18th century Virginia," says one historian. The family patterns, the religious, social, and educational homogeneity of the House of Commons were duplicated in the House of Burgesses. An examination of six pre-Revolutionary legislatures shows that the "economic elite" comprising the top 10 percent of the population held 85 percent of the seats.

Even the town meeting was not in fact the hotbed of democracy of popular myth: Samuel Eliot Morison has called "political democracy" in colonial Massachusetts a "sham," and a recent study has detailed the devices which the powerful used to control the town meeting. Boston meetings were often called with whole wards unnotified, and Brown's contention that actual qualifications were less rigid than legal qualifications bears ironic fruit when the evidence is examined more closely: we find not only informal enfranchisement but also informal *disfranchisement*, all depending not on some conception of democracy but rather on how those with power thought people might vote on a particular issue.

Those who might suppose that the rise of the lower houses of the colonial legislatures was equivalent to a rise in popular control of government would do well to undertake a critical examination of the laws which they wrote. First of all, regardless of the extent of disfranchisement, it did not just happen: one group — the legislators — had to take deliberate steps to deprive others of the vote. Sometimes legislation was a blatantly one-sided expression of class interest. . . . If the assemblies stood for popular control, why was there so much conflict between the people and the legislatures on questions of civil liberties? Leonard Levy has characterized the image of a colonial America "which cherished freedom

of expression" as "a sentimental hallucination that ignores history."

If colonial legislatures seemed in many ways like the House of Commons, this was no accident: they strove to be, and they were elected in the same way — publicly and loudly, with influential candidates on hand to note how their dependents were voting and sometimes to thank them. . . . Although this is hardly free voting, some historians believe that many elections might not have turned out noticeably differently even if the ballot had been secret. For throughout the colonies they see a habit of *deference* on the part of the lower and middle classes disposing them to accept the upper class as their rulers.

Did the people defer to their rulers? Certainly we know that their rulers expected them to defer. Obedience was fully within the Lockean tradition. The *Second Treatise* is full of reassurance lest Locke's reader fear that the assertion of a right of revolution might lead to the overthrow of government "as often as it shall please a busie head, or turbulent spirit." Revolution is permissible only after "a long train of Abuses" convinces the *majority* that the time has come for an "Appeal to Heaven." Until that time the stress is on *"Obedience to the Legislative"*: the premature dissenter is "the common Enemy and Pest of Mankind" and deserves "ruine and perdition." Obedience is mandatory until the majority concludes that the government has broken its trust. Developing within this tradition, the political theory of the colonial elite saw the people as subordinate to their legislators. As Richard Buel, Jr. has put it: the people could apply the brakes when their rulers went off the track, but they could not dictate to them so long as they were still on the track. And when rulers went off the track—as the British did in 1776—the people were bound to obey the new governments which replaced them. . . .

The men who wrote and signed the Declaration of Independence were far from literal in their interpretation of the phrase "all men are created equal." Jefferson's belief that urban workingmen were "the panders of vice and the instruments by which the liberties of a country are generally overturned" suggests the narrow limits of his faith in the ability of what he unashamedly called "the swinish multitude" to govern itself. And although the Congress rejected his condemnation of the slave *trade*, it did let stand his attack on the King who had excited insurrection by offering slaves their freedom if they would desert their masters. It seems entirely likely that the Negro never even entered Jefferson's mind as he wrote of the equality of men: his later statements on the Negro characterize him as a definitely inferior being, and possibly inferior by nature rather than merely by condition.

The meaning of Jefferson's egalitarianism in 1776 can be better understood if we examine its institutional implementation in his drafts for a constitution for Virginia. His plan resembled that presented in Adams' *Thoughts on Government:* a bicameral legislature, with only the lower house directly elected, and with senators elected for lengthy terms, possibly for life. A similar antipopulism expressed itself in most of the other state constitutions: all but three provided for bicameral legislatures; property qualifications were prescribed in most; qualifications for electors and members of the upper houses were higher than for the lower houses and terms were generally longer.

Some of the state constitutions went against this trend: Pennsylvania's was the most notable. Here a convention led by men who put "personal liberty and safety" ahead of "the possession and security of property" drew up a constitution on the principle that "any man, even the most illiterate, is as capable of any office as a person who has had the benefit of education." An early draft of a bill of rights spoke of the dangers of large concentrations of wealth in the hands of a few and saw the discouragement of such concentrations as a proper role for government. The constitution as finally adopted was only slightly less populist. Its enemies called it a poor man's constitution: the people cherished their copies as they did the Bible, and they would later take up arms against its domestic opponents. . . . Property qualifications were abolished for both voters and officeholders. Power was centered in a single legislature, annually elected, checked, and balanced by the people themselves, to whom the doors of the assembly hall were to be open and who were to participate in lawmaking through a device resembling the referendum. Various officeholders were made more accountable—to meet "the danger of Establishing an inconvenient Aristocracy"—by rotation in office and limits on terms, while other provisions abolished imprisonment for debt and established the right of conscientious objection.

The Pennsylvania Constitution of 1776 shows the mark of Tom Paine's thought, if not his authorship. In *Common Sense* Paine had been concerned that "the *elected* might never form to themselves an interest separate from the *electors*"; he ridiculed the idea of checks and balances in England and proposed for each colony a single-house legislature, to meet annually; elections must be held often, in order that a "frequent interchange [among electors and elected] will establish a common interest." Later, he defended the Pennsylvania Constitution, calling it good for rich and poor alike and supporting the elimination of property qualifications and the establishment of a unicameral legislature: *"bolts, bars,* and *checks"* were only an obstacle to freedom. All in all, Paine is one man whom we should not be timid about calling a "democrat": when he spoke of freedom or rights, he meant "a perfect equality of them," and he was quite literal about it. A unicameralist in an age of checks and balances, he was also an abolitionist, an internationalist, something of a feminist and anticolonialist, and one of the few leaders of the American Revolution to apply his egalitarianism to the plight of the poor. He was in the tradition of the Levellers, and his thought presents an alternative and a standard by which to judge the thought of the other leaders of the Revolution, for most of whom Locke went far enough.

Although Paine clearly represents a minority strain in American political thought, he was not alone in 1776. Others, many of them anonymous pamphleteers, felt that the people, who "best know their own wants and necessities," were "best able to rule themselves." . . .

In the midst of the ferment of the year 1776 the Philadelphia Yearly Meeting of the Society of Friends decided to bar from membership those who continued to own slaves. The decision of 1776 was the outcome of over a century of antislavery agitation among Quakers. In 1688 the Germantown Quakers had condemned slavery as a violation of the freedom to which all men were entitled, and two decades before the Declaration of Independence the New Jersey Quaker John Woolman had applied to slavery the observation that "liberty [is] the natural right of all men equally." That the Quakers thought these thoughts demonstrates that others could have, as well; the range of thought among such groups as the Quakers gives us another perspective from which to examine early American values. Quakers had disobeyed unjust laws long before the American Revolution. They steered clear of the American mainstream in their increasingly humane treatment of Negroes and were usually equally deviant and equally humane in their conduct toward Indians, other religious and ethnic groups, women, and the poor. Few more striking alternatives to the American business ethos can be found than John Woolman, aged thirty-six, telling his customers to go elsewhere, so that he could lessen an increasingly prosperous business in order better to seek "the real substance of religion, where practice doth harmonize with principle." This absolutism, this literalism, is in a sense definitive of radicalism in a culture which has had no lack of high principles but a great deal of difficulty realizing those principles. . . .

In order to demonstrate that humane and democratic thoughts, in some ways more in tune with a later age, could be conceived in 1776, we need find only one man who thought them; in fact there were many such men. Surely the intellectual and empirical ingredients which produced the thought of a Paine or a Woolman were available to an Adams or a Jefferson. (Even if the *ingredients* of such thought were not available, the *product* was, in the form of personal conduct and published writings.) Thus we cannot explain the failure of the Revolution's leaders to choose more democratic and humane ways on grounds that the ideas' time had not yet come. The ideas were in the marketplace; the leaders' failure to buy them constitutes a choice, even if they did not conceive of it as such. Against this background, the meaning of the phrase "all men are created equal" to the men who signed the Declaration becomes clearer: they interpreted it in a limited way, and in doing so, rejected alternatives offered by their contemporaries and their predecessors. Those who have cried out for "liberty" have often sought no more than the liberty of a few, intending nothing in the way of social revolution: the liberties spoken of by Coke and Pym were primarily, as Christopher Hill has suggested, "the rights of the propertied." . . . Thus, those who, like Daniel Boorstin, have asserted that the Revolution aimed only at separation from Great Britain and not at social revolution are quite right, but only insofar as they have described the attitudes of the elite: what the common people and articulate radicals made of the Declaration of Independence may have been quite a different matter.

The evidence presented thus far suggests that in 1776 confidence in "established modes" was far from a universal sentiment. To say that Paine, Woolman, and the others mentioned above took the egalitarianism of the Declaration more literally than did those who signed the document is to say that there existed in 1776 a body of political thought which did not endorse deference. To detect such a body of thought is not necessarily to demonstrate that the people who were supposed to defer refused to do so. However, it is suggestive: people less articulate than those mentioned thus far might have developed similar ideas directly out of the actual experience of their lives. . . .

During the period of the American Revolution there was just such an expression from below: the powerless refused to stay in the places to which a theory of deference and subordination assigned them. Among the most blatant cases are those of Negroes who petitioned for that freedom to which, *"as men,"* they claimed they had "a naturel [sic] right"; they reminded their masters that their struggle was merely "[In imitat]ion of the Lawdable [sic] Example of the Good People of these States" who were "nobly contending, in the Cause of Liberty," and lectured them on "the inconsistancey [sic] of acting themselves the part which they condem [sic] and oppose in others." Merrill Jensen has ably described the pursuit of expanded political power by disfranchised whites and has presented clear evidence of conflict between rich and poor. Staughton Lynd has seen "government-from-below" in the conduct and "ideology" of New York's mechanics on the eve of the Revolution. In 1774 Gouverneur Morris observed New York's "mob" beginning "to think and to reason," debating with the rich on whether government should henceforth be "aristocratic or democratic." In 1776 much of the impetus for the movement to overthrow Pennsylvania's old government and draw up a new constitution came from below, in mass meetings and in the activities of privates in the militia.

Insofar as activities such as these focused on questions of voting, they reflect a striking failure of the lower class to provide the deference which their rulers expected of them. John Adams might boast of the respect of the Massachusetts electorate for what he later called the "natural aristocracy," and later writers might assure us that colonials did not suppose that they should govern: according to Tom Paine, voters too poor to vote would borrow or lie their way up to the property qualifications and they would do it without hesitation. Let John Adams boast about the freeness of elections in Massachusetts: in 1770 Philadelphia mechanics would refuse to rubberstamp tickets set in advance by "leading men," while their brothers in New York would rebel against the coercions which *made* them vote, again and again, for the same families. . . . If deference ever existed, it was clearly gone when Americans began to describe the supporters of open balloting as "the great and the mighty, and the rich, and the long Wiggs and the Squaretoes, and all Manner of Wickednesses in high places."

"In Pursuance of the Declaration for Independency . . .," and within less than a week, New York's debtors had been released from prison. The freeing of these "oppressed" indicates that some took their egalitarianism literally and extended their literalism to economics: Paine and Woolman were not alone in identifying economic subordination with lack of freedom. Ever since Thomas Morton's "partners and consociates" had rejected servitude in Virginia to "live together as equals" amidst the pleasures of Merrymount, many Americans had made the same identification and chosen freedom. . . . Bound servants conspired to run away, to strike and to rebel, aiming "either [to] be free or dye for it," and crying out for those *"who would be for liberty and freed from bondage"* to join them. Slaves, too, displayed what Cotton Mather called "a *Fondness* for *Freedom*": they revolted, ran away, and governed themselves in runaway communities from which they launched attacks against their former masters; they fought for "Liberty & Life" and marched "with Colours displayed, and . . . Drums beating"—a black Spirit of '76. And long

before the first trade unions, free white workers had engaged in strikes, slowdowns, and other protests, in some cases directly opposing laws which punished them for disobedience. "Mutiny" is a poor word to describe those seamen who seized their ship, renamed it *Liberty*, and chose their course and a new captain by voting. Many colonial laborers, white and Negro alike, expressed their refusal to defer by protests in which the economic grievance is hardly distinguishable from the social and political.

"Colonials" meant many people, often people in . conflict with one another: there was, from the very beginning, something of a struggle over who should rule at home. The people on the bottom of that conflict were also involved in the struggle for home rule, but their activities have been made to seem an extension of the conduct of the more articulate, who have been seen as their manipulators. The inarticulate could act on their own, and often for very sound reasons. It is time that we examined the coming of the American Revolution from their perspective. What follows is an attempt to sketch some of the kinds of events and considerations which should be explored if we are to understand what opposition to the British meant to those who were to bear the burden of the fighting and dying.

Late in October of 1765 the Stamp Act Congress added its Declarations to those of the individual colonies: the Act was unconstitutional. As Edmund and Helen Morgan have put it, "it would have been difficult to find an American anywhere who did not believe in them [Declarations of the Stamp Act Congress]—as far as they went." The problem was that many Americans did not think that they went far enough. . . .

The Stamp Act Congress had adjourned without answering the question,

What is to be *done?* The Stamp Act riots showed that the mob had begun to think and reason. Historians have been hesitant to acknowledge it. Instead they have preferred to accept the testimony of British officials who attributed the riots to "the Wiser and better Sort," who stirred up the lower class in behalf of a cause in which that class had no real interest; thus they easily turned to plunder and violence for its own sake. But gentlemen of property associated themselves with mob violence only under the most extreme conditions. Those conditions had not been achieved in 1765. British officials assumed that the lawyers and property owners were the riots' secret leaders partly because of a bias which said that leaders *had* to be people of "Consequence." In addition, these officials were accustomed to confronting members of the upper class as political adversaries in the courts and in the assembly halls. But a new politics—a politics of the street—was replacing the old politics—the politics of the assembly hall. British officials failed to understand these new politics. Wherever they went—and most of them did not go very far—they saw lawyers, merchants, and men of substance. When events which displeased them took place in the streets, they understood them only in their limited frame of reference. Transferring events to that frame, they saw only their old enemies.

The upper classes may not have been pulling the strings in the Stamp Act riots. The assumption that an uninterested mob had to be artificially aroused—created—disregards the ability of the people to think for themselves; like everyone else in the colonies, they had real grievances against the British. Unlike others, they had fewer legal channels through which to express their grievances. So they took to the streets in pursuit of political goals. Within that context, their "riots" were really extremely orderly and expressed a clear purpose. Again and again, when the mob's leaders lost control, the mob went on to attack the logical political enemy, not to plunder. They were led but not manipulated: to dismantle the puppet show is not to do away with the whole concept of leadership, but instead of cynical fomentors, we find direction of the most rudimentary sort, a question of setting times, of priorities, and in the heat of the riot, of getting from one street to another in the quickest way possible.

The struggle against the Stamp Act was also a struggle against colonial leadership. Declarations had not prevented the Act's taking effect. Those who had *declared* now had to *do,* but they could do no better than a boycott: the cessation of all business which required the use of stamps. This strategy put pressure on the English merchants, but it also increased the pressure on the American poor, the hungry, the prisoners in city jails who could not hope for release so long as the lawyers refused to do business.

Radicals protested against the absurdity of American blustering about liberty and then refusing to do anything about it: if the law was wrong, then it was no law and business ought to go on as usual without the use of stamps. They urged disobedience. Upper-class leaders demanded legality and tried, sometimes by shady means, to suppress or distort this dissent. But the radicals continued their pressure, and they were supported by the self-defeating character of the boycott strategy. The more time that passed without ship sailings, the more attractive a policy of disobedience became to merchants, and they began to send their ships out without stamped papers. British officials began to cave in: they were worried about "an Insurrection of the Poor against the Rich," united action by unemployed artisans and the increasing numbers of unruly seamen who were pouring into the colonial cities and finding no way to get out. The seamen—"the ... people ... most dangerous on these Occasions"—especially worried customs officials; instead of waiting for them to force their captains to sail without stamps, the officials yielded, giving way before enormous pressures and allowing a radical triumph. Then the Parliament itself backed down, repealing the Stamp Act. The poor people of the colonies had reason to congratulate themselves: word of their actions had thrown a scare into Parliament, and they might even suspect that the economic rationale which Parliament offered for repeal covered its fear of a challenge not so much to its view of the constitution as to its actual authority in the colonies. Thus the meaning of the Stamp Act crisis goes beyond the pursuit of constitutional principles. The lower class had spoken out against the British, against deference, and against colonial leadership, and they had won.

The repeal of the Stamp Act left the Sugar Act of 1764 still on the books, and in 1767 Parliament added a new revenue act. Oliver M. Dickerson has described the activities of the new American Board of Customs Commissioners in enforcing these acts beginning in 1768 as "customs racketeering" and has blamed the Board for transforming "thousands of loyal British subjects into active revolutionists." Corrupt customs officers made seizures on technicalities and pocketed the proceeds. The Hancocks and the Laurenses suffered greatly, but the poor suffered more. Even the pettiest of woodboats in purely local trade were seized; even the common seaman had his chest rifled and its contents confiscated. Seamen, small traders, and rich merchants all came to identify British authority with corruption and injustice.

Customs racketeering was on the wane by mid-1770. This was due in large part to popular opposition and especially to the withdrawal of troops from Boston: the Commissioners could not survive without armed support. The troops left Boston after the street fight which came to be known as the Boston Massacre. The Massacre, in turn, grew out of an antagonism between the troops and the population which has been given too little attention. Long-standing practice in the British army allowed off-duty soldiers to take civilian employment, and they did so at wages which undercut those given to American workingmen: soldiers in New York in 1770 worked for between 37.5 percent and 50 percent of the wages offered to Americans for the same work. As might be expected, this situation led to great antagonisms, especially in hard times. . . . On the evening of March 5 one of the ropemakers who had been wounded in the earlier encounter led a mob which took on the rampaging soldiers. "Come on you rascals, you bloody backs, you lobster scoundrels, fire if you dare, G[o]d damn you, fire and be damned, we know you dare not." Somebody did dare: when the smoke cleared, the ropemaker was dead along with two others and several wounded. . . .

The British Navy was as unpopular in the colonies as was the Army. One of the reasons for the Navy's unpopularity has been almost entirely missed by historians who have shown too little concern for those matters which concern the inarticulate. Impressment, previously seen as significant only in connection with the War of 1812, also played a role in bringing on the Revolution. . . . The poor were the press gang's peculiar victims. . . . Their numbers mounted into the tens of thousands. The complaints of American governmental bodies spoke for the merchant, not the seaman; they focused on the harmful effects of the practice on colonial trade and seemed almost as critical of those who violently resisted as of the Royal Navy. So the seamen and poor people of the colonies were on their own. Historians have failed to see the significance of their active opposition to impressment: one seems to put blame on seamen for escaping and fighting back, much as one might blame slaves for the same offenses; another, admitting that colonial crowds became "political" in 1765, sees the innumerable impressment riots before that date as "ideologically inert." But the seamen were fighting, literally, for their life, liberty, and property, and their violence was all the politics they could have. . . .

Excessive attention to *Common Sense* for its propaganda values has obscured its substantive meaning as an expression of populist democracy. Indeed, the very concept of "propaganda" has perhaps hindered us more than it has helped us to understand the causes of the American Revolution. "We know today," wrote Philip Davidson in 1941, "that large bodies of people never cooperate in any complex movement except under the guidance of a central machine operated by a comparatively few people. . . ." Davidson found a few people—men like Tom Paine and Sam Adams—managing such a campaign: "'By their fruits ye shall know them.'" The assumption here is that one can read back from the "fruits" —the Revolution—to the efforts of propagandists, that is, that Paine and Adams in some sense *caused* the Revolution. . . . All of this smacks of unproved conspiracy and utterly ignores the fact that Paine did speak "common sense": the Revolution has substantive causes and is rooted

in genuine grievances; to explain it as the result of efficient propaganda is to belittle the reality of the grievances and to suggest that the Americans were largely content until they were aroused by a few demagogues.

The final test of the agency of the lower class is their conduct in the Revolution: if they had been tricked into rebellion by demagoguery and propaganda, we might expect them to have had second thoughts when the fighting became bloody. From April 19, 1775, the war was fought, on the American side, by a people in arms, understanding and interpreting their war goals in their own way. The American technique was frequently that of guerrilla warfare, depending on mobility, withdrawal, and unexpected counterattack: they fled when they could not win and turned and fought only when they had a good chance of victory. The Revolution was like modern guerrilla wars in another sense. In guerrilla warfare, according to the aphorism, the people are the water and the troops are the fish who inhabit that water. The troops must live off the people, retaining their support not by coercion but rather because the people believe in and support the cause for which the troops fight. Although the analogy with guerrilla warfare is only an analogy, it is suggestive. As long as the Americans continued to fight, it was impossible for the British to win the war. Mere military conquest was insignificant: to win, the British would have had to occupy simultaneously the entire populated area of the thirteen colonies, and even then their victory would have been unstable, a peace maintained only by force. The British could not win precisely because the Americans were fighting a popular war.

Although an analogy with guerrilla warfare can give us some suggestion as to the extent of patriotism during the

Revolution, we need more specific information. One fruitful technique for evaluating the loyalties of the inarticulate is to look at them under pressure—in prison. With little chance of exchange, amidst starvation and disease, and ruled over by cruel and corrupt administrators, captured American seamen were offered a way out: they could join the Royal Navy. Most remained patriots, and they were very self-conscious about it. Instead of defecting, they resisted, escaping, burning their prisons, and defiantly celebrating the Fourth of July. Separated from their captains and governing themselves for the first time, on their own they organized into disciplined groups with bylaws: in microcosm the prisoners went through the whole process of setting up a constitution. . . .

If the American Revolution was a popular war, still, support for it was far from universal. John Adams later estimated that "nearly one third" of the Americans sided with the British. Who were the Loyalists? Social class may have had nothing to do with the phenomenon of Loyalism, but we will never know if we foreclose research on the matter; we continue to need studies which at least pose the question. A recent study generalizes about Loyalists, including under the heading "Artisans and craftsmen" such diverse groups as an owner of salt works, managers, and manufacturers undifferentiated from laborers and waiters. Any conceivable difference between merchants and their clerks, captains and common seamen, doctors and their apprentices is obliterated by the categorization. So long as our techniques of research foreclose the possibility of our finding anything but consensus the case for consensus will be unproved.

Finally, we need studies which will use Loyalism as a touchstone for a more precise definition of the Revolution. Loyalists had very little faith in man and reveled in the inequalities among men. Wealthy Massachusetts judge Peter Oliver distinguished between such "Men of Sense" as John Adams and the common people, whom he repeatedly dismissed as "Rabble." Maryland clergyman Jonathan Boucher had resolved, before his twelfth birthday, not to "pass through life like the boors around me"; the people were "fickle," "false," "wrongheaded," and "ignorant." The Loyalist view of the American Revolution built on their view of the nature of man. The "Mobility of all Countries," said Oliver, were "perfect Machines" which could be "wound up by any Hand who might first take the Winch." Sam Adams, he said, "understood human Nature, in low life, so well, that he could turn the Minds of the great Vulgar as well as the small into any Course that he might chuse"; the people were "duped," "deceived," and "deluded" by demagogues who were motivated by ambition and pride and aimed to satisfy "private grudges." . . . "Many, if not most of you," said Oliver to the rebellious people of Massachusetts, "were insensible of the ambitious views of your leaders" and would have spurned those leaders but for ignorance.

There seems to be a common theme in Loyalism: a rejection of the idea that all men are created equal. If those who opposed the Revolution rejected egalitarianism, this suggests that what they rejected—the Revolution itself—might have been in some sense egalitarian. On the other hand, how much difference would one find, in regard to egalitarianism, between the views of an Oliver or a Boucher and a Hamilton? or even an Adams? When egalitarianism is the point of division, men such as Hamilton and Adams appear closer to the Loyalists than they do to Paine. Such a conclusion would strengthen the theory that the Revolution was a fight over "the true constitution of the British Empire" rather than a social movement—*on the level of leadership*. Regardless of the result, studies comparing the leaders of the Revolution with the right-wing alternatives available to them would bring us much closer to the meaning of the Revolution.

In neither the French Revolution nor the American Civil War did a losing cause do so well on the battlefields of historiography as has Loyalism. While the Loyalists themselves may not have too many friends, their accents—manipulation, propaganda, and the mindlessness of the people—reign largely unchallenged, albeit in somewhat different language, in the recent historiography of the American Revolution. Perhaps underlying this remarkable congruence is a modern lack of faith in man, echoing the Loyalists' dim view of human nature. Regardless of the cause, our historiography has taken on a flavor of unintentional partisanship; this has given rise to a one-sided history which must be reexamined.

The American Revolution can best be re-examined from a point of view which assumes that all men are created equal, and rational, and that since they can think and reason they can make their own history. These assumptions are nothing more nor less than the democratic credo. All of our history needs re-examination from this perspective. The history of the powerless, the inarticulate, the poor has not yet begun to be written because they have been treated no more fairly by historians than they have been treated by their contemporaries.

J. FRANKLIN JAMESON (1859–1937) served as managing editor of the *American Historical Review* from its founding in 1895 to 1928, except for a four-year interval. After a teaching career at Johns Hopkins, Brown University, and The University of Chicago, Jameson served as Director of Historical Research in the Carnegie Institution of Washington and as Chief of the Division of Manuscripts in the Library of Congress. Jameson's work, *The American Revolution Considered as a Social Movement*, stresses the extent of the social reforms won at home during the war. Both Jameson and Schlesinger emphasize class conflict in the Revolution. Which selection is the more moderate in its approach?*

J. Franklin Jameson

The Revolution as a Social Movement

It is indeed true that our Revolution was strikingly unlike that of France, and that most of those who originated it had no other than a political programme, and would have considered its work done when political independence of Great Britain had been secured. But who can say to the waves of revolution: Thus far shall we go and no farther? The various fibres of a nation's life are knit together in great complexity. It is impossible to sever some without also loosening others, and setting them free to combine anew in widely different forms. The Americans were much more conservative than the French. But their political and their social systems, though both were, as the great orator said, still in the gristle and not yet hardened into the bone of manhood, were too intimately connected to permit that the one should remain unchanged while the other was radically altered. The stream of revolution, once started, could not be confined within narrow banks, but spread abroad upon the land. Many economic desires, many social aspirations were set free by the political struggle, many aspects of colonial society profoundly altered by the forces thus let loose. The relations of social classes to each other, the institution of slavery, the system of landholding, the course of business, the forms and spirit of the intellectual and religious life, all felt the transforming hand of revolution, all emerged from under it in shapes advanced many degrees nearer to those we know. . . .

*From J. Franklin Jameson, *The American Revolution Considered as a Social Movement* (Princeton, N.J.: Princeton University Press, 1940), pp 9–38, *passim*.

If then it is rational to suppose that the American Revolution had some social consequences, what would they be likely to be? It would be natural to reply that it depends on the question, who caused the Revolution, and that therefore it becomes important to inquire what manner of men they were, and what they would be likely, consciously or unconsciously, to desire. In reality, the matter is not quite so simple as that. Allowance has to be made for one important fact in the natural history of revolutions, and that is that, as they progress, they tend to fall into the hands of men holding more and more advanced or extreme views, less and less restrained by traditional attachment to the old order of things. Therefore the social consequences of a revolution are not necessarily shaped by the conscious or unconscious desires of those who started it, but more likely by the desires of those who came into control of it at later stages of its development. . . .

All things considered, it seems clear that in most states the strength of the revolutionary party lay most largely in the plain people, as distinguished from the aristocracy. It lay not in the mob or rabble, for American society was overwhelmingly rural and not urban, and had no sufficient amount of mob or rabble to control the movement, but in the peasantry, substantial and energetic though poor, in the small farmers and frontiersmen. And so, although there were men of great possessions like George Washington and Charles Carroll of Carrollton who contributed a conservative element, in the main we must expect to see our social changes tending in the direction of levelling democracy.

It would be aside from the declared purpose of these lectures to dwell upon the political effects which resulted from the victory of a party constituted in the manner that has been described. There are, however, some political changes that almost inevitably bring social changes in their wake. Take, for instance, the expansion of the suffrage. The status in which the electoral franchise was left at the end of the Revolutionary period fell far short of complete democracy. Yet during the years we are considering the right of suffrage was much extended. The freeholder, or owner of real estate, was given special privileges in four of the new state constitutions, two others widened the suffrage to include all owners of either land or personal property to a certain limit, and two others conferred it upon all tax-payers. Now if . . . we are considering especially the status of persons, we must take account of the fact that the elevation of whole classes of people to the status of voters elevates them also in their social status. . . .

A far more serious question, in any consideration of the effect of the American Revolution on the status of persons, is that of its influence on the institution of slavery, for at this time the contrast between American freedom and American slavery comes out, for the first time, with startling distinctness. It has often been asked: How could men who were engaged in a great and inspiring struggle for liberty fail to perceive the inconsistency between their professions and endeavors in that contest and their actions with respect to their bondmen? How could they fail to see the application of their doctrines respecting the rights of man to the black men who were held among them in bondage far more reprehensible than that to which they indignantly proclaimed themselves to have been subjected by the King of Great Britain? . . .

There is no lack of evidence that, in

the American world of that time, the analogy between freedom for whites and freedom for blacks was seen. If we are to select but one example of such evidence, the foremost place must surely be given to the striking language of Patrick Henry, used in 1773, when he was immersed in the struggle against Great Britain. It is found in a letter which he wrote to one who had sent him a copy of Anthony Benezet's book on slavery.

Is it not amazing [he says] that at a time, when the rights of humanity are defined and understood with precision, in a country above all others fond of liberty, that in such an age and in such a country we find men professing a religion the most humane, mild, gentle and generous, adopting a principle as repugnant to humanity as it is inconsistent with the Bible and destructive to liberty? . . . Would anyone believe I am the master of slaves of my own purchase! I am drawn along by the general inconvenience of living here without them. I will not, I can not justify it. However culpable my conduct, I will so far pay my devoir to virtue, as to own the excellence and rectitude of her precepts, and lament my want of conformity to them. I believe a time will come when an opportunity will be offered to abolish this lamentable evil. . . .

Along with many examples and expressions of individual opinion, we may note the organized efforts toward the removal or alleviation of slavery manifested in the creation of a whole group of societies for these purposes. The first anti-slavery society in this or any other country was formed on April 14, 1775, five days before the battle of Lexington, by a meeting at the Sun Tavern, on Second Street in Philadelphia. The members were mostly of the Society of Friends. . . . The New York "Society for Promoting the Manumission of Slaves" was organized in 1785, with John Jay for its first president. In 1788 a society similar

to these two was founded in Delaware, and within four years there were other such in Rhode Island, Connecticut, New Jersey, Maryland, and Virginia, and local societies enough to make at least thirteen, mostly in the slave-holding states.

In actual results of the growing sentiment, we may note, first of all, the checking of the importation of slaves, and thus of the horrors of the trans-Atlantic slave trade. The Continental Congress of 1774 had been in session but a few days when they decreed an "American Association," or non-importation agreement, in which one section read: "That we will neither import nor purchase any slave imported after the first day of December next, after which we will wholly discontinue the slave trade, and will neither be concerned in it ourselves, nor will we hire our vessels nor sell our commodities or manufactures to those who are concerned in it"; and the evidence seems to be that the terms of this agreement were enforced throughout the war with little evasion.

States also acted. Four months before this, in July 1774, Rhode Island had passed a law to the effect that all slaves thereafter brought into the colony should be free. . . . A similar law was passed that same year in Connecticut. Delaware prohibited importation in 1776, Virginia in 1778, Maryland in 1783, South Carolina in 1787, for a term of years, and North Carolina, in 1786, imposed a larger duty on each negro imported.

Still further, the states in which slaves were few proceeded, directly as a consequence of the Revolutionary movement, to effect the immediate or gradual abolition of slavery itself. Vermont had never recognized its existence, but Vermont was not recognized as a state. Pennsylvania in 1780 provided for gradual abolition, by an act which declared that no negro born after that date should be held in any sort of bondage after he became twenty-eight years old, and that up to that time his service should be simply like that of an indented servant or apprentice. Now what says the preamble of this act? That when we consider our deliverance from the abhorrent condition to which Great Britain has tried to reduce us, we are called on to manifest the sincerity of our professions of freedom, and to give substantial proof of gratitude, by extending a portion of our freedom to others, who, though of a different color, are the work of the same Almighty hand. Evidently here also the leaven of the Revolution was working as a prime cause in this philanthropic endeavor.

The Superior Court of Massachusetts declared that slavery had been abolished in that state by the mere declaration of its constitution that "all men are born free and equal." In 1784 Connecticut and Rhode Island passed acts which gradually extinguished slavery. In other states, ameliorations of the law respecting slaves were effected even though the abolition of slavery could not be brought about. Thus in 1782 Virginia passed an act which provided that any owner might, by an instrument properly attested, freely manumit all his slaves, if he gave security that their maintenance should not become a public charge. It may seem but a slight thing, this law making private manumission easy where before it had been difficult. But it appears to have led in eight years to the freeing of more than ten thousand slaves, twice as great a number as were freed by reason of the Massachusetts constitution, and as many as there were in Rhode Island and Connecticut together when the war broke out. . . .

Thus in many ways the successful struggle for the independence of the United States affected the character of American society by altering the status of persons. The freeing of the community led not unnaturally to the freeing of the individual; the raising of colonies to the position of independent states brought with it the promotion of many a man to a higher order in the scale of privilege or consequence. So far at any rate as this aspect of life in America is concerned, it is vain to think of the Revolution as solely a series of political or military events. . . .

If anything should occur which should administer a great shock to the entire social system of the country, it would dislodge and shake off from the body politic, as an outworn vesture, such institutions as no longer met our needs. Now this is just what the Revolution did. It broke up so much that was traditional and customary with the Americans, in dissolving their allegiance to a monarchy for which they had felt a most loyal attachment, that whatever else was outgrown or exotic seemed to be thrown into the melting-pot, to be recast into a form better suited to the work which the new nation had before it. The hot sun of revolution withered whatever was not deeply rooted in the soil. There was no violent outbreak against the land-system, for there had been no grinding oppressions or exactions connected with it. No maddened and blood-stained peasants rushed furiously from château to château, burning court-rolls and shedding the blood of seigneurs and châtelains. But in a quiet, sober, Anglo-Saxon way a great change was effected in the land-system of America between the years 1775 and 1795.

In the first place, royal restrictions on the acquisition of land fell into abeyance. The king's proclamation of 1763, forbidding settlement and the patenting of lands beyond the Alleghenies, and those provisions of the Quebec Act of 1774 which in a similar sense restricted westward expansion and the formation of new, interior colonies had, it is true, never been executed with complete rigidity, but they, and the uncertainties of the months preceding the war, had certainly checked many a project of large colonization and many a plan for speculation in land. Now these checks were removed. Moreover, all the vast domains of the Crown fell into the hands of the states, and were at the disposal of the state legislatures, and it was certain that these popular assemblies would dispose of them in some manner that would be agreeable to popular desires. Whether the land law in respect to old holdings should be altered by the Revolution or should remain unchanged, it was certain that in respect to new lands, on which the future hopes of American agriculture and settlement rested, a more democratic system would be installed.

Then there was the matter of the quit-rents, which in most of the colonies, according to the terms on which lands were granted to individual occupants, were to be paid to the crown or to the proprietary of the province. They ranged from a penny an acre to a shilling a hundred acres per annum. It is true that payment was largely evaded, but since the amount received at the time when the Revolution broke out was nearly $100,-000, we may count the quit-rent as something of a limitation upon the ready acquisition of land. So at any rate the colonists regarded it, for in making their new constitutions and regulations respecting lands they abolished quit-rents with great emphasis and vigor, and forbade them for the future.

Another encumbrance on land-tenure which the Revolution removed was the provision, by British statute intended to ensure an adequate supply of masts for the royal navy, that no man should cut white-pine trees on his land till the king's surveyor of woods had surveyed it and designated the trees, sometimes many in number, which were to be reserved for the king's use. It is true that the law was not rigorously enforced; it could not be, with such staff as the surveyors had. But John Wentworth, the last royal governor of New Hampshire and the last surveyor of the king's woods in New England, tried diligently to enforce it, and, though he did it tactfully, he found it everywhere exceedingly unpopular. With the coming of the Revolution, the restriction came to an end, and fee simple was fee simple.

In the fourth place, great confiscations of Tory estates were carried out by the state legislatures, generally in the height of the war. New Hampshire confiscated twenty-eight estates, including the large property of its governor, Sir John Wentworth. In Massachusetts a sweeping act confiscated at one blow all the property of all who had fought against the United States or had even retired into places under British authority without permission from the American government. . . . In New York, all lands and rents of the crown and all estates of fifty-nine named persons were confiscated, the greatest among them, probably, being that of the Phillipse connection. . . .

The largest estate confiscated was that of the Penn family, proprietaries of Pennsylvania, which they estimated at nearly a million pounds sterling. The commissioners of the state of Maryland who sold confiscated property in that state took in more than £450,000 sterling. In Georgia the single estate of Sir James Wright was valued at $160,000. The broad lands of the sixth Lord Fairfax, the genial old man in whose service

Washington had first practised as a surveyor, and those of Sir John Johnson in the Mohawk country, 50,000 acres, are other examples of Tory confiscation on the grand scale. In one colony and another, hundreds of estates were confiscated. Altogether, it is evident that a great deal of land changed hands, and that the confiscation of Tory estates contributed powerfully to break up the system of large landed properties, since the states usually sold the lands thus acquired in much smaller parcels. . . .

If, as I have suggested, nothing was more important in the American social system than its relation to the land, and if the Revolution had any social effects at all, we should expect to see it overthrowing any old-fashioned features which still continued to exist in the land laws. What, then, was the old land-law in the American colonies? The feudal ages had discovered that, if men desired to give stability to society by keeping property in the hands of the same families generation after generation, the best way to do this was to entail the lands strictly, so that the holder could not sell them or even give them away, and to have a law of primogeniture, which, in case the father made no will, would turn over all his lands to the eldest son, to the exclusion of all the other children. There could not be two better devices for forming and maintaining a landholding aristocracy. When the Revolution broke out, Pennsylvania and Maryland had abolished primogeniture, and South Carolina had abolished entails. But in New York, New Jersey, Virginia, North Carolina, and Georgia, entails and primogeniture flourished almost as they did in old England. Indeed, Virginian entails were stricter than the

English. The New England colonies had a peculiar rule of their own for the descent of land in case a man left no will. They liked a democratic distribution, and yet they could not feel quite comfortable to cut away entirely from the old English notions about the eldest son. Moreover, their Puritanical feeling for the law of Moses (Deut. xxi 17) was very strong. Accordingly, they arranged that in such a case all the children should inherit equally, except that the eldest son should have a double share. Then came the Revolution. In ten years from the Declaration of Independence every state had abolished entails excepting two, and those were two in which entails were rare. In fifteen years every state, without exception, abolished primogeniture and in some form provided for equality of inheritance, since which time the American eldest son has never been a privileged character. It is painful to have to confess that two states, North Carolina and New Jersey, did not at once put the daughters of the Revolution upon a level with the sons. North Carolina for a few years provided for equal distribution of the lands among the sons alone, and not among daughters save in case there were no sons. New Jersey gave the sons a double share. But elsewhere absolute equality was introduced. Now I submit that this was not an accident. How hard Washington found it to get these thirteen legislatures to act together! And yet here we find them all with one accord making precisely the same changes in their land-laws. Such uniformity must have had a common cause, and where shall we find it if we do not admit that our Revolution, however much it differed from the French Revolution in spirit, yet carried in itself the seeds of a social revolution?

MERRILL JENSEN (1905–1980) who taught at the University of Wisconsin, inherited the mantle of earlier Progressive historians such as Beard, Becker, and Jameson. In two major works, *The Articles of Confederation* and *The New Nation*, Jensen sharply revised the traditional view of the so-called "critical" period. In contrast to Jameson, who stresses social and economic reforms during the Revolution, Jensen emphasizes advances in political democracy. Does Jensen believe the Revolution was a democratic movement in its origins?*

Merrill Jensen

The Revolution as a Democratic Movement

The historian who ventures to talk about democracy in early America is in danger because there are almost as many opinions as there are writers on the subject. The Puritans have been pictured as the founders of American democracy, and it is vigorously denied that they had anything to do with it. Some have seen in Roger Williams the father of American democracy, and others have denied that he was a democrat, whatever his putative progeny may be. The conflict is equally obvious when it comes to the American Revolution, and the problems of solution are far more complex than they are for the seventeenth century. The difficulty is compounded, for all too often men's emotions seem to become involved.

It is sometimes suggested that we avoid the use of the word "democracy" when discussing the seventeenth and eighteenth centuries. It seems to me that this is a flat evasion of the problem, for the Americans of those centuries used the word and they meant something by it. Our task, then, is not to avoid the issue but to try to understand what they meant, and understand what they meant in the context of the times in which they lived. What we must not do is to measure the seventeenth and eighteenth centuries in terms of our own assumptions about what democracy is or should be. This is all the more important since many of us do not seem to be too clear about our assumptions, even for the century in which we live.

---

* Merrill Jensen, "Democracy and the American Revolution," *Huntington Library Quarterly*, XX (August, 1957), pp. 321–341. Reprinted by permission of the *Huntington Library Quarterly*.

A number of years ago I took the position that "in spite of the paradoxes involved one may still maintain that the Revolution was essentially, though relatively, a democratic movement within the thirteen American colonies, and that its significance for the political and constitutional history of the United States lay in its tendency to elevate the political and economic status of the majority of the people." And then, with a somewhat rhetorical flourish which I have sometimes regretted but have not as yet withdrawn, I went on to say that "the Articles of Confederation were the constitutional expression of this movement and the embodiment in governmental form of the philosophy of the Declaration of Independence."[1] One thing can be said for this statement at least: reviewers read it and quoted it, some with raised eyebrows, and some with approval, whether or not they said anything at all about the rest of the book.

During most of the present century historians have assumed that democracy was involved somehow or other in the American Revolution. They have assumed also that there were conditions within the American colonies that were not satisfactory to at least some of the American people. The causes of internal discontent were various, ranging all the way from religious to economic differences. The discontent was of such intensity that in certain colonies it led to explosive outbreaks in the 1760's such as the Regulator movements in the Carolinas, the Paxton Boys' uprising in Pennsylvania, and the tenant farmer revolt in New York, outbreaks that were suppressed by the armed forces of the colo-

nial governments and with the help of British power.

Most historians have agreed also that the individual colonies were controlled politically by relatively small groups of men in each of them, allied by family, or economic or political interests, or by some combination of these. The colonial aristocracies owed their position to many things: to their wealth and ability, to their family connections and political allies, and to the British government which appointed them to office. As opposed to Britain, they had won virtual self-government for the colonies by 1763. Yet in every colony they were a minority who managed to maintain internal control through property qualifications for the suffrage, especially effective in the growing towns, and through refusal or failure to grant representation in any way proportional to the population of the rapidly growing frontier areas. Probably more important than either of these was the fact that in most colonies the aristocracies manned the upper houses of the legislatures, the supreme courts, and other important posts—all by royal appointment. Beyond this, their control extended down through the county court system, even in Massachusetts. In short, colonial political society was not democratic in operation despite the elective lower houses and the self-government which had been won from Great Britain.[2]

This is a brief but, I think, fair summary of a widely held point of view concerning the political actualities at the beginning of the revolutionary era.

1 Merrill Jensen, *The Articles of Confederation: An Interpretation of the Social-Constitutional History of the American Revolution, 1774–1781*, reprint with new foreword (Madison, Wis., 1948), pp. 15, 239.

2 *Ibid.*, ch. iii, "The Internal Revolution"; Leonard W. Labaree, *Conservatism in Early American History* (New York, 1948); and Robert J. Taylor, *Western Massachusetts in the Revolution* (Providence, 1954), as examples. For methods of local control see Charles S. Sydnor, *Gentlemen Freeholders: Political Practices in Washington's Virginia* (Chapel Hill, 1952).

This view has been challenged recently. A writer on Massachusetts declared that "as far as Massachusetts is concerned, colonial society and the American Revolution must be interpreted in terms something very close to a complete democracy with the exception of British restraints." It was not controlled by a wealthy aristocracy. There was little inequality of representation, and property was so widely held that virtually every adult male could vote.[3] The assumption that Massachusetts was an idyllic democracy, united in the fight against British tyranny, will be somewhat surprising to those who have read the letters of Francis Bernard and the diary of John Adams, not to mention the history of Thomas Hutchinson, and, I suspect, would be even more surprising to those gentlemen as well. Elsewhere, this writer has implied that what was true for Massachusetts was probably true for other colonies and for the United States after the Revolution.[4]

On the other hand it is asserted that democracy had nothing to do with the Revolution. Such an assertion made in connection with Pennsylvania is a little startling, for ever since C. H. Lincoln's work of more than a half century ago, down to the present, it has been held that there was a democratic movement in Pennsylvania during the revolutionary era. Not so, says a reviewer of the most recent study. He declares that "the attribution of democratic motivations and ideas to eighteenth century colonists is a common fault among many historians of the colonial period. . . ." He

argues that the struggle in Pennsylvania before 1776 was one between "radical and conservative variants of whiggism," which he defines as one between "those who held privilege most dear and those who valued property above all." The Pennsylvania Constitution of 1776 itself was not democratic, but a triumph of "colonial radical whiggism."[5]

It is clear that a considerable diversity of opinion prevails. It is also clear that the time has come to set forth certain propositions or generalizations which seem to me to have a measure of validity.

First of all, a definition of democracy is called for. And just to face the issue squarely, I will offer one stated at Newport, Rhode Island, in 1641 when a meeting declared that "the government which this body politic doth attend unto . . . is a democracy or popular government; . . . that is to say: It is in the power of the body of freemen, orderly assembled, or the major part of them, to make or constitute just laws, by which they will be regulated, and to depute from among themselves such ministers as shall see them faithfully executed between man and man." That such an idea was not confined to Newport was shown six years later when the little towns in Rhode Island formed a confederation, the preamble of which states: "It is agreed, by this present assembly thus incorporate, and by this present act declared, that the form of government established in Providence Plantations is democratical; that is to say, a government held by the free and voluntary consent of all, or the greater part of the free inhabitants."

These are simple but, I think, adequate definitions. I will go even further

---

[3] Robert E. Brown, "Democracy in Colonial Massachusetts," *New England Quarterly*, XXV (1952), 291–313, and at length in *Middle Class Democracy and the Revolution in Massachusetts, 1691–1780* (Ithaca, N.Y., 1955).
[4] Robert E. Brown, "Economic Democracy Before the Constitution," *American Quarterly*, VII (1955), 257–274.

[5] Roy N. Lokken, review of Theodore Thayer, *Pennsylvania Politics and the Growth of Democracy, 1740–1776* (Harrisburg, 1953), in *William and Mary Quarterly*, XII (1955), 671.

and offer as a theoretical and philosophical foundation for democracy the statement by Roger Williams in the *Bloudy Tenent* of 1644. After describing civil government as an ordinance of God to conserve the civil peace of the people so far as concerns their bodies and goods, he goes on to say: "The sovereign, original, and foundation of civil power lies in the people (whom they must needs mean by the civil power distinct from the government set up). And if so, that a people may erect and establish what form of government seems to them most meet for their civil condition. It is evident that such governments as are by them erected and established have no more power, nor for no longer time, than the civil power or people consenting and agreeing shall betrust them with. This is clear not only in reason, but in the experience of all commonweals where the people are not deprived of their natural freedom by the power of tyrants."[6]

The central issue in seventeenth-century New England was not social equality, manhood suffrage, women's rights, or sympathy for the Levellers, or other tests which have been applied. The central issue was the source of authority for the establishment of a government. The English view was that no government could exist in a colony without a grant of power from the crown. The opposite view, held by certain English dissenters in New England, was that a group of people could create a valid government for themselves by means of a covenant, compact, or constitution. The authors of the Mayflower Compact and the Fundamental Orders of Connecticut operated on this assumption, although they did not carry it to the logical conclusion and

call it democracy as did the people in Rhode Island. It is the basic assumption of the Declaration of Independence, a portion of which reads much like the words of Roger Williams written 132 years earlier.

The second proposition is that colonial governments on the eve of the Revolution did not function democratically, nor did the men who controlled them believe in democracy. Even if we agree that there was virtually manhood suffrage in Massachusetts, it is difficult, for me at least, to see it as a democracy. In 1760 the government was controlled by a superb political machine headed by Thomas Hutchinson, who with his relatives and political allies occupied nearly every important political office in the colony except the governorship. The Hutchinson oligarchy controlled the superior court, the council, the county courts, and the justices of the peace; with this structure of appointive office spread throughout the colony, it was able to control the house of representatives elected by the towns. For six years after 1760 the popular party in Boston, led by Oxenbridge Thacher and James Otis, suffered one defeat after another at the hands of the Hutchinson machine. The popular leaders in the town of Boston tried everything from slander to mob violence to get control of the government of the colony but it was not until after the Stamp Act crisis that they were able to win a majority of the house of representatives to their side. Even then, men like James Otis did not at first realize that the Stamp Act could be turned to advantage in the fight against the Hutchinson oligarchy.[7] In terms of political support between 1760 and 1765, if Massachusetts had a democratic

---

6 *English Historical Documents*, IX, *American Colonial Documents to 1775*, ed. Merrill Jensen (London and New York, 1955), pp. 168, 226, 174.

7 See Ellen E. Brennan, *Plural Office Holding in Massachusetts 1760–1780* (Chapel Hill, 1945), and "James Otis: Recreant and Patriot," *New England Quarterly*, XII (1939), 691–725.

leader, that man was Thomas Hutchinson, a charge to which he would have been the first to issue a horrified denial.

The third proposition is that before 1774 or 1775 the revolutionary movement was not a democratic movement, except by inadvertence. The pamphleteers who wrote on political and constitutional questions, and the town and county meetings and legislatures that resolved endlessly between 1763 and 1774, were concerned with the formulation of constitutional arguments to defend the colonies and their legislatures from interference by parliament.

The colonial theorists wrote much about the British constitution, the rights of Englishmen, and even of the laws of nature, but they accepted the British assumption that colonial governments derived from British charters and commissions. Their essential concern was with the relationship that existed, or ought to exist, between the British government and the colonial governments, and not with the relationship between man as man, and government itself. Such writers showed no interest in domestic problems, and when it was suggested that the arguments against taxation by parliament were equally applicable to the taxation of under-represented areas in the colonies, or to dissenting religious groups, such suggestions were looked upon as being quite out of order.

The same indifference was displayed in the realm of political realities. The ardent leaders of the fight against British policies showed no interest in, or sympathy for, the discontent of back-country farmers or religious groups such as the Baptists. Instead, they temporarily joined with their political enemies to suppress or ignore it. Such sympathy as the discontented got, they got from the British government, or from colonial leaders charged with being tools of the British power.

The fact is that the popular leaders of the revolutionary movement had no program of domestic reform.[8] Instead, their program was a combination of a continuous assault on the local office-holding aristocracies and an ardent attack on British policies; and in the course of time they identified one with the other. It is sometimes difficult to tell with which side of the program the popular leaders were more concerned. In Massachusetts, for instance, before 1765 they were so violent in their attack on Hutchinson that they prevented Massachusetts from joining the other colonies in making formal protests against British legislation.

The fourth proposition is related to the third. It is that although the popular leaders in the colonies showed no interest in internal political and social change, they were still able to build up a political following, particularly in the seacoast towns. They were superb organizers, propagandists with a touch of genius, and possessed of an almost demonic energy in their dual fight against the local political aristocracies and British policies. After a few false starts such as that of James Otis, who at first called the Virginia Stamp Act Resolves treason,[9] the popular leaders took an extreme stand on the subject of colonial rights. The political aristocracies might object to British policies, as most of them did, but considering what they owed to British backing, they displayed an understandable caution, a caution

[8] For example, see Irving Mark, *Agrarian Conflicts in Colonial New York, 1711–1775* (New York, 1940); *The Carolina Background on the Eve of the Revolution,* ed. Richard J. Hooker (Chapel Hill, 1953); and Elisha Douglass, *Rebels and Democrats* (Chapel Hill, 1955).

[9] Brennan, "James Otis: Recreant and Patriot," p. 715.

that made it impossible for them to pose as patriotic leaders.

The popular leaders were also willing to take extreme measures in practical opposition to British policies, ranging all the way from mob violence to non-importation agreements forced upon unwilling merchants. And with ever more force and violence they accused Americans who did not agree with them or their methods of knuckling under to British tyranny and of readiness to sell the liberties of their country for a little pelf. In the course of this campaign they appealed to the people at large. Men who normally could not or did not take part in political life, particularly in the cities, were invited to mass meetings where the rules of suffrage were ignored and where they could shout approval of resolutions carefully prepared in advance by their leaders. In addition, the mob was a constant factor in political life, particularly in Boston where it was efficiently organized. Mobs were used to nullify the Stamp Act, to harass British soldiers, to hamper the operations of the customs service, and to intimidate office holders.

All these activities on the part of the disfranchised, or the hitherto politically inactive, accustomed men to taking part in public affairs as never before; and it gave them an appetite for more. From the beginning of the crisis in 1774 onward, more and more "new men," which was the politest name their opponents called them, played an ever more active role, both on the level of practical politics and on the level of political theory. They began writing about and talking about what they called "democracy." And this was a frightening experience, not only to the conservative-minded leaders of the colonies, but to many of the popular leaders as well.

For instance, when a New York mass meeting gathered in May 1774 to answer the letter of the Boston Town Meeting asking for a complete stoppage of trade with Britain as an answer to the Boston Port Act, the people talked about far more than letter writing. One alarmed observer wrote: "I beheld my fellow-citizens very accurately counting all their chickens, not only before any of them were hatched, but before above one half of the eggs were laid. In short, they fairly contended about the future forms of our government, whether it should be founded upon aristocratic or democratic principles." The leaders had "gulled" the mob for years, and now, said Gouverneur Morris, the mob was waking up and could no longer be fooled. The only salvation for the aristocracy of New York was peace with Britain at almost any price.[10]

Another witness to the stirrings among the people was John Adams. Unlike Gouverneur Morris, he never wavered in his belief in independence, but at the same time he was constantly concerned with the danger of an internal upheaval. Years later in his "Autobiography," he recalled as vividly as if it had happened the day before an event that took place while he was home in Massachusetts in the fall of 1775. While there he met a man who had sometimes been his client. "He, though a common horse jockey, was sometimes in the right, and I had commonly been successful in his favor in our courts of law. He was always in the law, and had been sued in many actions at almost every court. As soon as he saw me, he came up to me, and his first salutation to me was, 'Oh! Mr. Adams, what great things have you and your colleagues done for us! We can never be grateful enough to you. There are no

10 Gouverneur Morris to [John] Penn, May 20, 1774, in *English Historical Documents*, IX, 861–863.

courts of justice now in this province, and I hope there never will be another.'" Then Adams goes on: "Is this the object for which I have been contending? said I to myself, for I rode along without any answer to this wretch. Are these the sentiments of such people, and how many of them are there in the country? Half the nation for what I know; for half the nation are debtors, if not more, and these have been, in all countries, the sentiments of debtors. If the power of the country should get into such hands, and there is great danger that it will, to what purpose have we sacrificed our time, health, and everything else? Surely we must guard against this spirit and these principles, or we shall repent of all our conduct."[11]

In May of 1776, with the talk of independence filling the air and the Virginia convention planning to draft a constitution, old Landon Carter of Virginia wrote to Washington bewailing the "ambition" that had "seized on so much ignorance all over the colony as it seems to have done; for this present convention abounds with too many of the inexperienced creatures to navigate our bark on this dangerous coast. . . ." As for independence, he said, "I need only tell you of one definition that I heard of Independency: It was expected to be a form of government that, by being independent of the rich men, every man would then be able to do as he pleased. And it was with this expectation they sent the men they did, in hopes they would plan such a form. One of the delegates I heard exclaim against the Patrolling Law, because a poor man was made to pay for keeping a rich man's slaves in order. I shamed the fool so much for it that he slunk away; but he got elected by it."[12]

One could go on endlessly giving examples like these from the hectic days between 1774 and 1776, examples of the fear among leaders of all shades of opinion that the people would get or were getting out of hand. Meanwhile there was an increasing amount of political writing in the newspapers, writing which was pointing in the direction of independence and the creation of new governments in America. More than a year before *Common Sense,* a piece which appeared first in the *Pennsylvania Packet* declared that "the history of kings is nothing but the history of the folly and depravity of human nature." "We read now and then, it is true, of a good king; so we read likewise of a prophet escaping unhurt from a lion's den, and of three men walking in a fiery furnace without having even their garments singed. The order of nature is as much inverted in the first as it was in the last two cases. A good king is a miracle."[13]

By early 1776 the debate over future governments to be adopted was in full swing. Disliking intensely the ideas of government set forth in *Common Sense,* John Adams drafted his *Thoughts on Government.* His plan was modeled on the old government of Massachusetts, with an elective rather than a royal governor, of course, but certainly contemplated no radical change in the political structure.[14] John Adams was no innovator. He deplored what he called "the rage for innovation" which had appeared in Massachusetts by June of 1776. The projects, said he, are not for repairing the building but for tearing it down. "The projects of county assemblies, town

11 John Adams, "Autobiography," *The Works of John Adams,* ed. Charles F. Adams (Boston, 1856), II, 420–421.

12 *American Archives,* ed. Peter Force, 4th ser. (Washington, 1837–1846), VI, 390–391, May 9, 1776.

13 *English Historical Documents,* IX, 816–817.

14 *Works of John Adams,* IV, 189–200.

registers, and town probates of wills are founded in narrow notions, sordid stinginess, and profound ignorance, and tend directly to barbarism."[15]

There was equal alarm in the south at demands for change and new governments. Among those who sought to defend the old order was Carter Braxton. In a long address to the Virginia convention he praised the British constitution and declared that it would be "perverting all order to oblige us, by a novel government to give up our laws, our customs, and our manners." The spirit of principles of limited monarchy should be preserved. Yet, he said, we daily see it condemned by the advocates of "popular governments. . . . The systems recommended to the colonies seem to accord with the temper of the times, and are fraught with all the tumult and riot incident to simple democracy. . . ." Braxton declared that democracies would not tolerate wealth, and that they could exist only in countries where all the people are poor from necessity. Nowhere in history could he find an example of a successful democracy. What he proposed for Virginia was a three-part government with a house of representatives elected by the voters for three years. The house, in turn, would choose a governor to serve during good behavior and a council of twenty-four to hold their places for life and to act as an upper house of the legislature.[16] Braxton in Virginia, like John Adams in Massachusetts, hoped to make the transition from dependence to independence without any fundamental political change.

But change was in the air, and writer after writer sought to formulate new ideas about government and to offer concrete suggestions for the theoretical foundations and political structures of the new states to be. In 1775, on hearing that congress had given advice to New Hampshire on the establishment of a government, General John Sullivan offered his thoughts to the revolutionary congress of his colony. All government, he wrote, ought to be instituted for the good of the people. There should be no conflicting branches in imitation of the British constitution "so much celebrated by those who understand nothing of it. . . . " The two houses of the legislature and a governor should all be elected by the people. No danger can arise to a state "from giving the people a free and full voice in their own government." The so-called checks upon the licentiousness of the people "are only the children of designing or ambitious men, no such thing being necessary. . . ."[17]

In the middle colonies appeared an address "To the People of North America on the Different Kinds of Government." After defining monarchy, aristocracy, oligarchy, and democracy, the anonymous writer said: "Popular government —sometimes termed democracy, republic, or commonwealth—is the plan of civil society wherein the community at large takes the care of its own welfare, and manages its concerns by representatives elected by the people out of their own body."

"Seeing the happiness of the people is the true end of government; and it ap-

[15] To John Winthrop, Philadelphia, June 23, 1776, in Mass. Hist. Soc. *Collections,* 5th ser. (Boston, 1878). IV, 310. This was in reply to a letter of John Winthrop, written on June 1, in which he reported to Adams on the various schemes afoot in Massachusetts. *Ibid.,* 305–308.

[16] *The Virginia Gazette* (Dixon and Hunter), June 8, 1776. This had been printed earlier in pamphlet form. For similar ideas see the letter of William Hooper, North Carolina delegate to the Continental Congress, to the North Carolina Provincial Congress, October 26, 1776, in *The Colonial Records of North Carolina,* ed. W. L. Saunders, X (1890), 866–869.

[17] John Sullivan to Meshech Weare, Winter Hill [Mass.], December 11, 1775, in *American Archives,* IV, 241–242.

pearing by the definition, that the popular form is the only one which has this for its object; it may be worth inquiring into the causes which have prevented its success in the world."

This writer then undertakes to explain the failure of former democracies. First of all, he says that past republics tried democracy too late and contained within them remnants of aristocracies and military cliques which disliked it. A second cause was that men did not have adequate knowledge of representation and that their large and tumultuous assemblies made it possible for unscrupulous men to charge all troubles to the constitution. A third cause of failure has been the political writers who from ignorance or ulterior motives have tried to discredit democracy. "This has been carried to such a length with many, that the mentioning a democracy constantly excites in them the idea of anarchy; and few, except such as have emancipated themselves from the shackles of political bigotry and prejudice, can talk of it with patience, and hearken to anything offered in its defence." Such are the causes of the destruction of former republics, but the Americans have the best opportunity ever open to mankind to form a free government, "the last and best plan that can possibly exist."[18]

In "The Interest of America," another writer says that new governments must soon be created in America and that "the good of the people is the ultimate end of civil government." Therefore, "we should assume that mode of government which is most equitable and adapted to the good of mankind . . . and I think there can be no doubt that a well-regulated democracy is most equitable." The annual or frequent choice of magistrates is most likely to prevent

usurpation and tyranny; and most likely to secure the privileges of the people. Legislatures should be unicameral for a plurality of branches leads to endless contention and a waste of time.[19]

In New England, where the revolutionary congresses of Massachusetts and New Hampshire were controlled by leaders along the seacoast, there was a growing discontent among the people of the backcountry counties. Out of it came one of the clearest democratic statements of the times: "The People are the Best Governors." The author starts with the premise that "there are many very noisy about liberty, but are aiming at nothing more than personal power and grandeur." "God," he said, "gave mankind freedom by nature, made every man equal to his neighbor, and has virtually enjoined them to govern themselves by their own laws." Representatives in legislatures should have only the power to make laws. They should not have power to elect officials or to elect councils or senates to veto legislation. Only the people have this power. If there must be senates, they should be elected by the people of the state at large and should have only advisory powers. Representation should not be according to taxable property, for "Nature itself abhors such a system of civil government, for it will make an inequality among the people and set up a number of lords over the rest." Representation according to population also has its difficulties. The solution is for each town to have one representative, with more for larger towns if the legislature thinks fit. So far as property qualifications for representatives are concerned, there should be none. "Social virtue and knowledge . . . is the best and only necessary qualification of the person before us." If we have property quali-

18 *American Archives*, V, 180–183. [March 1776.]

19 *Ibid.*, VI, 840–843. [June 1776.]

fications "we root our virtue; and what will then become of the genuine principle of freedom?" "Let it not be said in future generations that money was made by the founders of the American states an essential qualification in the rulers of a free people." The writer proposed annual elections of a one-house legislature, of a governor, and of the judges of the superior court. The people in the counties should elect annually all their own officials—judges, sheriffs, and others —as should the inhabitants of the towns. And in all elections "any orderly free male of ordinary capacity" should have the right to vote if he has lived in a town for a year.[20]

From such discussions one may sum up certain of the essential ideas. (1) They agree that the "good" or the "happiness" of the people is the only end of government. (2) They agree that "democracy" is the best form of government to achieve that end. (3) They show a distrust of men when in power—a distrust shared with far more conservative-minded writers of the times.

As to details of government there are variations, but they do agree on fundamentals. (1) The legislatures, whether one or two houses, are to be elected by the people. (2) Public officials, state and local, are to be elected by the people or by their representatives in the legislatures. (3) There should be annual elections. (4) Some argue for manhood suffrage, and one writer even advocated that tax-paying widows should vote. (5) There should be freedom of religion, at least for Protestants; in any case, freedom from taxation to support established churches.

One may well ask: did such theoretical discussions have any meaning in terms of practical politics, or were they idle speculations by anonymous writers without influence? The answer is that they did have meaning. I have already cited the discussion of the principles of government in New York in the spring of 1774, and the litigious jockey in Massachusetts in 1775 who hoped that the courts would remain closed forever. These are not isolated examples. By the end of 1775 all sorts of organized activity was under way, ranging in place from North Carolina to New Hampshire, and from militia groups to churches.

In North Carolina the defeat of the Regulators in 1771 had not ended discontent but merely suppressed it. By September 1775 Mecklenburg County was instructing its delegates in the provincial congress to work for a plan of government providing for equal representation and the right to vote for every freeman who supported the government, either in person or property. Legislation should not be a "divided right"; no man or body of men should be "invested with a negative on the voice of the people duly collected. . . ."[21] By November 1776, when North Carolina elected a congress to write its first state constitution, Mecklenburg County was even more specific in its instructions. It told its delegates that they were to endeavor to establish a free government under the authority of the people of North Carolina, and that the government was to be a "simple democracy, or as near it as possible." In fixing fundamental principles, the delegates were to "oppose everything that leans to aristocracy or power in the hands of the rich and chief men exercised to the oppression of the poor."[22]

In the middle colonies militia organ-

---

[20] Reprinted in Frederick Chase, *A History of Dartmouth College and the Town of Hanover, New Hampshire* (Cambridge, 1891), I, Appendix D, 654–663.

[21] *Colonial Records of North Carolina*, X, 239–242. [Sept. 1775.]

[22] *Ibid.*, 870, a-f. [Nov. 1776.]

izations made demands and suggestions. Pennsylvania was in turmoil, with the assembly controlled by the opponents of independence and the revolutionary party working in large measure through a voluntary militia organization called the Associators. In February 1776 a committee of privates from the Philadelphia Associators told the assembly "that it has been the practice of all countries, and is highly reasonable, that all persons . . . who expose their lives in the defense of a country, should be admitted to the enjoyment of all the rights and privileges of a citizen of that country. . . ." All Associators should be given the right to vote.[23]

In June the committee of privates again protested to the legislature. This time they denied the right of the assembly to appoint two brigadier generals for the Associators as recommended by the Continental Congress. The privates declared that since many of them could not vote, they were not represented in the assembly. Furthermore, many counties where the Associators were most numerous did not have proportional representation. And for that matter, since many members of the assembly were members of a religious profession "totally averse to military defense," they could not possibly be called representatives of the Associators.[24]

While such ideas were being expounded in Pennsylvania, some militia in Maryland were proposing a new constitution. There was a growing discontent in Maryland with the revolutionary convention which was opposed to independence, and whose members were appointing one another to military posts. Government by convention should stop,

said one writer, and regular government be instituted.[25]

Late in June 1776 disputes from the militia battalions in Anne Arundel County met and proposed a constitution to be submitted to the people of the county. They started out with the declaration that the right to legislate is in "every member of the community," but that for convenience the right must be delegated to representatives chosen by the people. The legislature must never form a separate interest from the community at large, and its branches must "be independent of and balance each other, and all dependent on the people." There should be a two-house legislature chosen annually "as annual elections are most friendly to liberty, and the oftener power reverts to the people, the greater will be the security for a faithful discharge of it." All provincial officials, including judges, should be elected annually by joint ballot of the two houses. All county officials should be chosen annually by the people of each county. Nothing is said of property qualifications for either voting or office-holding. So far as taxes are concerned, "the unjust mode of taxation by poll" should be abolished, and all monies raised should be according to a fair and equal assessment of people's estates.[26]

In New Jersey the revolutionary congress, like that in other colonies, was trying to prevent change and was maintaining the land qualification for voting for its members. But the complaints grew so loud that it was forced to yield. One petition in 1776, for instance, declared that "we cannot conceive the wise author of our existence ever designed that a certain quantity of earth on which we tread should be annexed to a man to

23 Votes and Proceedings of the Assembly, Feb. 23, 1776, in *Pennsylvania Archives*, 8th ser. [Harrisburg, 1935], VIII, 7406.

24 *Ibid.*, 7546–47. June 14, 1776.

25 "An American" in "To the People of Maryland," *American Archives*, VI, 1094–96.

26 *Ibid.*, 1092–94. June 26–27, 1776.

complete his dignity and fit him for society. Was the sole design of government either the security of land or money, the possession of either or both of these would be the only necessary qualifications for its members. But we apprehend the benign intentions of a well regulated government to extend to the security of much more valuable possessions—the rights and privileges of freemen, for the defense of which every kind of property and even life itself have been liberally expended."[27]

In Massachusetts the Baptists were quick to draw a parallel between the fight for civil liberty against England and their own fight to religious liberty. Baptists were being jailed for refusal to pay taxes to support churches. Their leader, the Reverend Isaac Backus, put Sam Adams squarely on the spot in January 1774, "I fully concur with your grand maxim," wrote Backus, "that it is essential to liberty that representation and taxation go together." Hence, since the representatives in the Massachusetts legislature have only civil qualifications, how can they levy ecclesiastical taxes? "And I am bold in it," Backus goes on, "that taxes laid by the British Parliament upon America are not more contrary to civil freedom, than these taxes are to the very nature of liberty of conscience. . . ." He hopes, he says, that Adams will do something about it so that a large number of peaceable people "may not be forced to carry their complaints before those who would be glad to hear that the legislature of Massachusetts deny to their fellow servants that liberty which they so earnestly insist upon for themselves. A word to the wise is sufficient."[28]

Samuel Adams was not interested in liberty of conscience, particularly for Baptists, and he did not reply. But Backus pursued him to the first Continental Congress in Philadelphia where a four-hour meeting was held in Carpenter's Hall one night. The Massachusetts delegation met with the Baptists, but with a large audience present, among whom were the Quaker leaders James and Israel Pemberton, and members of congress like Joseph Galloway. The Backus diary gives a picture of Sam and John Adams quite literally squirming as the Baptists cited the facts of religious life in Massachusetts.[29] One can well imagine with what delight Galloway and the Pembertons looked on as the Massachusetts delegation vainly tried to wriggle out of a dilemma produced by the contradiction between their theory and their practice.

The Declaration of Independence was taken seriously by many Americans, or at least they found its basic philosophy useful in battling for change in the new states. Nowhere was this done more neatly than in Grafton County, New Hampshire. The Provincial Congress was in the control of eastern leaders and they refused to grant representation that the western towns thought adequate. In calling elections in the fall of 1776, the Congress grouped various towns together for electing representatives and told them that the men they elected must own real estate worth £200 lawful money. Led by professors at an obscure little college at Hanover, the people of Grafton County went on strike. They refused to hold elections, and town after town met and passed resolutions. The whole procedure of the Congress was unconstitutional. No plan of representation had been adopted since the Declaration of Independence. By the Declaration, said Hanover and

27 Richard P. McCormick, *The History of Voting in New Jersey . . . 1664–1911* (New Brunswick, 1953), pp. 66–68.

28 To Samuel Adams, Jan. 19, 1774, in Alvah Hovey, *A Memoir of the Life and Times of the Rev. Isaac Backus* (Boston, 1859), pp. 195–197.

29 *Ibid.*, ch. XV.

two other towns in a joint statement, "we conceive that the powers of government reverted to the people at large, and of course annihilated the political existence of the Assembly which then was. . . ." Six other towns joined together and declared it to be "our humble opinion, that when the declaration of independency took place, the Colonies were absolutely in a state of nature, and the powers of government reverted to the people at large. . . ." Such being the case, the Provincial Congress has no authority to combine towns, each of which is entitled to representation as a corporate entity. And it has no right to limit the choice of representatives to the owners of £200, said the people of Lyme, because "every elector in free states is capable of being elected."[30]

It seems clear, to me at least, that by 1776 there were people in America demanding the establishment of democratic state governments, by which they meant legislatures controlled by a majority of the voters, and with none of the checks upon their actions such as had existed in the colonies. At the same time there were many Americans who were determined that there should be no changes except those made inevitable by separation from Great Britain.

The history of the writing of the first state constitutions is to a large extent the history of the conflict between these two ideals of government. The conflict can be exaggerated, of course, for there was considerable agreement on structural details. Most of the state constitutions worked out in written form the structure of government that had existed in the colonies, all the way from governors, two-house legislatures, and judicial systems, to the forms of local government.

In terms of structure, little that is revolutionary is to be found. Even the much maligned unicameral legislature of Pennsylvania was only a continuation of what Pennsylvania had had since the beginning of the century.

The significant thing is not the continuity of governmental structure, but the alteration of the balance of power within the structure, and in the political situation resulting from the break away from the supervising power of a central government—that of Great Britain.

The first and most revolutionary change was in the field of basic theory. In May 1776, to help bring about the overthrow of the Pennsylvania assembly, the chief stumbling block in the way of independence, Congress resolved that all governments exercising authority under the crown of Great Britain should be suppressed, and that "all the powers of government [be] exerted under the authority of the people of the colonies. . . ." John Adams described it as "the most important resolution that ever was taken in America."[31] The Declaration of Independence spelled it out in terms of the equality of men, the sovereignty of the people, and the right of a people to change their governments as they pleased.

Second: the Revolution ended the power of a sovereign central government over the colonies. Britain had had the power to appoint and remove governors, members of upper houses of legislatures, judges, and other officials. It had the power to veto colonial legislation, to review cases appealed from colonial supreme courts, and to use armed force. All of this superintending power was wiped out by independence.

Third: the new central government created in America by the Articles of Confederation was, in a negative sense

30 *American Archives*, 5th ser. (Washington, 1848–1853), III, 1223–24, and Chase, *History of Dartmouth*, I, 426–433.

31 *Warren-Adams Letters*, I (Boston, 1917), 245; in Mass. Hist. Soc. *Collections*, Vols. 72, 73.

at least, a democratic government. The Congress of the United States had no power over either the states or their citizens. Hence, each state could govern itself as it pleased, and as a result of some of the new state constitutions, this often meant by a majority of the voters within a state.

Fourth: in writing the state constitutions, change was inevitable. The hierarchy of appointed legislative, executive, and judicial officials which had served as a check upon the elective legislatures was gone. The elective legislature became the supreme power in every state, and the lower houses, representing people however inadequately, became the dominant branch. The appointive houses of colonial times were replaced by elective senates, which in theory were supposed to represent property. They were expected to, and sometimes did, act as a check upon the lower houses, but their power was far less than that of pre-war councils.

Fifth: the office of governor underwent a real revolution. The governors of the royal colonies had, in theory at least, vast powers, including an absolute veto. In the new constitutions, most Americans united in shearing the office of governor of virtually all power.

Sixth: state supreme courts underwent a similar revolution. Under the state constitutions they were elected by the legislatures or appointed by governors who were elected officials. And woe betide a supreme court that tried to interfere with the actions of a legislature.

What such changes meant in terms of political realties was that a majority of voters within a state, if agreed upon a program and persistent enough, could do what it wanted, unchecked by governors or courts or appeals to a higher power outside the state.

There were other areas in which changes took place, although they were only beginnings. A start was made in the direction of ending the property qualification for voting and office-holding. A few states established what amounted to manhood suffrage, and a few years later even women voted in New Jersey although that was stopped when it appeared that woman suffrage meant only a means of stuffing ballot boxes. A few states took steps in the direction of representation according to population, a process as yet unsolved in the United States. A large step was taken in the direction of disestablishing state churches, but on the whole one still had to be a Protestant, and a Trinitarian at that, to hold office.

In connection with office-holding, there is one eighteenth-century American idea that is worthy of a whole study by itself, and that is the concept of rotation in office. Many Americans were convinced that office-holding bred a lust for power in the holder. Therefore there must be frequent, if not annual, elections; and there must be a limitation on the time one might spend in certain offices. There is probably no more remarkable self-denying ordinance in the history of politics than the provision in the Articles of Confederation that no man could be a member of Congress more than three years out of any six. I have often been accused of wanting to go back to the Articles of Confederation, which is nonsense, but there are times when I do wish that this one provision might be revived in the twentieth century.

What I have done in this paper is to set before you some of the reasons for believing that the American Revolution was a democratic movement, not in origin, but in result. Certainly the political leaders of the eighteenth century thought the results were democratic. Whether they thought the results were good or bad is another story.

DANIEL J. BOORSTIN (b. 1912), Director of the Library of Congress, and trained as a lawyer in both England and the United States, is highly qualified to evaluate the constitutional issues of the Revolution. Boorstin in his book of essays, *The Genius of American Politics*, views the Revolution as a conservative movement aimed at maintaining those traditional liberties that Americans had long enjoyed under the British constitution. He rejects the thesis that ideas of the European Enlightenment exercised great influence in the Revolution and concludes that the framers of the Declaration of Independence based their arguments instead on law and history. Why, in Boorstin's opinion, did American Patriot leaders fail to formulate any revolutionary dogma to justify their separation from Britain?*

Daniel J. Boorstin

Revolution Without Dogma

We are accustomed to think of the Revolution as the great age of American political thought. It may therefore be something of a shock to realize that it did not produce in America a single important treatise on political theory. Men like Franklin and Jefferson, universal in their interests, active and spectacularly successful in developing institutions, were not fertile as political philosophers. . . .

We have been slow to see some of the more obvious and more important peculiarities of our Revolution because influential scholars on the subject have cast their story in the mold of the French Revolution of 1789. Some of our best historians have managed to empty our Revolution of much of its local flavor

by exaggerating what it had in common with that distinctively European struggle. This they have done in two ways.

First, they have stressed the international character of the intellectual movement of which the French Revolution was a classic expression—the so-called "Enlightenment." They speak of it as a "climate of opinion" whose effects, like the barometric pressure, could no more be escaped in America than in Europe. As Carl Becker put it in his *Heavenly City of the Eighteenth-Century Philosophers:* "The Enlightenment . . . is not a peculiarly French but an international climate of opinion . . . and in the new world Jefferson, whose sensitized mind picked up and transmitted every novel vibration in the intellectual air, and

*Reprinted from *The Genius of American Politics* by Daniel J. Boorstin by permission of The University of Chicago Press. Copyright 1953 by The University of Chicago, pp. 66–98 *passim*.

Franklin of Philadelphia, printer and friend of the human race—these also, whatever national or individual characteristics they may have exhibited, were true children of the Enlightenment. The philosophical empire was an international domain of which France was but the mother country and Paris the capital."

Second, they have treated ours as only a particular species of the genus "Revolution"—of what should perhaps more properly be called *revolutio Europaensis*. Since the French Revolution has been made the model, from that European revolution historians have borrowed the vocabulary in which ours is discussed and the calendar by which it is clocked. "Thermidor," for example, is the name used in one of our best college textbooks to introduce its chapter on the federal Constitution.

It goes on:

There comes a time in every revolutionary movement when the people become tired of agitation and long for peace and security. They then eliminate the radicals, troublemakers and warmongers, and take measures to consolidate their government, hoping to secure what has already been gained through turmoil and suffering. *Thermidor* this time is called in leftist language, from the counterrevolution in France that overthrew Robespierre and ended the reign of terror. Thus, the establishment of Cromwell as Lord Protector was the Thermidor of the English Revolution in the seventeenth century; and the Stalin dictatorship and exile of Trotsky marks the Thermidor of the Russian Revolution. Every taking of the Bastille, it may be said, is inevitably followed by Thermidor, since human nature craves security, and the progress of a revolution must be stopped somewhere short of anarchy [Morison and Commager, *Growth of the American Republic* (3rd ed.; New York, 1942), I, 277].

The effect of all this has been to emphasize—or rather exaggerate—the similarity of ours to all other modern revolutions.

In so doing, historians have exaggerated the significance of what is supposed to have been the ideology of the Revolution. Such an emphasis has had the further attraction to some "liberal" historians of seeming to put us in the main current of European history. It has never been quite clear to me why historians would not have found our revolution significant enough merely as a victory of constitutionalism.

The most obvious peculiarity of our American Revolution is that, in the modern European sense of the word, it was hardly a revolution at all. The Daughters of the American Revolution, who have been understandably sensitive on this subject, have always insisted in their literature that the American Revolution was no revolution but merely a colonial rebellion. The more I have looked into the subject, the more convinced I have become of the wisdom of their naïveté. "The social condition and the Constitution of the Americans are democratic," De Tocqueville observed about a hundred years ago. "But they have not had a democratic revolution." This fact is surely one of the most important of our history.

A number of historians (J. Franklin Jameson and Merrill Jensen, for example) have pointed out the ways in which a social revolution, including a redistribution of property, accompanied the American Revolution. These are facts which no student of the period should neglect. Yet it seems to me that these historians have by no means succeeded in showing that such changes were so basic and so far-reaching as actually in themselves to have established our national republican institutions. When we speak of the Revolution therefore, we are still fully justified in referring to something other than what Jameson's disciples mean by "the American Revolution as a social movement." If we consider the American Revolution in that sense, it would not be a great deal more notable than a number of other social movements in our history, such as Jacksonianism, populism, progressivism, and the New Deal. Moreover, in so far as the American Revolution was a social movement, it was not much to be distinguished from European revolutions; and the increasing emphasis on this aspect of our history is but another example of the attempt to assimilate our history to that of Europe.

The Revolution, as the birthday of our nation, must mean something very different from all this. It is the series of events by which we separated ourselves from the British Empire and acquired a national identity. Looking at our Revolution from this point of view, what are some features which distinguish it from the French Revolution of 1789 or the other revolutions to which western European nations trace their national identity? And, especially, what are those peculiarities which have affected the place of theory in our political life?

1. First, and most important, the United States was born in a *colonial* rebellion. Our national birth certificate is a Declaration of Independence and not a Declaration of the Rights of Man. The vast significance of this simple fact is too often forgotten. Compared even with other colonial rebellions, the American Revolution is notably lacking in cultural self-consciousness and in any passion for national unity. The more familiar type of colonial rebellion—like that which recently occurred in India—is one in which a subject people vindicates its local culture against foreign rulers. But the American Revolution had very little of this character. On the contrary, ours was one of the few conservative colonial rebellions of modern times.

We should recall several of the peculiar circumstances (most of them obvious) which had made this kind of revolution possible. At the time of the Revolution, the major part of the population of the American colonies was of British stock. Therefore, no plausible racial or national argument could be found for the superiority either of the inhabitants of the mother-country or of the continental American colonies. Even when Jefferson, in his *Notes on Virginia,* went to some trouble to refute Buffon and the Abbe Raynal and others who had argued that all races, including man, deteriorated on the American continent, he did not go so far as to say that the American races were distinctly superior.

Since the climate and topography of substantial parts of the American colonies were similar to those of the mother-country (and for a number of other reasons), there had been a pretty wholesale transplantation of British legal and political institutions to North America. Unlike the Spanish colonies in South America, which were to rebel, at least in part, because they had had so little home rule, the British colonies in North America were to rebel because, among other reasons, they had had so much. Finally, the North American continent was (except for sparse Indian settlements) empty of indigenous populations, hence barren of such local institutions and traditions as could have competed with what the colonists had brought with them.

All these facts were to make it easy, then, for the American Revolution to seem in the minds of most of its leaders an affirmation of the tradition of British institutions. The argument of the best theorists of the Revolution—perhaps we should call them lawyers rather than theorists—was not, on the whole, that America had institutions or a culture superior to that of the British. Rather their position, often misrepresented and sometimes simply forgotten, was that the British by their treatment of American colonies were being untrue to the ancient spirit of their own institutions. The slogan "Taxation without Representation Is Tyranny" was clearly founded on a British assumption. As James Otis put it in his pamphlet, *The Rights of the British Colonies* (1764), he believed "that this [British] constitution is the most free one, and by far the best, now existing on earth: that by this constitution, every man in the dominions is a free man: that no parts of His Majesty's dominions can be taxed without their consent: that every part has a right to be represented in the supreme or some subordinate legislature: that the refusal of this would seem to be a contradiction in practice to the theory of the constitution."

According to their own account, then, the Americans were to have forced on them the need to defend the ancient British tradition; to be truer to the spirit of that tradition than George III and Lord North and Townshend knew how to be. They were fighting not so much to establish new rights as to preserve old ones: "for the preservation of our liberties . . . in defence of the freedom that is our birthright, and which we ever enjoyed till the late violation of it" (Declaration of Causes of Taking up Arms, July 6, 1775). From the colonists' point of view, until 1776 it was Parliament that had been revolutionary, by exercis-

ing a power for which there was no warrant in English constitutional precedent. The ablest defender of the Revolution—in fact, the greatest political theorist of the American Revolution—was also the great theorist of British conservatism, Edmund Burke.

2. Second, the American Revolution was *not* the product of a nationalistic spirit. We had no Bismarck or Cavour or any nationalist philosophy. We were singularly free from most of the philosophical baggage of modern nationalism.

Perhaps never was a new nation created with less enthusiasm. To read the history of our Revolution is to discover that the United States was a kind of *pis aller*. This fact explains many of the difficulties encountered in conducting the Revolution and in framing a federal constitution. The original creation of a United States was the work of doubly reluctant men: men reluctant, both because of their local loyalties—to Virginia, Massachusetts, Rhode Island, and New York—and because of their imperial loyalty. The story of the "critical period" of American history, of the Articles of Confederation and the Constitution, tells of the gradual overcoming of this reluctance. It was overcome not by any widespread conversion to a nationalist theory —even the *Federalist* papers are conspicuously lacking in such a theory—but by gradual realization of the need for effective union.

In the period of the American Revolution we do discover a number of enthusiasms: for the safety and prosperity of Virginia or New York, for the cause of justice, for the rights of Englishmen. What is missing is anything that might be called widespread enthusiasm for the birth of a new nation: the United States of America. Until well into the nineteenth century, Jefferson—and he was not alone in this—was using the phrase "my country" to refer to his native state of Virginia.

3. Our Revolution was successful at the first try. This is equally true whether we consider it as a revolt against British rule or as a movement for republican federalism. There was no long-drawn-out agitation, no intellectual war of attrition, of the sort which breeds dogmas and intransigence. Thomas Paine's *Common Sense,* which is generally considered "the first important republican tract to be issued in America . . . the first to present cogent arguments for independence," did not appear until January 10, 1776. Down to within six months of the break, few would have considered independence; and even then the colonists had only quite specific complaints. There had been no considerable tradition in America either of revolt against British institutions or of republican theorizing.

The political objective of the Revolution, independence from British rule, was achieved by one relatively short continuous effort. More commonly in modern history (take, for example, the European revolutions of the nineteenth century) any particular revolt has been only one in a long series. Each episode, then, ends on a note of suspense which comes from the feeling that the story is "to be continued." Under those circumstances, challenges to constituted authority follow one another, accumulating their ideological baggage.

In France, for example, 1789 was followed by 1830 and 1848 and 1870; a similar list could be made for Italy, Germany, and perhaps Russia. Such repetition creates a distinctive revolutionary tradition, with continued agitation keeping alive certain doctrines. Repeated efforts provide the dogmatic raw material for a profusion of later political parties, each of which rallies under the banner of one or another of the defeated revolutions or of a revolution yet to be made. But, properly speaking, 1776 had no sequel, and needed none. The issue was separation, and separation was accomplished.

The student who comes for the first time to the literature of our Revolution is liable to be disappointed by the dull and legalistic flavor of what he has to read. Although the American Revolution occurred in an age which throughout Europe was laden with philosophic reflection and important treatises, our Revolution was neither particularly rich nor particularly original in its intellectual apparatus.

Orators, textbook-writers, and other tradition-makers have been hard put to it to find those ringing phrases, the battle-cries and philosophical catchwords, which slip smoothly off the tongue, remain fixed in the memory, and uplift the soul. This helps explain why a few phrases and documents have been overworked and why even these have always been read only in part or out of context. The first two paragraphs of the Declaration of Independence have been worn thin; few bother to read the remaining thirty. People have grasped at "life, liberty, and the pursuit of happiness," forgetting that it was two-thirds borrowed and, altogether, only part of a preamble. We have repeated that "all men are created equal," without daring to discover what it meant and without realizing that probably to none of the men who spoke it did it mean what we would like it to mean. Or we have exploited passages in the "speeches" of Patrick Henry, which were actually composed less by Henry than by his biographers.

The proper slogan of the Revolution— if, indeed, there was a slogan—was "No Taxation without Representation." Such words are far too polysyllabic, far too legalistic, to warm the popular heart. But if we compare them with the "Liberty, Equality, Fraternity" of the French Revolution and the "Peace, Bread and Land," of the Russian, we have a clue to the peculiar spirit of the American Revolution. It is my view that the major issue of the American Revolution was the true constitution of the British Empire, which is a pretty technical legal problem. This notion is supported by Professor Charles H. McIlwain, who, in his admirable little book on the American Revolution, comes closer than any other recent historian to the spirit of our Revolutionary age.

In that age men were inclined to take their opponents at their word; the Revolutionary debate seems to have been carried on in the belief that men meant what they said. But in this age of Marx and Freud we have begun to take it for granted that, if people talk about one thing, they must be thinking about something else. Ideas are treated as the apparatus of an intellectual sleight-of-hand, by which the speaker diverts the audience's attention to an irrelevant subject while he does the real business unobserved. To study the Revolutionary debate is then to try to see (in the phrase of one historian) how "the colonists modified their theory to suit their needs." From such a point of view, there is perhaps never much political or legal thought worth talking about; to be realistic we should focus our discussion on hormones and statistics.

But such an approach would bleach away the peculiar tone of our history and empty our Revolution of its unique significance. Therefore, even at the risk of seeming naïve, I should like to consider the outlandish possibility that men like Jefferson and Adams all along meant what they were saying, that is, that the Revolution had something to do with the British constitution. . . .

The feature to which I want to direct your attention might be called the "conservatism" of the Revolution. If we understand this characteristic, we will begin to see the Revolution as an illustration of the remarkable continuity of American history. And we will also see how the attitude of our Revolutionary thinkers has engraved more deeply in our national consciousness a belief in the inevitability of our particular institutions, or, in a word, our sense of "givenness."

The character of our Revolution has nourished our assumption that whatever institutions we happened to have here (in this case the British constitution) had the self-evident validity of anything that is "normal." We have thus casually established the tradition that it is superfluous to the American condition to produce elaborate treatises on political philosophy or to be explicit about political values and the theory of community.

I shall confine myself to two topics. First, the manifesto of the Revolution, namely, the Declaration of Independence; and, second, the man who has been generally considered the most outspoken and systematic political philosopher of the Revolution, Thomas Jefferson. Of course, I will not try to give a full account of either of them. I will attempt only to call your attention to a few facts which may not have been sufficiently emphasized and which are especially significant for our present purpose. Obviously, no one could contend that there is either in the man or in the document nothing of the cosmopolitan spirit, nothing of the world climate of opinion. My suggestion is simply that we do find another spirit of at least equal, and perhaps overshadowing, importance and that this spirit may actually be more characteristic of our Revolution.

First, then, for the Declaration of Independence. Its technical, legalistic, and conservative character, which I wish to emphasize, will appear at once by contrast with the comparable document of the French Revolution. Ours was concerned with a specific event, namely, the separation of these colonies from the mother-country. But the French produced a "Declaration of the Rights of Man and the Citizen." When De Tocqueville, in his *Ancien Régime* (Book I, chap. iii), sums up the spirit of the French Revolution, he is describing exactly what the American Revolution was not:

> The French Revolution acted, with regard to things of this world, precisely as religious revolutions have acted with regard to things of the other. It dealt with the citizen in the abstract, independent of particular social organizations, just as religions deal with mankind in general, independent of time and place. It inquired, not what were the particular rights of the French citizens, but what were the general rights and duties of mankind in reference to political concerns.
>
> It was by thus divesting itself of all that was peculiar to one race or time, and by reverting to natural principles of social order and government, that it became intelligible to all, and susceptible of simultaneous imitation in a hundred different places.
>
> By seeming to tend rather to the regeneration of the human race than to the reform of France alone, it roused passions such as the most violent political revolutions had been incapable of awakening. It inspired proselytism, and gave birth to propagandism; and hence assumed that quasi religious character which so terrified those who saw it, or, rather, became a sort of new religion, imperfect, it is true, without God, worship, or future life, but still able, like Islamism, to cover the earth with its soldiers, its apostles, and its martyrs [trans. John Bonner (New York, 1856), pp. 26 f.].

In contrast to all this, our Declaration of Independence is essentially a list of specific historical instances. It is directed not to the regeneration but only to the "opin-

ions" of mankind. It is closely tied to time and place; the special affection for "British brethren" is freely admitted; it is concerned with the duties of a particular king and certain of his subjects.

Even if we took only the first two paragraphs or preamble, which are the most general part of the document, and actually read them as a whole, we could make a good case for their being merely a succinct restatement of the Whig theory of the British revolution of 1688. Carl Becker himself could not overlook this fact. "In political theory and in political practice," he wrote parenthetically, "the American Revolution drew its inspiration from the parliamentary struggle of the seventeenth century. The philosophy of the Declaration was not taken from the French. It was not even new; but good old English doctrine newly formulated to meet a present emergency." To be understood, its words must be annotated by British history. This is among the facts which have led some historians (Guizot, for example[1]) to go so far as to say that the English revolution succeeded twice, once in England and once in America.

The remaining three-quarters—the unread three-quarters—of the document is technical and legalistic. That is, of course, the main reason why it remains unread. For it is a bill of indictment against the king, written in the language of British constitutionalism. "The patient sufferance of these Colonies" is the point of departure. It deals with rights and franchises under British charters. It carefully recounts that the customary and traditional forms of protest, such as "repeated Petitions," have already been tried.

The more the Declaration is reread in context, the more plainly it appears

---

[1] François Guizot (1787–1874), leading French historian and statesman, who wrote extensively on the Puritan Revolution in England—*Ed.*

a document of imperial legal relations ~~rather than a piece of high-flown~~ polit-~~ical philosophy~~. The desire to remain true to the principles of British consti-tutionalism up to the bitter end explains why, as has been often remarked, the document is directed against the king, despite the fact that the practical griev-ances were against Parliament; perhaps also why at this stage there is no longer an explicit appeal to the rights of Eng-lishmen. Most of the document is a bald enumeration of George III's failures, excesses, and crimes in violation of the constitution and laws of Great Britain. One indictment after another makes sense only if one presupposes the frame-work of British constitutionalism. How else, for example, could one indict a king "for depriving us in many cases, of the benefits of Trial by Jury"?

We can learn a great deal about the con-text of our Revolutionary thought by examining Jefferson's own thinking down to the period of the Revolution. We need not stretch a point or give Jefferson a charismatic role, to say that the flavor of his thought is especially important for our purposes. He has been widely con-sidered the leading political philosopher of the Revolution. Among other things, he was, of course, the principal author of the Declaration of Independence itself; and the Declaration has been taken to be the climax of the abstract philosophizing of the revolutionaries. Because he is sup-posed to be the avant-garde of revolu-tionary thought, evidence of conservatism and legalism in Jefferson's thought as a whole is especially significant.

We now are beginning to have a defin-itive edition of Jefferson's papers,[2] . . . which is one of the richest treasures ever amassed for the historian of a particular period. This helps us use Jefferson's thought as a touchstone. Neither in the letters which Jefferson wrote nor in those he received do we discover that he and his close associates—at least down to the date of the Revolution—showed any con-spicuous interest in political theory. We look in vain for general reflections on the nature of government or constitutions. The manners of the day did require that a cultivated gentlemen be acquainted with certain classics of political thought; yet we lack evidence that such works were read with more than a perfunctory inter-est. To be sure, when Jefferson prepares a list of worthy books for a young friend in 1771, he includes references to Montes-quieu, Sidney, and Bolingbroke; but such references are rare. Even when he ex-changes letters with Edmund Pendleton on the more general problems of institu-tions, he remains on the level of legality and policy, hardly touching political theory. Jefferson's papers for the Revolu-tionary period (read without the hind-sight which has put the American and the French revolutions in the same era of world history) show little evidence that the American Revolution was a goad to higher levels of abstract thinking about society. We miss any such tendency in what Jefferson and his associates were reading or in what they were writing.

On the other hand, we find ample evi-dence that the locale of early Jeffersonian thought was distinctly *colonial;* we might even say *provincial.* And we begin to see some of the significance of that fact in marking the limits of political theorizing in America. By 1776, when the irreversi-ble step of revolution was taken, the colo-nial period in the life of Jefferson and the other Revolutionary thinkers was tech-nically at an end; but by then their minds had been congealed, their formal educa-

[2] Julian P. Boyd (ed.) *The Papers of Thomas Jef-ferson* (19 vols.; Princeton, N.J., 1950–)—*Ed.*

tion completed, their social habits and the cast of their political thinking determined. The Virginia society of the pre-Revolutionary years had been decidely derivative, not only in its culture, its furniture, its clothes, and its books, but in many of its ideas and—what is more to our purpose—in perhaps most of its institutions. . . .

The importance of this colonial framework in America, as I have already suggested, was to be enormous, not only from the point of view of Revolutionary thought, but in its long-run effect on the role of political theory in American life. The legal institutions which Americans considered their own and which they felt bound to master were largely borrowed. Jefferson and John Adams, both lawyers by profession, like their English contemporaries, had extracted much of their legal knowledge out of the crabbed pages of Coke's *Institutes.*[3] . . .

We begin to see how far we would be misled, were we to cast American events of this era in the mold of European history. The American Revolution was in a very special way conceived as both a vindication of the British past and an affirmation of an American future. The British past was contained in ancient and living institutions rather than in doctrines; and the American future was never to be contained in a theory. The Revolution was thus a prudential decision taken by men of principle rather than the affirmation of a theory. What British institutions meant did not need to be articulated; what America might mean

was still to be discovered. This continuity of American history was to make a sense of "givenness" easier to develop; for it was this continuity which had made a new ideology of revolution seem unnecessary. . . .

The experience of our Revolution may suggest that the sparseness of American political theory, which has sometimes been described as a refusal of American statesmen to confront their basic philosophical problems, has been due less to a conscious refusal than to a simple lack of necessity. As the British colonists in America had forced on them the need to create a nation, so they had forced on them the need to be traditional and empirical in their institutions. The Revolution, because it was conceived as essentially affirming the British constitution, did not create the kind of theoretical vacuum made by some other revolutions. . . .

The Revolution itself, as we have seen, had been a kind of affirmation of faith in ancient British institutions. In the greater part of the institutional life of the community the Revolution thus required no basic change. If any of this helps to illustrate or explain our characteristic lack of interest in political philosophy, it also helps to account for the value which we still attach to our inheritance from the British constitution: trial by jury, due process of law, representation before taxation, habeas corpus, freedom from attainder, independence of the judiciary, and the rights of free speech, free petition, and free assembly, as well as our narrow definition of treason and our antipathy to standing armies in peacetime. . . .

---

[3] Sir Edward Coke, the great English jurist, published his *Institutes* in 1628.—*Ed.*

ROBERT A. GROSS (b. 1945), who teaches at Amherst College represents the breed of "new social historians." They seek to reconstruct the
past from less traditional sources such as town and church records, genealogies, tax lists, wills, deeds and petitions. By resorting to statistical
methods and by using computers to manipulate the data extracted from
such sources, Gross is able to capture the life of a single community in
intimate detail. Why had Concord's Minutemen gone to war in 1775,
and what was the effect of the Revolution on their lives? In what way
is Gross's approach similar to that of Jesse Lemisch? In what ways is it
different?*

Robert A. Gross

The New Social History
and the Revolution

The town of Concord has always occupied a special place in the minds of
Americans, and naturally so. It was the
starting point of the Revolution: the site
of the battle of April 19, 1775, at the old
North Bridge. And in the nineteenth
century, as the home of Emerson and
Thoreau, it became the intellectual
capital of the new republic. Concord
thus played a leading part in the achievement of our political and cultural independence as a people. In turn, the
town has come to symbolize devotion to
liberty, intellectual freedom, and the
stubborn integrity of rural life.

Many writers have told Concord's
story. For the most part, theirs have been
tales of great events and great men—of
the "embattled farmers" and the distinguished writers who have brought
fame to the town. This book takes a
different approach. It sets the Concord
Fight, as it used to be known, in the context of the townspeople's ordinary lives,
before and after April 19, 1775. It ex-
amines how the citizens farmed the land,
raised their families, and carried on their
politics at the end of the colonial period.
Within this setting, it then asks what
brought them to the bridge, and it shows
how the peculiar tensions and social
patterns of the town shaped both its
response to revolution and what men
did on April 19. Finally, it traces the
townspeople through the Revolution and
the war into the new republic and links

*A selection from *The Minutemen and Their World* by Robert A. Gross, pp. vii–viii, and 171–
191. Reprinted without footnotes with the permission of Hill and Wang (Now a division of Farrar,
Straus and Giroux, Inc.).

the world of the Minutemen to that of Emerson and Thoreau. In this way, the Minutemen emerge as real people, with hopes and fears, ambitions and doubts, ideals and interests. Without such a connection between the soldiers at the bridge and the people of the town, it is difficult to comprehend the human meaning of the Revolution—to see it as a social force in men's lives, affecting what they would plant, where they would live, and what they could hope to achieve. Freedom, they knew, and we need to recall, is an intensely practical matter.

This study is part of the "new social history." It is based on a reconstruction of eighteenth-century Concord from such sources as vital records, genealogies, tax and assessment lists, wills, deeds, petitions, and the minutes of town meetings. Through the use of statistical methods and with the aid of a computer, such records can reveal the life of a whole community in surprisingly intimate detail. They allow one to write history "from the bottom up"—to tell the story of ordinary men and women who have left behind few of the diaries and letters on which historians have long relied. Unfortunately, quantitative social history can be dull and tedious work, and at times it requires technical knowledge and skills. In this book, I have chosen to relate Concord's response to revolution directly and simply, without flogging the evidence. The detailed support for my conclusions and the sometimes dry methodological issues of this research have been left to the notes. Social history, like any other branch of history, should be accessible to as wide an audience as possible, for it deals with everyday, fundamental experiences of human life—with work and play, with growing up and raising families, with growing old and

facing death. It thereby provides us with our closest points of contact with men and women of the past. By seeing how earlier Americans have lived and struggled in their daily lives, we can come to recognize them as people like ourselves and gain a new understanding of our society and our heritage. . . .

Fewer than twenty years after the American Revolution, the people of Concord pulled down the venerable North Bridge. They were looking ahead to the future and not toward symbols of the past, and as a result of highway improvements, the old bridge was obsolete. Its planks were removed a few hundred yards down river to a new bridge near John Flint's farm. Only the stone abutments remained to remind passers-by of the stirring scenes that had happened there. Having served its historic purpose, "the rude bridge that arched the flood" was cast away, an early victim of progress.

Concord took on a fresh look in the 1790s, the look of prosperity. As George Washington was assuming the presidency, trade was picking up, and by the time he left office, it was booming. Owing to the outbreak of war in Europe, neutral Americans became merchants to the world—the indispensable middlemen for everything from Jamaican sugar to Mocha coffee to Sumatran pepper—and as Boston and Salem got rich, so did their country cousins. The roads from Concord to the seaboard were filled with oxcarts, creaking under loads of barreled beef and pork, destined for West Indian plantations, and surpluses of wood, rye, and hay to build and feed the expanding port cities. Flourishing as never before, Concord farmers spent freely in the numerous stores and craft shops that dominated the village. Money passed over the counter so fast that deacon John

White, a mediocre merchant, had only to buy his stock of goods "with ordinary care, mark them at the desired profits, and the sales would assuredly be made." The handsome profits of trade lured Boston merchant John Thoreau to open a store near White's on the common. A clock industry sprang up on the mill dam; it was brought to town by such newcomers as Asaph Whitcomb, who manufactured watches and also pulled teeth "bunglingly." On the Bay Road, Jonathan Fay, a Westborough native who had spent his senior year in Concord as part of the Harvard class of 1776, replaced Daniel Bliss as the town lawyer. Fay was conveniently located to argue cases in the elegant new county courthouse or to console losing clients in the new stone jail, the two buildings facing on opposite sides of the common.

So active was business in the town center that a description of Concord in 1792 read much like a present-day Chamber of Commerce pamphlet. William Jones, the young Harvard-educated son of blacksmith Samuel Jones, boasted that "there are but few towns in the country where every mechanical branch of business is carried on with greater skill or industry. . . . The people are very industrious, enterprising, hospitable and patriotick." In all, a quarter of the townsmen earned an income from a trade or a profession. But no visitor to Concord could forget that the town's prosperity was based on agriculture. From eleven slaughterhouses and six tanneries came the periodic, heavy stench of offal and hides, which must have made many men eager to chop trees in the woods.

With the coming of good times, the citizens began to create a new town for a new republic. New and straighter roads were but one sign of a growing spirit of improvement: the inhabitants faced up to obstacles they had previously gone out of their way to avoid. Men were beginning to sense that they could make their own world—that just as they had waged a revolution, broken with the past, and formed a new government, so they could start afresh in all their affairs. America would be a "New Order of the Ages." In Concord men set out to realize that dream by reversing the long decline of the town and directing the course of their social and economic evolution.

At long last, farmers were taking up agricultural reforms. Wealthy gentlemen like Thomas Hubbard, Jr., kept in touch with the new Massachusetts Society for Promoting Agriculture and introduced the latest innovations. Frequently reminding his neighbors that "whatever is worth doing is worth doing well," Hubbard was patient whenever his farming experiments failed. "Well," he would say, "it is better to use money so, than to spend it for new rum." The example of Hubbard and other gentlemen-farmers apparently inspired their fellow townsmen. By 1801 most crop yields had risen above prewar levels. Yeomen were putting more labor into the land and rotating crops more carefully. More English clover was planted, which added nitrogen to the soil even as it produced better hay. And although its pastures still looked "indifferent" to one visitor in 1796, Concord was no longer fated to become a dilapidated home for undernourished cows. More than ever, farmers fattened their cattle on upcountry pastures, then drove them back to slaughter in town. Inevitably, more intensive farming brought an end to the easygoing habits of the past. Pigs lost the liberty to run at large, and each taxpayer was allowed to pasture only one cow along the public ways. A town pound stood on the common to pick up strays.

A new social landscape took shape, too, as a result of the drive for improvements. Before the Revolution a man could go to church once a week, attend a few town meetings, and drill with the militia four times a year and he would have exhausted nearly all the organized social outlets in town. But now opportunities were expanding for a richer social life. The townspeople had discovered the secret of the voluntary association. "Two are better than one," announced the founders of the Charitable Library Society in 1795, "and a threefold cord is not easily broken." The Library Society was one application of this principle. To spread knowledge and virtue—without which, it was believed, the republic could not survive—the fifteen wealthy members made available to all of their neighbors, for a small fee, an impressive collection of books that included religious tracts, *Paradise Lost, Washington's Letters, The Wealth of Nations,* and a volume called the *Ladies' Library.* Even the inhabitants of the county jail could borrow books, although they were limited to heavily moralistic fare. Prisoners might also gain inspiration from the town's Corinthian Lodge of Masons, whose members strove to practice harmony, love, and order in all their affairs and thus to set an example for others. On a more mundane level, a Fire Society was organized to put out fires and a Harmonic Society to improve singing in church. These organizations were open to men in all parts of town, but it was principally residents of the village who joined. Outlying farmers could not or would not travel into the center simply to borrow a book or observe the fraternal rituals of Masonry.

The founding of these societies owned much to another new association, the Social Circle. Established "to promote the social affections and disseminate useful communications among its members," the group was a gathering of the town political and social elite. David Brown belonged, as did Jonas Heywood, Joseph Hosmer, and Ephraim Wood. They were joined by such up-and-coming younger men as Reuben Brown, Jonathan Fay, John White, and Dr. Isaac Hurd, another graduate in the Harvard class of 1776. There was a total of twenty-five members, all residents of the town center and nearly all engaged in trade. Every Tuesday evening, from the first of October to the last of March, the men assembled in a member's parlor to enjoy each other's company. The group had originally grown out of the Committee of Safety, which was little more than a club by the end of the war, but it had broken up for a while, in part because of rivalry between merchants Elnathan Jones and Duncan Ingraham over who could throw more extravagant suppers for the members. Re-forming in 1794, the club settled for less lavish entertainment and perhaps more substantial conversation. The participants talked freely about the common subjects of the day—political news, religious ideas, farming reforms—and considered the needs of the town. In the process, the Circle effectively became a general improvement society. Most of the members sponsored the Charitable Library and helped found the Fire Society; Isaac Hurd joined every voluntary association in town. In the future the Social Circle would have a hand in all the important measures to come before the town.

Even as it promoted the public welfare, the Social Circle weakened the old colonial community. Once, nearly everybody had a place in all the activities of the town—at least ideally. But now social leaders were distinguished from the common run öf mankind not only by wealth or breeding but by membership in a formal organization. They were developing a distinctive identity as a group and potentially special interests of their own. Indeed, all of the voluntary associations served to set neighbors off from one another, to nurture attachments separate from the whole community. From one viewpoint, Concord had gained a livelier, more diverse social life. From another, the community had lost a certain moral unity.

Shops and stores, taverns, clubs, courts, the post office opened in 1795 at William Parkman's place, the new brick grammar school on the common—all imparted an urban flavor to life in the bustling town center. Indeed, Concord was linked more closely than ever to Boston and the cosmopolitan world it represented. A regular stage began running from Boston through Concord in 1791 along improved highways that shortened the journey. The routes carried not only men and goods but also ideas and institutions. High style came to town around 1790 in newcomer Jonathan Hildreth's sophisticated Federal-style house, with its brick ends, hipped roof, and four chimneys. The Social Circle was probably modeled upon the Boston Wednesday Club, a similar association. And when a town committee recommended rules for schoolmasters in 1799, it could think of "none more suitable than those expressed by the school committee of the town of Boston, in the year 1789." The suspicions that had flared between country and city during the postwar depression were gone. Boston influenced Concord's politics, its trade, and its culture—even its homes: young people now frequently took brides and grooms from the metropolis.

But Concord was not content to be a satellite of the city. It aimed to be Boston's rival. During the postwar depression, Massachusetts farmers, angry at the unresponsive financial policies of the state, had demanded relocation of the capital in the countryside, and the townspeople of Concord had jumped on the bandwagon. What better capital could there be in a country of farmers than strategically located Concord, birthplace of the Revolution? In 1787 a legislative committee recommended Concord as a "suitable place" for the General Court to sit, but the full House turned down the suggestion. The issue did not die with the return of prosperity. In November 1792, as a gesture to the yeomanry, the legislature convened in Concord. It departed after two weeks, perhaps because smallpox had erupted in town. This was to be the last time the General Court sat in Concord, but Boston remained uneasy. Many years later a writer in the Concord *Yeomen's Gazette* recalled that Boston representatives had undercut a proposal in the 1790s to erect a monument to the Revolution in Concord. "Everything . . . which had the smallest tendency to bring Concord into notice and consequence, was strenuously, not to say artfully opposed. . . ."

If Concord could not be state capital, it bid fair to become the governmental center of Middlesex County. Since the Revolution, the county courts had met chiefly in Concord, and the Supreme Court came to town on circuit once a year. In the 1790s, with wide support in the countryside, the townspeople revived the colonial campaign to capture all the county institutions from Cambridge and Charlestown—with no greater success.

The town's future seemed boundless. A writer in the *Massachusetts Magazine* in 1794 predicted that someday the name of Concord would bear the luster of "imperial Rome," and tourists were already coming to visit the first battle site of the Revolution. "From the plains of Concord," Yale College President Timothy Dwight mused in 1796, "will henceforth be dated a change in human affairs, an alteration in the balance of human power, and a new direction to the course of human improvement. Man, from the events which have occurred here, will in some respects assume a new character, and experience in some respects a new destiny." The people of Concord evidently agreed. They were beginning to translate these hopes into reality. . . .

The changes that came to Concord after 1790 were largely the work of a new generation. Most of the old faces were gone. Colonel Barrett, Colonel Prescott, Squire Cuming, Honest John Beatton: all had passed away. Colonel John Buttrick died in 1791, memorialized as a Cincinnatus at the plow. Dr. Joseph Lee lived on till 1797; he actively managed his farm—still the largest in town—lent out money, and worried about the state of the world until his death at age eighty-one, too soon to see his son Jonas realize the father's political ambitions. Those Revolutionary leaders who remained stepped aside for younger men. Ephraim Wood left the selectmen in 1795 after a quarter century of service; he would spend the rest of his public career as a judge of the Court of Common Pleas, a justice of the peace, and an occasional moderator of town meetings. Joseph Hosmer retired from the State Senate to become high sheriff of Middlesex County. In all, only a third of the men who paid taxes just before the Revolution were still in town by 1795. They were overshadowed by their sons and by the many citizens—nearly a third of the town—who had moved in since the war.

Even the Minutemen—the young men of the Revolution—had sought other fields far from home. By the mid-1790s more than half had departed the town they once fought to defend. Purchase Brown went back on the road to Ticonderoga, testing several places in Vermont before ending up in the town of Swanton on Lake Champlain, having endured the hardships of pioneering along the way. His first wife died in childbirth, he himself was "soarly visited with sickness," and once he nearly lost a leg when a ladle of "Scalding hot potash" fell on his foot. But it was worth the struggle. By 1800 he had acquired what he could not get in Concord: an "excellent" hundred acres of his own.

Purchase Brown was not alone. Despite the commercial boom and the revival of agriculture, there was still not enough land in Concord for all the would-be farmers in town. As a result, families like the Browns continued to send their sons and daughters to the frontier. Purchase's brother Reuben joined him in Vermont, as did one sister for a while. Two sisters went with their husbands to Winchendon, Massachusetts; two brothers settled on their father's wild land in Barrettstown (now Baldwin), Maine, a community promoted by a successful Concord emigrant, the wealthy speculator Charles Barrett of New Ipswich, New Hampshire. The dispersal took its emotional cost. Though the family tried valiantly to keep in touch, visits inevitably became less frequent, and by 1798 sixty-five-year-old Captain David Brown simply hoped to see his sons in Maine "once more before I die." But for the Browns who moved it was a necessary change. They did fairly well—the sons in Barrettstown became selectmen, like their father—while the family's fortunes sank in Concord. Left on the homestead were two spinster daughters, a son who died young, a mentally deranged son, and Joseph, the youngest, who inherited the farm at his father's death in 1802. Joseph took over a good estate, but he fell on hard times and had to mortgage the property; after his death in 1821 the run-down farm was sold to pay his debts. The feeble-minded son, William, lasted in Concord the longest, the charge first of his family and then the town. When he died in 1849, Henry David Thoreau wrote to Ralph Waldo Emerson's daughter Ellen, "William Brown of the poor house is dead—the one who used to ask for a cent—'Give me a cent?' I wonder who will have his cents now!' . . .

For the Minutemen and their leaders who remained in Concord, life generally went on in traditional ways. Joseph Hosmer attended meetings of the Social Circle and the Library Society dressed in a ruffled shirt and breeches and with his light hair, which never grayed, brushed back and curling on his neck. Hosmer and his contemporaries were poised between the old and the new. They were ready to improve their farming or to sponsor libraries, but in the interest of maintaining the world they had fought to preserve. Social values changed more slowly than the means to carry them out. Squire Barrett, Jonas Heywood, and Ephraim Wood were still seating the meetinghouse in 1792, assigning people to places according to their stations in life. The selectmen were still regulating individual morality, as the notorious tippler Oliver Wheeler discovered when tavern-keepers were barred from accepting his trade. And if the new school regulations emphasized reason over "threatenings and promises" in the education of children, they still taught the old virtues—belief in God and religious obligations, duty to parents and masters, "ye beauty and excellence of truth, justice, and mutual love," and "ye duty which they owe their country, and ye necessity of strict obedience to the laws." Ultimately, however, the application of reason could not be contained. Over the next generation, young people, born into a new republic and thinking for themselves, would cut their hair, adopt new fashions, and insist on carving out their own places in the world, free from the conventions of the past and the dictates of their parents. They would carry out a social revolution which the men of 1775 had not meant to inspire and which only a handful of Revolutionary veterans would live to see completed.

The Barretts remained Concord's premier political family down to the Age of Jackson. They retained their influence, in large part, through well-calculated marriages; as much as ever, family ties furnished the bonds of political alliance and the means of access to office. Squire Barrett's daughter Patty married Joseph Hosmer's son Cyrus, and when Squire Barrett died in 1799, his widow wed Ephraim Wood. With his brother's death, it was Stephen Barrett's turn to carry the family's banner in town politics. Lieutenant Barrett, as he was known, entered the board of selectmen in 1802, serving for six straight terms before making way for his nephew, Major James Barrett, and going on to his father's and brother's seat in the General Court. By then he was a man of substance: a tanner and farmer, with eighty acres in Concord, another fifty nearby, and a half share in some four hundred acres in the town of Holden, in Worcester County, where he pastured large herds of cattle. He was indeed living much the same life his father had lived —just as he had always expected. And he, in turn, planned to pass on to his children the same advantages he had inherited. He raised his two eldest sons to be tanners like himself, married his three daughters off well—one to a son of Ephraim Wood—and settled all but one of his six children near him. On the surface, the passage from one generation to the next was unbroken.

But Stephen Barrett could not repeat the past. He could not continue the family political dynasty in his own right nor assure his son's fortunes in the world. And even the Barretts now had to cope with rebellious sons. Although economic opportunities were increasing, young people, especially farmboys, were still dependent on their fathers for their start in life. But the fathers, who as youths had been in a hurry to grow up, were in no hurry to make way for the next generation. Indeed, having won their birthright only after a struggle, the middle-aged men of the 1790s clung more tightly to their property than even their own fathers had. And as a result of the Revolution, with its stress on natural rights, eldest sons had lost their privileges and now gained no better treatment than their brothers.

For Stephen Barrett, getting land proved easy, but it did not for his sons. Neither Stephen, Jr., nor Emerson, nor Cyrus Barrett ever received from their father a gift of land "in Consideration of Love and good will toward my sons." Lieutenant Barrett apparently intended to take his time before distributing his estate. But events intervened.

In the summer of 1799, Sally Barrett, the unmarried daughter of the lieutenant's first cousin Samuel, became pregnant, and the father turned out to be Stephen, Jr., age twenty-three. The news probably occasioned no great shock among the parents—premarital sex remained epidemic—but it hastened the young man's coming of age. Within less than a year after the marriage, Lieutenant Barrett provided his son with $1,400 to buy a farm and tannery in the western town of Shirley. The baby, born on April 19 at the opening of a new century, had secured its parents' independence.

Gradually, over the first decades of the nineteenth century, the contest between the generations abated. Young men began to leave home sooner. They might spend winters clerking in a store, serving a short apprenticeship in a mill or shop, attending an academy, or lumbering in Maine before returning in the spring to work on the family farm. Although their fathers normally helped them out, the sons would take responsibility for their economic lives, choose their own occupations, and settle when and where they pleased. And if they ultimately established themselves on the paternal estate, they would pay their own way. This is what Emerson Barrett, the lieutenant's second son, eventually did. For years he worked as a tanner, probably in partnership with his father, saving his earnings and investing in land until he was ready to wed. Then in 1810, at age thirty-two, he married, moved into a house next door to his father, and five months later bought the house, fifteen acres, and the family tannery for $1,200 from the sixty-year-old lieutenant. The father had gained a retirement fund and the son his independence, free and clear. The tensions between the generations were resolved in a free and rational economic exchange.

As it turned out, none of the lieutenant's sons did very well economically, however they came of age. Cyrus, the only child of Stephen Barrett's second marriage, died young and single before getting any land of his own. Stephen, Jr., abandoned economic striving altogether and joined a Shaker community. And for all his patient labors, Emerson could not hold onto what he had earned. Within two years of his father's death in 1824, his property was reduced to the house he and his family occupied. He never amassed much more. The standard of the Barretts passed to other branches of the family.

Major Joseph Hosmer probably bridged the gap between the colonial world and the new republic as well as any of the Revolutionary leaders in town. He was, in many ways, a born activist, as the dramatic events of his career attest: he had quietly subverted Jonathan Barnes, had agitated against the Barretts, had challenged Daniel Bliss, fought the British, and defied the haughty Hancock. And in later years he was still occasionally refusing to resign himself to the word of authority. A friend once lay ill from typhoid fever, and the doctors had given him up for dead. Hosmer went to the sickbed, inserted a penknife between his friend's teeth, and poured in a few drops of brandy. Then he paused to consult his watch. Every few minutes he continued the remedy until the patient showed signs of improvement. The man got well and lived another twenty years. Hosmer was a natural candidate for the Library Society and the Social Circle: doing good, he had learned from boyhood, brought eternal rewards, no matter what parson Daniel Bliss might say.

Yet, life taught Hosmer a sense of limits—two of his children died in infancy, and he outlived a third—and a stronger respect for authority and hierarchy than many in the rising gen-

eration would show. In politics he became a "federalist of the old school" and a lifelong admirer of Alexander Hamilton—"the first man in America," he thought. In his role as high sheriff, Hosmer would improve where he could but accept what he must. Often, after his deputies had seized a man's goods for debt, he would ride after them the next day and give "a sorrowing and distressed" wife $5, $10, or $20—whatever he could spare. "It is a hard law," he would say, "but the laws must be obeyed. Here is a little for your present necessity." And once he was required to oversee the hanging of a poor wretch condemned to die, under an old English law, for stealing a watch. He spent the night before the execution consoling the widow-to-be and suffered intensely throughout the entire ordeal. When he returned home, his son recalled, "a deep gloom fell upon the household and for days after they hardly spoke above a whisper." Still, for all his pains, Hosmer never protested aloud; his good works were done in private. Another generation would campaign against the death penalty.

Within his own family, Hosmer could take pride in his four children. His two daughters married comfortably fixed farmers; his older son farmed successfully on the family domain; and the younger son, Rufus, attended Harvard, became a lawyer, and, settling in neighboring Stow, rose to prominence in the Middlesex bar and eventually won election to the Governor's Council. The major, once the leader of "all the young men in town," never lost touch with the next generation. He could often be seen, smoking his pipe, at the center of an admiring circle of young people, and on court days the young lawyers would gather about his chair to hear his predictions on the pending cases. "I never knew him make a wrong guess," recalled one. Hosmer also had a vast store of anecdotes about the Revolutionary war, which he constantly replenished. Whenever an old soldier wandered into town, the owner of the Middlesex Hotel would make him welcome at the bar and send for Hosmer to hear his stories— although sometimes the innkeeper's daughter protested, "Father, don't send for Major Hosmer; if you do, they will never go away." The major was the last of Concord's Revolutionary leaders to go, a vigorous and eloquent figure to his end at age eighty-five in 1821. "Patty," he told his daughter-in-law in what were supposedly his last words, "surely goodness and mercy have followed us all the days of our lives, and we will dwell in the house of our God forever."

Lucy Hosmer had died three years before the major, but long before then she had apparently faded into the background of her husband's career. When Joseph received guests at the homestead in 1798, his favorite daughter-in-law, and not his wife, was on his arm: Patty Hosmer, the daughter of Squire Barrett, occupies the anecdotes in Hosmer's later life. Lucy is remembered only as an old woman grumbling about "those dark Concord woods" and reliving for her granddaughter her brief moment of rebellion—the one time she had dared to claim her freedom in a male-dominated society—before she took her subordinate place as the wife of the major and mother of his children.

Like mother, like daughter. Lavinia— born "Lovina"—Hosmer was five months' pregnant on her wedding day in 1782, and her sister Lucinda may have continued the tradition in the next decade. Perhaps the young women were defying their father. Or better, perhaps the mother had prepared her daughters

to assert their will in the one major life decision they could control—as a contemporary poem suggests:

> Some maidens say, if through the nation,
> Bundling should quite go out of fashion,
> Courtship would lose its sweets; and they
> . Could have no fun till wedding day.
>
> * * *
>
> Some mothers too, will plead their cause,
> And give their daughters great applause,
> And tell them 'tis no sin nor shame,
> For we, your mothers did the same.

In any case, after the marriages were made, the daughters, too, were caught up in bearing and rearing children—a dozen to Lavinia, eight to Lucinda. The Revolution initially made little difference in the lives and social position of New England women. Not until the early decades of the nineteenth century did courtship and marriage change, as young people came to exercise greater control over their own destiny. Women now chose their own mates, subject to their parents' veto, and not the other way around. They took their chances in the marriage market, where "fallen" women lost their value and where middle-class men, bent on establishing careers, were in no hurry to wed. Hence, chastity came back into fashion, and courtship lost its "sweets." Within marriage, too, prudence and reason held sway. Yankee couples no longer passively accepted the arbitrary decree that some families were fated to have a dozen children and others none at all. By 1820 they were consciously practicing birth control, limiting their families to a desired goal of four or five children. They thereby resolved the dilemma of too many children and not enough land for all. In the process—indeed, perhaps as a deliberate result—married women were liberated from wearying, foreshortened lives of one pregnancy after another. Self-repression became the means to the new freedom.

For the blacks of Concord, the Revolution brought the most formal change but the least in substance. A series of court decisions, ruling that under the Massachusetts Constitution all men were "free and equal," gave the *coup de grace* to slavery. By 1790 there were no slaves in Concord or anywhere else in Massachusetts. That year the census taker did count twenty-nine blacks in town, almost double the number just before the war. Many were longtime residents or their wives and children; the black population was as strongly rooted in Concord as the white and perhaps even more so. Philip Barrett never came back from the war, but Brister Freeman and Caesar Minot did, and so, surprisingly, did Casey Whitney. Cato Ingraham and Cato Lee were still working for their former masters.

Concord's freedmen now enjoyed the liberty to move about when and where they pleased, and a few even became accepted in white society. Thomas Dugan, a runaway slave from Virginia, came to Concord around 1791; after seven years of working as a farm laborer, he owned a house and two acres of land. Dugan, a mulatto, was an expert grafter of apple trees and supposedly harvested rye with the first cradle used in Massachusetts. His wife, Jenny, "a full-blooded Guinea Negro," made clothes. They were respectable folk, as was the family of Caesar Robbins, a former slave of Simon Hunt, on whom white ladies occasionally came calling for tea. But the success of these few only emphasizes the limits of possibility for most of Concord's blacks.

A small plot of land, a good house, decent clothes, and a full stomach: this was the best blacks could do in the new republic, and it was not much better than John Jack had done in a land of slavery.

Other blacks were worse off. They lived and worked at the edges of white society, on back lanes to the Great Meadows and Fields and in the vicinity of Walden Pond, an area reserved for town outcasts long before Henry David Thoreau took up residence in the woods. Of course, those freedmen who stayed with their former owners were well housed and well fed and were assured support for the rest of their lives. Dr. Joseph Lee directed his heirs to provide for "my faithful Servant" Cato, even after his laboring days were done—though on the condition that Cato remain "as diligent in business, and faithful to the family as he hath hitherto been." But when a black declared his independence, he lost his security in the white world. Cato gained Duncan Ingraham's permission to marry, only after agreeing to give up his claims on the former master. The wealthy Ingraham shortly thereafter moved to Medford, where his third wife lived. Cato continued in Concord and fell in need. Soon the former slave was paying a visit to Medford. When Ingraham reminded him of the agreement, Cato replied heatedly, "I don't want to hear any more about that; I tell you I am out of everything." The black was understandably desperate, for most likely Concord recognized no obligation for his support.

Freedom could mean not only cold and hunger but also exposure to the malice of whites, with no hope of redress. Brister Freeman once passed by Peter Wheeler's village slaughterhouse minutes after a ferocious bull had been, with enormous effort, finally driven inside. As Wheeler and his men were wondering how they would ever kill the beast, they spied the hapless Freeman. Wheeler, "giving his men the wink," cheerfully asked after the Negro's health and told him "if he would go into the slaughterhouse and get an axe, he should have a little job to do." The unsuspecting Brister opened the door and walked into a fight for his life. Meanwhile, Wheeler, son of the quick-thinking miller Timothy, and his laborers watched through the knotholes and cheered their victim on with roars of laughter. When the battle was over, a victorious Freeman emerged, his face "literally white with terror," and fled the scene without waiting for congratulations. As the frequent butt of such humor, it is no surprise that Freeman gained a reputation as "a very passionate man and often got into quarrels with the boys who loved to insult and plague him."

The possibility of random abuse and violence must have hung over the lives of most blacks in Concord, keeping them always on their guard. But in their everyday comings and goings, they were more likely to encounter the sullen indifference of a world they inhabited only on sufferance. For years John Jack's tombstone, with Daniel Bliss's antislavery inscription, lay broken and overgrown with weeds next to the grave—a symbol of the town's unconcern for its blacks. It was not until the beginning of the abolitionist movement that a campaign was launched to procure a facsimile and restore the stone to its proper place. Ironically, the man who initiated that effort was Rufus Hosmer, the son of Bliss's old antagonist. The Tory lawyer's elegant lines were destined to become "the most famous epitaph in America," frequently copied by nineteenth-century

visitors to town and printed in newspapers throughout the world. But that was small comfort for Concord's blacks. Though the white inhabitants were adopting all sorts of reforms and changing their most intimate habits within the family, they moved far more slowly to improve their treatment of their black townsmen. Racism remained the last stand of tradition and unreason.

On September 2, 1824, the Marquis de Lafayette passed through Concord on his way from Boston to New York. The aging French warhorse of the American struggle for independence was just beginning a triumphal progress through the United States to receive the tributes of a grateful republic and to stand in, as it were, for his old friend George Washington at the fiftieth anniversary of the Revolution. Concord welcomed this opportunity to pay its respects to the past. A town committee arranged a reception in an open tent on the common, in front of the meetinghouse. But not everyone was invited within. Only town officials, the welcoming committee, a few old soldiers, and the women who served the cake and punch at the festivities were allowed into the presence of "the nation's guest." The rest of the townspeople had to catch a glimpse of the general from a distance, from outside the ropes that cordoned off the tent and were guarded by soldiers.

In their eagerness to get close, many inhabitants pressed against the barriers, the soldiers pushed them back, and as the crowd grew dense, tempers rose. Some people began to complain out loud that although "they were not as well dressed nor as educated in society . . . as those within . . . their fathers had served the country, some had fought with Lafayette at the battles of the Revolution, and they were as grateful for his services."

Luckily, there was no riot. Lafayette departed within an hour or two. But the visit by the French aristocrat left bitterness toward Concord's own "aristocracy" in its wake.

Lafayette had come to a very different community from the one the Redcoats entered on April 19, 1775. Then the townspeople accepted the existence of rank and privilege as part of the natural order of things. Now they no longer went quietly to their assigned places in life, whether at patriotic celebrations or on Sabbaths at the meetinghouse. Between the two attitudes lay a social and intellectual revolution that had transformed the town.

In 1775, Concord was a community in decline. The economy was stagnant, the land was worn out, the town was losing its young. Yet, men barely sought to reverse the course of decay. They were accustomed to resign themselves to circumstances. Their lives were determined by many forces—the weather, the changing seasons, the whims of death, the twists and turns of an international market—over which they had no influence and to which they adapted as best they could. In matters close to home, which they could control, they largely deferred to the wisdom of the past. The townsmen dressed old and thought old, choosing their magistrates from proven families and proven classes and turning naturally in a crisis to men of great years and experience. Even in their rebellions they looked backward. Young people were in a hurry to be like their mothers and fathers. Feuding leaders blamed each other for violating ancestral ideals. And the greatest rebellion of all was proudly undertaken in the name of tradition. They owed it to their forefathers, William Emerson had told them, to defy the assault on New England's sacred heritage.

Fifty years later the colonial world had nearly vanished, along with powdered wigs and silver-buckled shoes. Concord was swept up in the new—economically, socially, intellectually. The townspeople bent their energies to improving and mastering all their affairs, to subjecting life itself to rational control. The economy was growing, decade by decade, farming was improving, and opportunities in trade were wider than ever, although it was true that young people continued to go West and, increasingly, to the city and factory. Politically, the dominance of the old families and of the wealthy elite that sat inside the tent during Lafayette's visit would soon come under attack. Newspapers, Bible societies, temperance societies, lyceums, and libraries all promoted reform. Thanks to its location "almost in the suburbs of the city," as the town newspaper put it, Concord was exposed to the intellectual fads of the day—to exhibitions of ventriloquism and parades of lions and dromedaries and elephants. And if Americans still looked to England for ideas and models, within a decade the grandson of Concord's Revolutionary parson would sit in the Old Manse, look out over the battle site, and compose a declaration of intellectual independence. "Build therefore your own world," Ralph Waldo Emerson told his countrymen. "As fast as you conform your life to that pure idea in your own mind, that will unfold its great proportions. A correspondent revolution in things will attend the influx of the spirit."

What explained the transformation? The men of 1775 had not gone to war to promote change but to stop it. Most would have preferred to ignore events in distant London—to pay loyalty to their king while going about their own squabbling business. But the outside world would not leave them alone. Boston kept sounding the tocsin, the British threat kept pressing closer and closer to home. Always in the background there was the town's downward slide, heightening the inhabitants' fears of the future and undermining their old, cherished ways— even a father's hold over his sons. Finally, they were forced to act if they wished to retain their traditional life. Indeed, they did. They rose in fury against the assault on their autonomy, and at the peak of the Revolutionary movement they were attached more strongly than ever to the ideals and values of the past. They would restore order to their lives by clinging to custom—and making revolution.

The strains of war deflated their hopes and made all their economic problems worse. At its end, the townspeople were once again on the defensive, struggling with financial depression and suspicious of the outside commercial interests they blamed for causing their plight. Yet, the war and revolution had opened the town to change. Army service exposed numerous individuals to new places and new ideas, while the flood of refugees from the metropolis brought Boston and Cambridge—the urban and intellectual capitals of the province—to Concord's doorstep, if only for a while. And as a result of the wartime mobilization, what the inhabitants did with their money and their lives was increasingly determined by decisions in Boston; they naturally responded by paying closer attention to state government than ever before. Most important of all, the people of Concord and the rest of Massachusetts had decisively and creatively broken with the past and established a new republican government, according to the most enlightened principles of the day Indeed, Concord contributed its own innovation to the novel work of making and changing governments—the idea of the constitutional convention. Popular government was a dynamic ideal. By the end of the war, the old deference to magistrates had weakened, and representatives were being treated not as "fathers" but as hired agents of the people. The citizens of Concord were taking control of their political lives.

The impact of that revolution in government was profound. It stood as an inspirational model of men's power to alter their own lives, to think new thoughts, to act on the best ideas of mankind, to liberate themselves from the dead weight of the past. When a new nation was securely established, when an unprecedented prosperity burst upon them, the people of Concord moved with remarkable energy to impress their will and their reason on all those forces that once held them in control. Thomas Jefferson declared that the earth belonged to the living, and after 1790 a new generation claimed possession.

The Revolution did not so much create the upsurge of confidence in human betterment as certify and encourage it and stimulate those dynamic, progressive forces that had been checked and submerged in colonial society. In war, men grow up quickly, and perhaps the young soldiers who did the fighting—those same young men who had been pressing against paternal authority—felt they had earned their own as well as a nation's independence. No doubt the timing of the boom, at the outset of the new national government, did much, too, to heighten the desire for improvement.

But the good times came to an abrupt end in Concord with the events leading to the War of 1812, and by 1820 the clockmakers were long gone, the cabinet-makers had returned to farming, and the townsmen were just beginning to climb their way back to prosperity and uninterrupted economic growth. What remained were a readiness to innovate, to search out opportunity, and a rich network of self-help groups. The age of progress had begun. And it was fitting that the town of Concord, where the Revolution had its start, would eventually produce in Ralph Waldo Emerson nineteenth-century America's greatest philosopher of that progress and in Henry David Thoreau its greatest critic.

ROBERT R. PALMER (b. 1909) is generally recognized as the dean of scholars who consider revolutions from the perspective of comparative history. In his two-volume work, *The Age of Democratic Revolution*, Palmer presents the American Revolution within the broad context of the numerous European revolutions that occurred throughout much of the Western world from the 1770s to the 1840s. In what ways does Palmer consider the American Revolution to be more radical than the French? In what ways does he view the American Revolution as conservative and nonrevolutionary?*

Robert R. Palmer

A Comparative History View

The Revolution: Was There Any?

It is paradoxical . . . to have to begin by asking whether there was any American Revolution at all. There may have been only a war of independence against Great Britain. The British lid may have been removed from the American box, with the contents of the box remaining as before. Or there may have been a mechanical separation from England, without chemical change in America itself. Perhaps it was all a conservative and defensive movement, to secure liberties that America had long enjoyed, a revolt of America against Great Britain, carried through without fundamental conflict among Americans, by an "Ameri-can consensus," in the words of Clinton Rossiter, or, as George Bancroft said a century ago, a revolution "achieved with such benign tranquillity that even conservatism hesitated to censure."

A populous country, much given to historical studies, has produced an enormous literature on the circumstances of its independence. Occupied more with European than with American history, I have been able only to sample this literature. It is apparent, however, that there is no agreement on what the American Revolution was. Differences reflect a different understanding of historical fact, a difference of attitude toward the concept of revolution, or a difference of

*Excerpts from Vol. I, *The Challenge* by R. R. Palmer, *The Age of Democratic Revolution: A Political History of Europe and America, 1769–1800* (Copyright © 1959 by Princeton University Press; Princeton Paperback, 1969), pp. 185–206 and 232–235. Reprinted by permission of Princeton University Press.

feeling on the uniqueness, if it be unique, of the United States.

The old patriotic historians, like Bancroft, who fumed against British tyranny, had no doubt that there had been a real revolution in America, even if "benignly tranquil." Writers of a liberal orientation in a twentieth-century sense, admitting that all revolutions are carried through by minorities and by violence, have said that the American Revolution was no exception. Some have seen a kind of bourgeois revolution in America, in which merchants and planters made a few concessions to the lower classes, but then, at the Philadelphia convention of 1787, rallied to the defense of property in a kind of Thermidor. Still others, of conservative temperament, sympathizing with the American loyalists, have found the ruthlessness of a true revolution in the American upheaval. It must be admitted that, for the purposes of the present book, it would be convenient to present the American part of the story in this way, on the analogy of revolutions in Europe.

But there is the contrary school that minimizes the revolutionary character of the American Revolution. Some in this school hold that there was no "democratic revolution" in America because America was already democratic in the colonial period. Thus, it has recently been shown that, contrary to a common impression, as many as ninety-five per cent of adult males had the right to vote in many parts of colonial Massachusetts. Others find the Revolution not very revolutionary because the country was still far from democratic when it became independent. They point to· the maintenance of property qualifications for voting and office-holding, or the fact that estates confiscated from loyalists found their way into the hands of speculators or well-to-do people, not of poor farmers. Those who discount the revolutionary character of the American Revolution seem to be gaining ground. For example, thirty years ago, J. F. Jameson in his little book, *The American Revolution Considered as a Social Movement*, suggested a variety of social changes that he said took place, in landholding and land law, in the disestablishment of churches and the democratizing tendencies in an aristocratic society. The book won followers and inspired research. F. B. Tolles described the aristocratic *ancien régime* of colonial Philadelphia, dominated by Quaker grandees whose social ascendancy, he said, came to an end in the American Revolution. But in 1954 the same Professor Tolles, reviewing the Jameson thesis and summarizing the research of recent decades, concluded that, while Jameson's ideas were important and fruitful, the degree of internal or social or revolutionary change within America, during the break with Britain, should not be unduly stressed.

Whether one thinks there was really a revolution in America depends on what one thinks a revolution is. It depends, that is to say, not so much on specialized knowledge or on factual discovery, or even on hard thinking about a particular time and place, as on the use made of an abstract concept. "Revolution" is a concept whose connotation and overtones change with changing events. It conveyed a different feeling in the 1790's from the 1770's, and in the 1950's from the 1930's.

No one in 1776, whether for it or against it, doubted that a revolution was being attempted in America. A little later the French Revolution gave a new dimension to the concept of revolution. It was the French Revolution that caused some to argue that the American Revolution had been no revolution at all. In 1800 Friedrich Gentz, in his *Historisches Journal* published at Berlin, wrote an essay comparing the French and American revolutions. He was an acute observer, whose account of the French Revolution did not suit all conservatives of the time, and would not suit them today; still, he made his living by writing against the French Revolution, and later became secretary to Metternich. He considered the French Revolution a bad thing, all the worse when compared to the American. He thought the American Revolution only a conservative defense of established rights against British encroachment. John Quincy Adams, then in Berlin, read Gentz's essay, liked it, translated it, and published it in Philadelphia in 1800. It served as a piece of high-toned campaign literature in the presidential election of that year, in which the elder Adams and the Federalist party were challenged by Jefferson and the somewhat Francophile democrats. The merit of Gentz's essay, said the younger Adams in his preface, was that "it rescues that revolution [the American] from the disgraceful imputation of having proceeded from the same principles as the French." In 1955 Adams' translation of Gentz was reprinted in America as a paper-back for mass distribution, with a foreword by Russell Kirk, known as a publicist of the "new conservatism." There was something in the atmosphere of 1955, as of 1800, which made it important, for some, to dissociate the American Revolution from other revolutions by which other peoples have been afflicted.

My own view is that there was a real revolution in America, and that it was a painful conflict, in which many were injured. I would suggest two quantitative and objective measures: how many refugees were there from the American Revolution, and how much property did they lose, in comparison to the French Revolution? It is possible to obtain rough but enlightening answers to these questions. The number of émigré loyalists who went to Canada or England during the American Revolution is set as high as 100,000; let us say only 60,000. The number of émigrés from the French Revolution is quite accurately known; it was 129,000, of whom 25,000 were clergy, deportees rather than fugitives, but let us take the whole figure, 129,000. There were about 2,500,000 people in America in 1776, of whom a fifth were slaves; let us count the whole 2,500,000. There were about 25,000,000 people in France at the time of the French Revolution. There were, therefore, 24 émigrés per thousand of population in the American Revolution, and only 5 émigrés per thousand of population in the French Revolution.

In both cases the revolutionary governments confiscated the property of counterrevolutionaries who emigrated. Its value cannot be known, but the sums paid in compensation lend themselves to tentative comparison. The British government granted £3,300,000 to loyalists as indemnity for property lost in the United States. The French émigrés, or their heirs, received a "billion franc indemnity" in 1825 during the Bourbon restoration. A sum of £3,300,000 is the equivalent of 82,000,000 francs. Revolutionary France, ten times as large as revolutionary America, confiscated only twelve times as much property from its émigrés, as measured by subsequent compensations, which in each case fell short of actual losses. The difference, even allowing for margins of error, is less great than is commonly supposed. The French, to be sure, confiscated properties of the church and other public bodies in addition; but the present comparison suggests the losses of private persons.

It is my belief also, John Quincy Adams notwithstanding, that the American and the French revolutions "proceeded from the same principles." The difference is that these principles were much more deeply rooted in America, and that contrary or competing principles, monarchist or aristocratic or feudal or ecclesiastical, though not absent from America, were, in comparison to Europe, very weak. Assertion of the same principles therefore provoked less conflict in America than in France. It was, in truth, less revolutionary. The American Revolution was, indeed, a movement to conserve what already existed. It was hardly, however, a "conservative" movement, and it can give limited comfort to the theorists of conservatism, for it was the weakness of conservative forces in eighteenth-century America, not their strength, that made the American Revolution as moderate as it was. John Adams was not much like Edmund Burke, even after he became alarmed by the French Revolution; and Alexander Hamilton never hoped to perpetuate an existing state of society, or to change it by gradual, cautious, and piously respectful methods. America was different from Europe, but it was not unique. The difference lay in the fact that certain ideas of the Age of Enlightenment, found on both sides of the Atlantic —ideas of constitutionalism, individual liberty, or legal equality—were more fully incorporated and less disputed in America than in Europe. There was enough of a common civilization to make America very pointedly significant to Europeans. For a century after the American Revolution, as is well known, partisans of the revolutionary or liberal movements in Europe looked upon the United States generally with approval, and European conservatives viewed it with hostility or downright contempt.

It must always be remembered, also, that an important nucleus of conservatism was permanently lost to the United States. The French émigrés returned to France. The émigrés from the American Revolution did not return; they peopled the Canadian wilderness; only individuals, without political influence, drifted back to the United States. Anyone who knows the significance for France of the return of the émigrés will ponder the importance, for the United States, of this fact which is so easily overlooked, because negative and invisible except in a comparative view. Americans have really forgotten the loyalists. Princeton University, for example, which invokes the memory of John Witherspoon and James Madison on all possible occasions, has been chided for burying in oblivion the name of Jonathan Odell, of the class of 1759, prominent as a physician, clergyman, and loyalist satirical writer during the Revolution, who died in New Brunswick, Canada, in 1818. The sense in which there was no conflict in the American Revolution is the sense in which the loyalists are forgotten. The "American consensus" rests in some degree on the elimination from the national consciousness, as well as from the country, of a once important and relatively numerous element of dissent.

Anglo-America before the Revolution

The American Revolution may be seen as a conflict of forces some of which were old, others brought into being by the event itself.

The oldest of these forces was a tradition of liberty, which went back to the first settlement of the colonies. It is true that half of all immigrants into the colonies south of New England, and two-thirds of those settling in Pennsylvania, arrived as indentured servants; but indentured servitude was not a permanent status, still less a hereditary one; the indentures expired after a few years, and all white persons soon merged into a free population.

Politically, the oldest colonies had originated in a kind of *de facto* independence from the British government. Even after the British made their colonial system more systematic, toward the close of the seventeenth century, the colonies continued to enjoy much local self-determination. Only five per cent of the laws passed by colonial assemblies were disallowed in Great Britain, and, while these often concerned the most important subjects, the infrequency of the British veto was enough to make it the exception. The elected assemblies, as already noted, were the most democratically recruited of all such constituted bodies in the Western World. In general, it was necessary to own land in order to have the right to vote for a member of the assembly, but small owner-farmers were numerous, most of all in New England; and recent studies all tend to raise the estimates of the proportion of those enjoying the franchise before the Revolution. It seems to have been above eighty per cent of adult white males in Massachusetts, half or more in New Jersey, perhaps a little under half in Virginia. Many who had the right to vote did not often use it, and this was in part because the procedure of elections was not made convenient for the ordinary hard-working man; but non-voting also suggests an absence of grievances, or perhaps only that the common man neither expected much nor feared much from government. The elected assemblies enjoyed what in Europe would be thought a dangerously popular mandate. By 1760, decades of rivalry for power between the assemblies and the governors had been resolved, in most of the colonies, in favor of the assemblies. The idea of government by consent was for Americans a mere statement of fact, not a bold doctrine to be flung in the teeth of government, as in Europe. Contrariwise, the growing assertiveness of the assemblies made many in England, and some in America, on the eve of the Revolution, believe that the time had come to stop this drift toward democracy—or, as they would say, restore the balance of the constitution. In sum, an old sense of liberty in America was the obstacle on which the first British empire met its doom. Here the most sophisticated latest researches seem to return to the old-fashioned American patriotic historical school.

From the beginnings of British America there had also been a certain rough kind of equality. Except for slaves, the poor were less poor than in Europe, and the rich were not so wealthy. Almost a quarter of the population of England were classified as paupers in 1688; almost a tenth in 1801. There was no pauperism in America, accepted and institutionalized as such; anyone not hopelessly shiftless, or the victim of personal misfortune, could make a living. At the other extreme, on the eve of the Revolution, there were men who owned hundreds of thousands of acres, mostly vacant, the main values being speculative and in the future. It is hard to say how wealthy a wealthy colonial was. A fortune of £30,000 was thought very large in Massachusetts; Joseph Galloway of Pennsylvania was said to possess £70,000. In England in 1801 there were probably 10,000 families with an average income of £1,500 a year or more, of which the capital value would be about £30,000. There is ground for believing that in England at this time, as in the United States in 1929, five per cent of the population received over thirty-five per cent of the income. The distribution of wealth in colonial America was far more equal.

There were recognized inequalities of social rank. But rank somehow lacked the magic it enjoyed in Europe. In the migration from England and Europe, the well-situated and the high-born had been notably absent. There were Americans of aristocratic pretensions, but the most ambitious genealogy led only to some middling English gentleman's manor house; most Americans were conscious of no lineage at all, American genealogy being largely a nineteenth-century science. No American could truthfully trace his ancestry to the mists of time or the ages of chivalry—nor, indeed, could many British peers or French noblemen. It was the complaint of Lord Stirling, as the New Jersey revolutionary, William Alexander, was called, that he was *not* recognized as a lord in England. A Swedish clergyman arriving in New Jersey in 1770, to take over the old Swedish congregation on the Delaware, found that well-to-do farmers were like lesser gentry in Sweden, in their use of fine linen and fondness for good horses. The significant thing for America was that people of this style of life did not, as in Sweden, consider themselves nobles. Everyone worked, and to the Swedish newcomer it seemed that "all people are generally thought equally good."

Whether religion acted as a force in the conflict of the American Revolution is disputed. Since the Worship of Reason at Notre-Dame de Paris in November 1793, there have always been those who have stressed the religious principles of the founders of the United States. It is a way of showing how different they were from Jacobins or Communists. The truth is that the age was not notably religious, and that the sentiments that burst out violently in Paris in 1793 were, as sentiments, not uncommon. We read, for example, of an Anglican rector in England who, about 1777, so admired the writings of Catherine Macaulay that "he actually placed her statue, adorned as the Goddess of Liberty, within the altar railing" of his parish church. "It will never be pretended," wrote John Adams in 1786, that the men who set up the new governments in America "had interviews with the gods, or were in any degree under the inspiration of Heaven, more than those at work on ships or houses, or laboring in merchandise or agriculture; it will forever be acknowledged that these governments were contrived by reason and the senses, as Copley painted Chatham . . . [or] as Paine exposed the mistakes of Raynal. . . ." John Adams, while differing with him in detail, had not yet broken with Thomas Paine.

Aggressive anti-Christianity did not develop in America, to the great good fortune of the future United States. It failed to develop, however, not because American revolutionary leaders were warmly religious, but because no religious body seriously stood in their way. Here again it was the weakness of conservative forces, not their strength, that made the Revolution "conservative." No church seriously opposed the political aims of the Revolution. No church figured as a first estate in colonial

America, none had its dignitaries sitting in the highest councils of government, and none lost vast tracts of material property, since none possessed any. The Anglican clergy generally opposed the Revolution, because of their close connection with British authority. Revolutionaries drove them out of their churches, for the same reason; worse would have happened to them had they not been so easily dislodged. In any case, even where the Anglican church was established, in New York and the South, Anglicans were not a majority of the population. At the opposite end of the religious spectrum the Quakers, because of their doctrine of non-resistance to established authority, were in effect a force to be reckoned on the British side. But they were unimportant politically outside of Pennsylvania. Over half the colonial Americans, and probably ninety per cent of New Englanders, were, vaguely or exactly, some species of Calvinists. No allegation was more common, from the British or the American loyalists, than that the whole Revolution had been stirred up by old Presbyterian disaffection. It is true that New England Congregationalists and Scotch-Irish Presbyterians did not admire some of the contemporary institutions of England, and that their ministers, when the time came, generally supported the Revolution. They probably infused, in a way hard to define, a certain religious atmosphere into the American patriot program.

A great many Americans, however, before and during the Revolution, belonged to no church at all. In conditions of constant movement, uprooting, settlement, and resettlement, probably a larger proportion of Americans were unchurched than in any European country. What aroused horror, when violently pursued as dechristianization in France a few years later, had gone pretty far, without violence, in America. As for the leaders of the American Revolution, it should be unnecessary to demonstrate that most of them were deists. They were strongly on the side of the best human virtues, or at least of those which were not ascetic; but they saw no connection between such virtues and religious practice. Like Jefferson in the Declaration of Independence, they appealed to the laws of Nature's God. They seem not to have felt, however, like Burke, that these laws placed serious limits upon their freedom of political action.

The simplicities in which British America had originated gave way to more complex forms of society in the eighteenth century. A liberty almost like that of the "state of nature," a liberty defined by the remoteness of government, gradually changed, especially after the British revolution of 1688, into the more organized and channelized liberty of British subjects under the British constitution. There was a bias toward equality in the foundations. The superstructure, as it was raised, exhibited palpable inequalities. As America became more civilized it began to have, like all civilized countries, a differentiation of social classes. Even the once unmanageable Quakers took on new social refinements. The Philadelphia Yearly Meeting of 1722 officially declared its "decent respect" for "ranks and dignities of men," and called for honor and obedience "from subjects to their princes, inferiors to superiors, from children to parents, and servants to masters." Increasingly there was a kind of native American aristocracy. No question was of more importance for the future than the way in which this new aristocracy would develop.

The colonial aristocracy, as it took form in the eighteenth century, owed a good deal to close association with government. From New Hampshire to the far South . . . there were intermarried families which monopolized seats in the governors' councils, in some cases, now, to the third and fourth generation. There were Americans, close to the British authorities, who regarded themselves as the natural rulers of the country. Sometimes, like Englishmen of the class to which they would compare themselves, they expected to draw a living from public offices, to which they need devote only part of their time. This practice has been most closely studied for Maryland, where there were a number of offices in which a man could live like a gentleman, with a good deal of leisure, for £150 a year.

More generally, the wealth of the growing American upper class came from early land grants, or from inheritance of land in a country where land values were always rising, or from mercantile wealth in the half-dozen seaboard cities, all of which except Charleston lay from Philadelphia to the North, or from the ownership of plantations and Negro slaves in the South. New York and the Southern provinces, because of their systems of landholding, were the most favorable to the growth of aristocratic institutions, but an upper class existed everywhere in the settled regions. In places where landed and mercantile wealth came together, as at New York and Charleston, people mixed easily with mutual regard; there was no standoffishness between "trade" and "gentry."

Without the rise of such a colonial aristocracy there could have been no successful movement against England. There had to be small groups of people who knew each other, who could trust each other in hazardous undertakings, who had some power and influence of their own, who could win attention and rally followers, and who, from an enlarged point of view, felt a concern for the welfare of the provinces as a whole. "While there are no noble or great and ancient families . . . they cannot rebel," as an observer of New England remarked in 1732. A generation later such "great" families, if not noble or very ancient, could be found everywhere in the colonies.

On the other hand, the rise of such an aristocracy brought class friction and internal tension. "In many a colony in 1764," according to Professor Rossiter (whose view of an "American consensus" I do not wish to misrepresent), "civil war seemed more likely than war with Britain." There was everlasting bickering over land titles, quit-rents, debts, and paper money. There was complaint, in the western part of several provinces, at under-representation in the elected assemblies, or at the long distances it was necessary to go to cast a vote or to be present in a court of law. Rich and poor were not so far apart as in Europe, but they were far enough apart to cause trouble. Western Massachusetts, suspicious of Boston, was not hostile to Britain until 1774. There was a great rent riot in the Hudson valley in 1766, directed against the manorial system on which the Van Rensselaers and the Livingstons grew wealthy. A thousand angry western Pennsylvania farmers marched on Philadelphia in 1764, enraged that the over-represented East, and its opulent and pacifistic Quaker aristocracy, begrudged them military protection at the time of Pontiac's Indian war. The best example was afforded by the Regulators of North Carolina.

This province, though scarcely a century old, had developed a fine system of decayed boroughs on the British model. The five oldest coastal counties, thinly inhabited, enjoyed a dozen times as much representation in the assembly, per capita, as the newer uplands, so that the bulk of the people, while having the vote, could get little accomplished. Political life was most active at the county level, and in each county a few families named the judges and sheriffs, who are estimated to have embezzled over half the public funds. The governing elite, if one may so term it, unabashedly made a living off the legal business that small farmers could not avoid. A group of these farmers founded an "association" for "regulating public grievances," and these Regulators began to refuse to pay taxes. The governor finally called out the militia against them, chiefly a mounted troop of Gentlemen Volunteer Light Dragoons, in which 8 "generals" and 14 "colonels" led less than 1,300 enlisted men. The Regulators were routed in the Battle of Alamance in 1771. Seven of them were hanged. Later, when the gentry led the province into the Revolution, the British found many loyalist strongholds in the back country of Carolina.

Conflicting forces were therefore at work in America, when the Stamp Act added the conflict between America and Great Britain. Americans all but universally opposed the Stamp Act. Most of those who eventually became loyalists disapproved of British policy in the ten years before the Revolution. The doctrine of parliamentary supremacy was an innovation, accepted in England itself only since the revolution of 1689; the trend toward centralization of the empire under parliamentary authority, with attendant plans for reordering the colonial governments, was a modern development, a new force, much less old than

the American liberties. On this Americans could agree. They began to disagree on the means used to uphold the American position. It was one thing to sit in meetings or submit petitions to Parliament; it was another to persist stubbornly in defiance, to insult or intimidate the King's officers, stop the proceedings of law courts, and condone the violence of mobs. Whether the British constitution really assured no taxation without representation was, after all, uncertain. It was far more certain that the British constitution secured a man against physical violence, against his having his house plundered and wrecked by political adversaries, or against being tarred and feathered for refusing to join a non-import agreement decided on by some unauthorized assembly which had no right to use force. As events unfolded, men took sides, and Americans found themselves disputing with each other on a new subject, the attitude to be taken to British law.

What happened to Plymouth Rock offers a parable. The stone on which the Pilgrims of 1620 had supposedly first set foot already enjoyed a local fame, as a symbol of what was most ancient and natively American in the New World. In 1774 a party of patriots decided to use it as the base for a liberty pole. They tried to haul it, with twenty oxen, from the shore to the town square. Under the strain, it broke in two.

The Revolution: Democracy and Aristocracy

Fighting between the King's troops and the people of Massachusetts began at Lexington and Concord in April 1775. In the following December the British government put the insurgent colonists outside the protection of the

British crown. The Americans were now in what they would call a state of nature, and what was in fact a condition of anarchy. Lawful authority melted away. Governors, unable to control their assemblies, undertook to disband them, only to see most of the members continue to meet as unauthorized congresses or associations; or conventions of counties, unknown to the law, chose delegates to such congresses for provinces as a whole; or local people forcibly prevented the sitting of law courts, or the enforcement of legal judgments by the sheriffs. Violence spread, militias formed, and the Continental Congress called into existence a Continental army, placing General George Washington in command.

In whose name were these armed men to act? To what civilian authority were they to be subordinated? How could the courts be kept open, or normal court decisions and police protection be carried out? If American ships, breaking the old navigation system, should enter the ports of Europe, in whose name should they appear? If diplomatic agents were sent to Versailles or the Hague, whom were they to say that they represented? If aid was to be sought from France, would the French give it for any purpose except to break up the British empire, and undo the British victory of 1763? These practical needs, together with the inflaming of feeling against England by war and bloodshed, and the extraordinary success of Thomas Paine's pamphlet, *Common Sense*, induced the Congress, more than a year after the battle of Lexington, to announce the arrival of the United States of America "among the powers of the earth," able to do "all acts and things which independent states may of right do."

With the Declaration of Independence, and the new constitutions which most of the states gave themselves in 1776 and 1777, the revolutionary colonials began to emerge from the anarchy that followed the collapse or withdrawal of British power. They sought liberty, it need hardly be said; but they also sought authority, or a new basis of order. A revolution, it has been wisely observed, is an unlawful change in the conditions of lawfulness. It repudiates the old definitions of rightful authority, and drives away the men who have exercised it; but it creates new definitions of the authority which it is a duty to obey, and puts new men in a position to issue legitimate commands. The new lawfulness in America was embodied in the new constitutions, which will be considered shortly. Meanwhile, what happened in America was against the law.

The Revolution could be carried out, against British and loyal American opposition, only by the use of force. Its success "was impossible without a revolutionary government which could enforce its will." Let us look simply at the case of New Jersey. Late in 1776 the danger to the patriots became very pressing, as the British pursued Washington's army across the state. One of the New Jersey signers of the Declaration of Independence was forced to recant; the man who had presided over the convention which had proclaimed independence of the state went over to the British. The state was full of open and hidden enemies of the new regime. Taxes were neither levied nor collected with any regularity; the paper money which financed the Revolution flooded the state, swollen by counterfeits that poured from loyalist presses in New York. Prices soared; price controls were imposed, but were generally ineffective. The new government had no means of enforcing its authority except the thirteen county courts carried over from colonial times. These proved ineffectual under conditions of civil war. Revolutionary leaders thereupon created a Council of Safety as a temporary executive. Its twelve members were chosen by the state legislature. They toured the state to arouse local patriots and speed up action of the courts. They took the law into their own hands wherever they wished, hunted out suspects, ordered arrests, exacted oaths of allegiance, punished evasion of militia service, and instituted proceedings to confiscate the property of those who openly joined the British. One member of this Council of Safety was William Paterson, born in Ireland, son of a storekeeper. His career had been made by the Revolution, during which he became attorney-general to the state. He became a heated revolutionary, detesting more than all others, as he once said, that "pernicious class of men called moderates." His position allowed him to buy confiscated lands on advantageous terms; he became a well-to-do man. He lived to be a justice of the United States Supreme Court, and a terror to democrats in the days of the Alien and Sedition laws.

Revolutionary government as a step toward constitutional government, committees of public safety, representatives on mission to carry revolution to the local authorities, paper money, false paper money, price controls, oaths, detention, confiscation, aversion to "moderatism," and Jacobins who wind up as sober guardians of the law—how much it all suggests what was to happen in France a few years later! With allowance for differences of scale and intensity, there was foreshadowed in the America of 1776 something of the *gouvernement révolutionnaire* and even the Terror of

France in 1793—except for the death sentences and the horrors that went with them, and except for the fact that the victims of these arbitrary proceedings never returned to political life as an organized force, to keep alive for all time an inveterate hatred of the Revolution.

It is not easy to say why some Americans warmly embraced the Revolution, or why others opposed it, or how many there were on each side. Independence made it in principle necessary to choose between loyalty and rebellion. But there were many who by isolation managed to avoid commitment, or whose inclinations swayed with the course of battle, or who, torn in their beliefs, prepared passively to accept whichever authority in the end should establish itself. Numbers therefore cannot be given. It has often been repeated, as a remark of John Adams, that a third of the American people were patriot, a third loyalist, and a third neutral; but this neat summary has gone into the attic of historical fallacies; what Adams meant, when he offered it in 1815, was that a third of the Americans in the 1790's had favored the *French* Revolution, a third had opposed it, and a third had not cared. The bulk of American opinion, after July 1776, seems to have been actively or potentially for independence. Positive and committed loyalists were a minority, but not therefore unimportant. They had the strength of the British empire on their side, and much also in the American tradition to support them. They believed in liberties for the colonies, and in old and historic rights under the British constitution, which, however, they felt to be less threatened by Parliament than by unruly new forces in America itself.

It is not possible to explain the division between patriot and loyalist by other or supposedly more fundamental divisions. The line coincided only locally or occasionally with the lines of conflict that had appeared before the war. Families divided, brothers often went different ways. Doubtless many a man marked himself for a lifetime by the impulsive decision of a moment. Economic and class motivations are unclear. The most firmly established merchants and lawyers tended to loyalism, but there were respected merchants and lawyers who embraced the revolution. New York and Virginia were both full of great landowners, but New York was the most loyalist province, Virginia one of the most revolutionary. Ironmasters, who had reason to object to British controls on the American iron industry, wound up in both camps. Debtors had reason to object to British attempts, over the previous half century, to limit paper money in America and stop inflation; but people do not always act from reason, and indebtedness in any case was scarcely a class phenomenon, since it was characteristic of the free-spending southern aristocracy, the businessmen in the towns, and farmers whose land was mortgaged, as well as of such actually poor people as may have been able to borrow any money. Religion of the Calvinist type was a force working against England, but the Presbyterians of the Carolina frontier, not eager to be governed by their own gentry, supplied many soldiers to the King. National origin had no general influence, for the Middle Colonies, the least English in origin, were stronger centers of loyalism than New England or the South. The young men, if we may judge by the infinitesimal proportion who were in the colleges, were ardently patriot. The colleges, from Harvard to William and Mary, were denounced by loyalists as hotbeds of sedition.

An obvious explanation, quite on the surface, is as good as any: that the patriots were those who saw an enlargement of opportunity in the break with Britain, and the loyalists were in large measure those who had benefited from the British connection, or who had organized their careers, and their sense of duty and usefulness, around service to the King and empire. These would include the American-born governors, Thomas Hutchinson in Massachusetts and William Franklin in New Jersey. There were also the families that customarily sat on the governors' councils or held honorific or lucrative offices under the crown. There were some in the rising American upper class who admired the way of life of the aristocracy in England, and who would imitate it as best they could. Such was surely their right as British subjects, but it might alienate them from Americans generally, even many of the upper class, who were willing to have social distinctions in America develop in a new way.

It is estimated that from half to two-thirds of those who had sat on the governors' councils became loyalists. For New Jersey we know exactly what happened. Of the twelve members of the provincial council in 1775, five became active and zealous loyalists, two became cautious or neutral loyalists, one went into retirement for age, and four became revolutionaries, one of whom made his peace with the British when he thought they were going to win. Massachusetts had as few loyalists as any province, but when the British troops evacuated Boston in 1776 they took over 1,100 civilians with them. Of these, 102 had been councillors or officials and 18 were clergymen, mainly Anglican; but 382 were farmers, 213 were merchants "and others," and 105 came from country towns. The rest were probably women and children. Like the émigrés from the French Revolution, the émigrés from America came from all classes. But those connected with the English government or English church, and identifying themselves with English society and the values of the British governing class, were more numerous among loyalists than in the general population. On the other hand, lest any one thesis be carried too far, it should be pointed out that Virginia, a very English province in some ways, was so solidly patriotic that only thirteen natives of the Old Dominion ever applied to Britain for compensation for loyalist losses.

The war itself polarized the issues. Each side needed strength, and the revolutionary leaders looked for it in the mass of the population, the loyalists among the ruling circles of Great Britain. In legal form, the struggle was between the sovereignty of the former colonies and the sovereignty of the British King-in-Parliament. Rebellious leaders, however, clothed themselves in the sovereignty of the "people," both in form and to a large degree in content. The social content of Parliament in the eighteenth century needs no further elaboration. The struggle, whatever men said, and whatever has been said since, was inseparable from a struggle between democratic and aristocratic forces. If the rebellion was successful, democracy in America would be favored. If it failed, if Parliament and the loyal Americans had their way, development in America would move in an aristocratic direction. In this respect the American Revolution resembled the revolutions in Europe.

That the war · favored democracy in America is apparent in many ways. In some places, notably Massachusetts, the suffrage was nearly universal before the Revolution; in others, notably Virginia, the Revolution did not extend it. But in Pennsylvania the pro-British leanings of the Quaker patriciate brought them into disrepute after hostilities began; and their aversion to military solutions, at a time when any solution was bound to be military, threw power into the hands of the western farmers, who by becoming soldiers made themselves indispensable to the infant state, so that Pennsylvania developed the most democratically organized government in the new union. In New Jersey the provincial congress, enjoying no legality and in rebellion against the legal authorities, sought to broaden its mandate by extending the voting franchise. In fact, petitions streamed into the Congress, urging that all householders or taxpayers should have the vote, the better to oppose enemies of the "American cause." The provincial congress in February 1776, five months before independence, granted the vote to all males at least twenty-one years old, resident in the state a year, and possessing goods worth £50 "proclamation money." With wartime depreciation of proclamation money, virtual universal manhood suffrage ensued. Voters also, after July 1776, were required to take an oath abjuring allegiance to George III, and some purists, pained by revolutionary illiberalism, have deprecated such restriction of political rights, as if the only feasible alternative would have been more democratic, and as if oaths did not exist in Britain itself, where men could still be obliged to abjure the House of Stuart.

An experience of Colonel Thomas Randolph of Virginia well illustrates the same spread of democracy. Randolph, one of the many Virginia aristocrats who fought for the Revolution, was entertaining a captured British officer in his home. Three farmers came in, sat down, took off their boots, did a little spitting, and talked business with the colonel. After they left, Randolph commented to his guest on how "the spirit of independency was converted into equality, and everyone who bore arms esteemed himself on a footing with his neighbor." He added, with distaste: "No doubt, each of these men conceives himself, in every respect, my equal." War, and a citizen army, had somewhat the same effects as in France after 1792. Leaders who did not fight for equality accepted it in order to win.

On the other hand, the American loyalists, who were in any case the Americans most inclined to favor hierarchic ideas, were made more so by the necessities of their position. William Eddis of Maryland, as early as 1770, thought that noblemen and bishops should be established in America as soon as possible. The commonest of all loyalist ideas was that the democratic branch, under the mixed British constitution in America, had gotten out of control. Their commonest allegation, during the war, was that the Revolution was the work of their social inferiors—"mechanics and country clowns," who had no right to dispute "what Kings, Lords, and Commons had done," as a South Carolina clergyman expressed it. He was driven out by his congregation.

The loyalists fully expected the British army to put down the rebellion very soon. They believed that the whole disturbance had been caused by a few troublemakers, from whom the bulk of the people in America were patiently awaiting liberation. Hence, they had plans ready for the government of America after the restoration of order. These plans parallelled some of the British ideas. . . . Like them, they called for the setting up in the colonies of something like a nobility. They expressed the idea that I have tried to show was so common in the eighteenth century, the idea of Blackstone and Gibbon and Montesquieu and the French parlements and many others, that some sort of nobility was a prerequisite to political liberty. There must be, in this view, an intermediate order of men having the personal right to take part in government, neither elected and hence under the influence of constituents, nor yet too amenable to influence by a king, so that they should be hereditary if possible, and at least hold office for life.

Loyal Americans congregated in New York, which was occupied by the British during most of the war. Here, as they talked over the sad state of their country, they found much on which they could agree. David Ogden of New Jersey was typical. He had served for twenty-one years on the New Jersey governor's council. After he fled to New York in January 1777, the revolutionary government in New Jersey confiscated from him twenty-three pieces of real estate, which he himself later valued at £15,231. He was one of the more prominent of the fugitives in New York, becoming a member of the Board of Refugees established there in 1779. He proposed that, after suppression of the rebellion, an American parliament be set up for all the colonies, subordinate to that of Great Britain, to consist of three branches, as in Britain: namely, a lord lieutenant, certain "barons" created for the purpose, and a house of commons chosen by the several colonial assemblies. The new parliament, incidentally, was to supervise the colleges, those "grand nurseries of the late rebellion."

The case of Joseph Galloway is more fully known. In 1774 he had tried to restrain the First Continental Congress by submitting a plan of American union, which that body had rejected as too favorable to parliamentary claims. During the war, after spending some time in New York, where he convinced himself that all Americans of any standing agreed with him, Galloway proceeded in 1778 to England, where for ten years he submitted a series of plans on colonial government to various persons in authority in London. These plans built on the plan of 1774, retaining its proposal for an autonomous inter-colonial parliament subordinate to the Parliament of Great Britain; but they added new ideas of structural reform.

The revolutionary states in America, according to Galloway, would be dissolved by the coming British victory, and the old forms of government would be forfeited by rebellion. There would therefore be a "state of nature without a civil constitution," or what he also called a Chart Blanche, "a perfect blank upon which a new policy shall be established." Opportunity would thus be afforded for certain longneeded changes. Temporarily, because of the war, there were two parties in America, the party of independence, "actuated by views of ambition and private interest," and the party favoring perpetual union with Great Britain. The former was "a mere republican party firmly attached to democratical government"; it had "vested the powers of all their new states originally and ultimately in the People." The other party, favoring union with England, preferred a "mixed form of government," to guard against abuse of power by either the sovereign or the

people. Most Americans, Galloway was persuaded, were tired of being pushed about by revolutionary cliques. Most of the colonists, and certainly most men of property, would therefore welcome his plan of reorganization.

In this reorganization, the old governments of the charter provinces (Connecticut and Rhode Island) and of the proprietary provinces (Pennsylvania and Maryland) were to be abolished, and all the provinces made to conform to the same model, the balanced government of the British constitution. If Britain and America were to remain long together, it was imperative that they should have "the same customs, manners, prejudices and habits." These would then give "the same spirit to the laws." There should be an American union with a lord lieutenant or governor general representing the crown, an upper house appointed for life and with "some degree of rank or dignity above the Commons," and a lower house chosen by the various colonial assemblies. The "weight and influence" of the crown would be assured by making all offices, "civil and military, honorable and lucrative," depend on royal appointment. Thus a group of Americans would be built up, hostile to pure democracy and with an interest in mixed government and the British connection. The Americans also, declared Galloway, recurring to the almost forgotten origin of the whole controversy, would willingly pay an agreed-upon share toward military and imperial expenses, by taxing themselves through such a parliament as he outlined.

As among Americans themselves, it is clear that the Revolution involved a contest between men committed either to a more popular or a more aristocratic trend in government and society. Had the loyalists returned, received back their property, and resumed the positions of prestige and public influence which many of them had once enjoyed, it seems unlikely that the subsequent history of the United States would have been like the history that we know. . . .

Ambivalence of the American Revolution

In conclusion, the American Revolution was really a revolution, in that certain Americans subverted their legitimate government, ousted the contrary-minded and confiscated their property, and set the example of a revolutionary program, through mechanisms by which the people was deemed to act as the constituent power. This much being said, it must be admitted that the Americans, when they constituted their new states, tended to reconstitute much of what they already had. They were as fortunate and satisfied a people as any the world has known. They thus offered both the best and the worst example, the most successful and the least pertinent precedent, for less fortunate or more dissatisfied peoples who in other parts of the world might hope to realize the same principles.

Pennsylvania and Georgia gave themselves one-chamber legislatures, but both had had one-chamber legislatures before the Revolution. All states set up weak governors; they had been undermining the authority of royal governors for generations. South Carolina remained a planter oligarchy before and after independence, but even in South Carolina fifty-acre freeholders had a vote. New York set up one of the most conservative of the state constitutions, but this was the first constitution under which Jews received equality of civil rights—not a very revolutionary departure, since Jews had been prospering in New York since 1654. The Anglican Church was dis-

established, but it had had few roots in the colonies anyway. In New England the sects obtained a little more recognition, but Congregationalism remained favored by law. The American revolutionaries made no change in the laws of indentured servitude. They deplored, but avoided, the matter of Negro slavery. Quit-rents were generally abolished, but they had been nominal anyway, and a kind of manorial system remained long after the Revolution in New York. Laws favoring primogeniture and entail were done away with, but apparently they had been little used by landowners in any case. No general or statistical estimate is yet possible on the disposition of loyalist property. Some of the confiscated estates went to strengthen a new propertied class, some passed through the hands of speculators, and some either immediately or eventually came into the possession of small owners. There was enough change of ownership to create a material interest in the Revolution, but obviously no such upheaval in property relations as in France after 1789.

Even the apparently simple question of how many people received the right to vote because of the Revolution cannot be satisfactorily answered. There was some extension of democracy in this sense, but the more we examine colonial voting practices the smaller the change appears. The Virginia constitution of 1776 simply gave the vote to those "at present" qualified. By one estimate the number of persons voting in Virginia actually declined from 1741 to 1843, and those casting a vote in the 1780's were about a quarter of the free male population over twenty-one years of age. The advance of political democracy, at the time of the Revolution, was most evident in the range of officers for whom voters could vote. In the South the voters generally voted only for members of the state legislatures; in Pennsylvania and New England they voted also for local officials, and in New England for governors as well.

In 1796, at the time of the revolution in Europe, and when the movement of Jeffersonian democracy was gathering strength in America, seven of the sixteen states then in the union had no property qualification for voters in the choice of the lower legislative house, and half of them provided for popular election of governors, only the seaboard South, and New Jersey, persisting in legislative designation of the executive. The best European historians underestimate the extent of political democracy in America at this time. They stress the restrictions on voting rights in America, as in the French constitution of 1791. They do so because they have read the best American historians on the subject and have in particular followed the school of Charles Beard and others. The truth seems to be that America was a good deal more democratic than Europe in the 1790's. It had been so, within limits, long before the revolutionary era began.

Nor in broad political philosophy did the American Revolution require a violent break with customary ideas. For Englishmen it was impossible to maintain, in the eighteenth century or after, that the British constitution placed any limits on the powers of Parliament. Not so for Americans; they constantly appealed, to block the authority of Parliament or other agencies of the British government, to their rights as Englishmen under the British constitution. The idea of limited government, the habit of thinking in terms of two levels of law, of an ordinary law checked by a higher constitutional law, thus came out of the

realities of colonial experience. The colonial Americans believed also, like Blackstone for that matter, that the rights of Englishmen were somehow the rights of all mankind. When the highest English authorities disagreed on what Americans claimed as English rights, and when the Americans ceased to be English by abjuring their King, they were obliged to find another and less ethnocentric or merely historical principle of justification. They now called their rights the rights of man. Apart from abstract assertions of natural liberty and equality, which were not so much new and alarming as conceptual statements as in the use to which they were applied, the rights claimed by Americans were the old rights of Englishmen—trial by jury, *habeas corpus*, freedom of the press, freedom of religion, freedom of elections, no taxation without representation. The content of rights was broadened, but the content changed less than the form, for the form now became universal. Rights were demanded for human beings as such. It was not necessary to be English, or even American, to have an ethical claim to them. The form also became more concrete, less speculative and metaphysical, more positive and merely legal. Natural rights were numbered, listed, written down, and embodied in or annexed to constitutions, in the foundations of the state itself.

So the American Revolution remains ambivalent. If it was conservative, it was also revolutionary, and vice versa. It was conservative because colonial Americans had long been radical by general standards of Western Civilization. It was, or appeared, conservative because the deepest conservatives, those most attached to King and empire, conveniently left the scene. It was conservative because the colonies had never known oppression, excepting always for slavery—because, as human institutions go, America had always been free. It was revolutionary because the colonists took the risks of rebellion, because they could not avoid a conflict among themselves, and because they checkmated those Americans who, as the country developed, most admired the aristocratic society of England and Europe. Henceforth the United States, in Louis Hartz's phrase, would be the land of the frustrated aristocrat, not of the frustrated democrat; for to be an aristocrat it is not enough to think of oneself as such, it is necessary to be thought so by others; and never again would deference for social rank be a characteristic American attitude. Elites, for better or for worse, would henceforth be on the defensive against popular values. Moreover the Americans in the 1770's, not content merely to throw off an outside authority, insisted on transmuting the theory of their political institutions. Their revolution was revolutionary because it showed how certain abstract doctrines, such as the rights of man and the sovereignty of the people, could be "reduced to practice," as Adams put it, by assemblages of fairly levelheaded gentlemen exercising constituent power in the name of the people. And, quite apart from its more distant repercussions, it was certainly revolutionary in its impact on the contemporary world across the Atlantic.

THOMAS C. BARROW (b. 1929) who is affiliated with Clark University takes the so-called "social science" approach to the Revolution. Seeking to make the Revolution relevant to events in our own time, he draws certain parallels between the American War of Independence and colonial wars of liberation in the twentieth century. Barrow holds that colonial societies share certain elements in common and bases his hypothesis upon an assumption of certain underlying laws of social behavior. Do you believe that his assumption is valid?*

Thomas C. Barrow

The Revolution as a Colonial War of Liberation

The current historiographical controversies over the American Revolution owe much to Carl Becker. From Becker's day to the present, historians have debated the question of the existence or non-existence of an "internal revolution" in American society. Some historians, following Becker's lead, search for traces of internal social or political turmoil. Others, disagreeing with Becker, stress the continuity of institutions and traditions during the Revolution. At issue is the basic question of just "how revolutionary was the American Revolution," and in the failure of historians to agree on an answer to that question lies the source of controversy. And so the great debate continues.

Unfortunately, there is no adequate definition of a "revolution." The dictionary description of a revolution as a "total or radical change" certainly provides no effective guideline. Since history is the study of change in human society, locating a revolution according to that formula becomes a matter of appraising just how much change is involved in a given event, which inevitably comes down to a question of where one wants to place the emphasis. In any case, precise definitions are somewhat beside the point. When the word *revolution* is used today in connection with a political system, its meaning, if not its precise definition, is abundantly clear. The image called to mind is inescapably that of the French

*Thomas C. Barrow, "The American Revolution as a Colonial War for Independence," *William and Mary Quarterly*, XXV (July, 1968), pp. 452–464. Reprinted by permission of the author. Some footnotes omitted.

and Russian revolutions, which have provided us with our classic formulas for revolutionary re-structurings of society. A revolution in these terms represents the replacement of an archaic, repressive regime or regimes with something new, something more open, more flexible, more adaptable. In effect, in the interests of "progress," within the political system stability is replaced by instability until some new synthesis is achieved. Only then is stability restored, at which point the revolutionary drama is closed.

For generations now American historians have struggled to fit their "revolution" into this classic mold.[1] The difficulties they have encountered in doing so are reflected in the present historiographical impasse. It is a problem that might have been avoided had we remembered that the American people were, until 1776, colonials. By its very nature, a colonial society must be, in certain vital ways, unstable. Unable to exercise complete political control, subject to continual external intervention and negative interference, a colonial society cannot achieve effective "maturity"— that is, cannot create and control a political system that will be suited to the requirements of the interests indigenous to that society. A colonial society is an "incomplete" society, and consequently an inherently unstable society. This was as true of American society prior to 1776 as it is today of the colonial societies

left in our world.[2] And, consequently, if instability is the given fact in American society at the beginning of the imperial crisis, it is hard to see how the classic pattern of "stability replaced by instability" can be imposed upon it. The answer, of course, is that it cannot, that in fact colonial wars for independence or "liberation" are generically different from revolutions of the French or Russian variety. And, after all, the American Revolution was just that—a colonial war of liberation. Given the widespread existence of such wars in today's world, it is odd that for so long a time we have overlooked the full implications of this fact.

Colonial wars for independence have an inner logic of their own. The first problem is to achieve self-determination. Once that is accomplished, it then becomes a matter of organization, about which, naturally, there always will be fundamental disagreement. What course this disagreement will take, and how bitter it will be, will be determined by the nature of the particular society. In former colonies which have emerged into nationhood in this century, the determining factor has largely been the heterogeneous nature of their societies; with little internal unity or coherence, these new nations generally have fallen back at first on authoritarian centralism. When this has

---

[1] The classic statement of the process of "revolution" and its application is Crane Brinton, *The Anatomy of Revolution*, rev. ed. (New York, 1952). See also the formula as worked out in Alfred Meusel, "Revolution and Counter-Revolution," Edwin R. A. Seligman, ed., *Encyclopedia of the Social Sciences* (New York, 1934), XIII, 367–375. But the work that has been most influential in relating the American Revolution to the European revolutionary tradition is Robert R. Palmer, *The Age of the Democratic Revolution: A Political History of Europe and America, 1760–1800,* I (Princeton, 1959).

[2] An example of the relationship between colonial status and instability in colonial America is the Regulator movement in South Carolina. As Richard M. Brown points out in *The South Carolina Regulators* (Cambridge, Mass., 1963), the coastal inhabitants were willing to adjust themselves to the needs of the interior sections but were prevented from doing so by English policy decisions and intervention. The result was social and sectional cleavage and controversy. Another more general example, common to all colonies, is that of the currency problem. Any American attempts to solve the riddle of how to obtain and maintain an adequate currency were frustrated by English intervention, so that the problem remained as a continuous source of friction and instability.

proved incapable of solving the complex problems confronting the society, it has been replaced usually by some kind of collective leadership, often based on the only effective national organization in existence, the military.[3] It is at this point that many of the emergent nations of today find themselves.

Americans were more fortunate in their escape from colonialism. Thanks to the nature of the First British Empire, with its emphasis on commercial growth rather than on imperial efficiency, its loose organization, and the high degree of self-government allowed to the colonists, Americans had developed effective political units which commanded the allegiance of most inhabitants and served as adequate vehicles for the transition from colonial status to nationhood. Given a common English inheritance and a common struggle against British "tyranny," these states made the transition with a minimum of disagreement and dissension. In effect, by 1760 self-government in America, while still incomplete, had gone far. A tightening of English imperial authority after the last war with France brought about a reaction within the colonies toward complete self-determination, which was achieved finally through military success.

Yet, whatever the difference of the American experience from other colonial wars of liberation, certain elements were of necessity shared in common. Within any colonial society there exists an establishment, a group of men whose interests and situation tie them to the existing structure and whose orientation is towards the preservation of the colonial status. When the issue of independence or self-determination begins to be debated, these men are caught in powerful crosscurrents. As natives to the society, they identify to some degree with its problems. At the same time, as beneficiaries of their privileged position within the existing colonial structure, they are not enthusiastic for change. Such men fall back on arguments of moderation, particularly stressing the economic benefits of association with the dominant country and also emphasizing the immaturity of their own society. The gains associated with independence are outweighed for them by the prospects of social and political disorganization. So these men cast their lot with their colonial rulers. Such a man was Thomas Hutchinson. So, too, were many of his Tory associates.

And men like Hutchinson found much to disturb them within American society. Actually, not only was American colonial society subjected to the instability normally inherent in colonial status but there were certain peculiar circumstances which complicated matters further. The melting-pot aspects of American society, the diversity of ethnic, religious, and cultural backgrounds to be found within it, created problems of communication.[4] And, of equal importance, American colonial society was, after all, an artificial creation. Unlike most other historic colonial episodes, the American case was not a matter of an indigenous native society

---

[3] For example, such has been the course of Ghana during and after Nkrumah, of Algiers during and after Ben Bella, and of Indonesia during and after Sukarno.

[4] The best case study of the melting-pot aspect of colonial America is Dietmar Rothermund, *The Layman's Progress* (Philadelphia, 1961). Rothermund's reference to "indirection" as the key to political success is particularly suggestive. *Ibid.*, 93, 134, 140. Interestingly, Rothermund views the Great Awakening as at least partially an effort to use religion to create a bridge, to form a common ground, between the various groups; when religion failed to accomplish this, logically the next development was the use of "patriotism," a "lay religion" acceptable on rational grounds, to fill the same need. *Ibid.*, 59, 62, 134.

being expropriated and exploited by outsiders. In such instances, the pre-existing patterns of such native societies provide a degree of internal continuity and stability. But the English colonies in North America had at their disposal no such pre-existence. They were created specifically and artificially to perform certain functions in relation to the mother country. Most particularly, from the very beginning their economy was geared to production for distant markets over which they had no control and little influence.

At the same time, while there were sizeable non-English elements within the colonial population which created special problems, nevertheless the majority of the colonists were of the same national origin as their "rulers." It was not an instance of a conquered native population forced to bow fatalistically before the superior skills and power of an alien culture. Rather, it was a case in large part of Englishmen being governed and exploited by Englishmen. The result was a high degree of friction between governed and governors—an insistence by the colonists on their rights as Englishmen—that gave a special flavor and complexity to colonial politics.

Thoughtful colonials were well aware of and influenced by these problems. Thomas Hutchinson and John Adams—Tory and Whig—disagreed not so much on the question of the eventual independence of the American colonies as on the question of timing. Hutchinson's toryism sprang in part from his conviction that American society was too immature, too unstable, to stand alone. External force and authority, it seemed to him, would be required for many years to maintain internal order and stability in America. Realistically, he understood that eventually independence was probable: "It

is not likely that the American Colonies will remain part of the Dominions of Great Britain another Century." But, Hutchinson added, until then, "as we cannot otherwise subsist I am consulting the best interest of my country when I propose measures for maintaining this subjection [to England]." What particularly disturbed Hutchinson about the changes in English policy after 1760 was that they tended to increase the instability and disorder inherent within American society: "Sieur Montesquieu is right in supposing men good or bad according to the Climate where they live. In less than two centuries Englishmen by change of country are become more barbarous and fierce than the Savages who inhabited the country before they extirpated them, the Indians themselves."

John Adams viewed American development in a different way. Contrasting the New World with the Old, he found the former far superior. The settlement of America had produced men who "knew that government was a plain, simple, intelligible thing, founded in nature and reason, and quite comprehensible by common sense. They detested all the base services and servile dependencies of the feudal system . . . and they thought all such slavish subordinations were equally inconsistent with the constitution of human nature and that religious liberty with which Jesus had made them free." The problem was that this purity of mind and behavior was always threatened by contact with the corruption of the Old World. Specifically, subordination of Americans to a distant Parliament which knew little of their needs and desires was not only frustrating but dangerous to the American experiment: "A legislature that has so often discovered a want of information concerning us and our country; a legislature interested to lay burdens upon us; a legislature, two branches of which, I mean the lords and commons, neither love nor fear us! Every American of fortune and common sense, must look upon his property to be sunk downright one half of its value, the moment such an absolute subjection to parliament is established." Independence was a logical capstone to such reasoning, although it took Adams some time to take that final step.

The differences between Hutchinson and Adams suggest that the divisions in American society between conservatives and radicals on the question of separation from Great Britain were related in part to a disagreement over the means to achieve coherence or stability within American society. For one side, continued tutelage under English authority was a necessity until such a time as maturity was achieved. For the other, it seemed that the major roadblock to maturity, to internal harmony and unity, was that selfsame English authority. In effect, it was a disagreement on means, not ends. And disagreements similar to that between Hutchinson and Adams can be found within any society—whether in the eighteenth or twentieth century—which is in the process of tearing itself loose from its colonial ties.

It is possible, too, to suggest certain similarities between American intellectual development in these years and the experience of other colonial peoples. From his study of politics in eighteenth-century America, and particularly from his analysis of the pamphlet literature of the Revolutionary years, Bernard Bailyn has concluded that the "configuration of ideas and attitudes" which comprised the "Revolutionary ideology could be found intact—completely formed—as far back as the 1730's" and that these ideas had their origin in the "transmission from England to America of the literature of political opposition that furnished the substance of the ideology of the Revolution." Colonial societies are both fascinated and yet antagonized by the culture of the dominant exploiting nation. They tend to borrow much from their rulers. The English background of a majority of the American colonists in their case made such borrowing a natural and easy process, particularly for those who, for one reason or another, identified themselves with British rule.

However, in colonial societies even many of those who are anxious to assert, or preserve, their native interests or culture cannot resist that fascination exerted by the dominant "mother country." These "patriots" borrow, too, but they are likely to borrow from the dissenting tradition within the dominant culture, from the literature of "opposition," to utilize in their own defense the language and literature of those elements within the ruling society which are critical, or subversive, of the governing traditions. In this way the prestige of the "superior" society can be used against that society itself. On the evidence of Bailyn's research, it seems that the Americans followed just such a line of development, fitting the "opposition" tradition into the framework of their own evolving institutions and traditions—a process which was facilitated by the natural connections between the American religious dissenting traditions and the "opposition" traditions of eighteenth-century English society.

Again, once the movement for independence enters its final phase within a colonial society and becomes an open contest of strength, other divisions tend to become obscured. The most determined supporters of the colonial rule are silenced or forced to rely increasingly on the military strength of their rulers to maintain their position. On the other side, the advocates of independence submerge momentarily whatever differences they may have and present a common front. It is a time of common effort, of mutual support within the forces interested in achieving self-determination. At the same time the "patriot" groups develop special organizations capable of coercing those elements within society, often a majority of the population, which are inclined towards neutrality or moderation. Such were the Sons of Liberty in the American Revolution, and the evidence suggests that they performed their work effectively. Partly because of their efforts, and more generally because of the peculiar character of American colonial society and the nature of the imperial conflict, American society weathered the crisis with relative stability and harmony. As John Adams put it, "The zeal and ardor of the people during the revolutionary war, supplying the place of government, commanded a degree of order, sufficient at least for the temporary preservation of society."

With independence come altered circumstances for a former colonial society. Victorious patriots, confronted with the task of creating a permanent political structure, gradually begin to disagree among themselves as to how it can best be done. Since the only effective central direction came previously from the colonial rulers, the problem in each newly independent society is to fit the surviving local units into some coherent national structure. Here the forces of localism and centralism come into conflict. Those men or interests firmly entrenched in their positions at the local level see in increased centralism a threat to their existence and power. On the other hand, those men or interests of a more cosmopolitan nature, geared to extra-local activ-

ities and contacts, can see the benefits that would accrue to them through the introduction of the smoother flow of communications and transactions that effective centralization would bring.[5] The disagreement pits the particularism of the entrenched local interests and individuals against the nationalism of the cosmopolitan interests and individuals. In most contemporary emergent societies these latter groups are by far the weaker. Fortunately, in America the cosmopolitan groups were stronger and more effective, partly again because of the unusual origin and nature of American colonial society. From the beginning the English colonies had been geared to production for European markets; it was the reason for their existence. The result was the development of an economy which had [internal] geographical variations but a common external orientation. Merchants and large-scale producers of items for export dominated this society. In the period after independence was achieved, these men provided a firm base for the construction of an effective national political system. Their success came with the substitution of the Constitution of 1787 for the Articles of Confederation.

Historians following the Becker-Beard approach put a different interpretation on the period following the achievement of de facto independence. For them, it was the moment of the triumph of radical democratic elements within American society. The wording of the Declaration of Independence, the constitutions of the

---

[5] The distinguishing characteristics of "cosmopolitan" and "local" elites as developed by Robert K. Merton, *Social Theory and Social Structure* (Glencoe, 1957), chap. 10, "Patterns of Influence: Local and Cosmopolitan Influentials," are useful. See also, Alvin W. Gouldner, "Cosmopolitans and Locals: Towards an Analysis of Latent Social Roles," *Administrative Science Quarterly*, II (1957–58), 281–306, 444–480.

new state governments, and particularly the drawing up of the Articles of Confederation represent for these historians the influence of a form of "radicalism." Yet, as Elisha Douglass has noted, in the formation of the governments for the new states, rather puzzlingly the one political reorganization that was subjected to the most democratic method of discussion and adoption—that of Massachusetts—turned out to be not only the most conservative of all the state constitutions but more conservative, in fact, than the previous system. Somehow in Massachusetts, at least, an excess of democracy seems to have led to an enthronement of conservatism. And, indeed, the new constitutions or systems adopted in all the states were remarkable generally for their adherence to known and familiar forms and institutions.

Obviously, given the disruption of the traditional ties to England, the interruption of the natural economic dependence on English markets, the division of American society into opposing Whig and Tory camps, and the presence on American soil of enemy troops (which occupied at different moments the most important commercial centers), some confusion and dissension was inevitable within American society. What is remarkable is how little upheaval and disagreement there actually was. Had American society been ripe for a social upheaval, had it been comprised of oppressing and oppressed classes, no better opportunity could have been offered. The conservative nature of the American response suggests that something other than a radical re-structuring of society was what was debated or desired.

Again, some historians have interpreted the decentralized political system created under the Articles of Confederation as a "triumph" of radical democracy.

However, if instability, associated with colonial status and with the peculiar character of American colonial society, was a recurrent problem, and if inability to achieve positive control of their own political system was a major irritant, then the decentralization of the Articles was a logical development. In effect, if home rule was the issue and the cure, it was only natural that each local unit should seek as much autonomy within the national framework as possible. Seemingly, decentralization was the best method to bring coherence and stability, or maturity, to American society. Each local unit could look to its own needs, could arrange for the effective solution of its own special problems, could work to create that internal balance and harmony of conflicting interests that are the earmark of stability and maturity.

The problem with the Articles was not an excess of democracy. What brought about an effective opposition to them was their failure to achieve their purpose. The history of the states under the Articles, at least in the eyes of many contemporaries, suggested that decentralization, rather than being a source of stability, was a source of confusion and turmoil. James Madison explained the nature of the mistake in his Tenth Federalist. In spite of independence, under the system created by the Articles, wrote Madison, "complaints are everywhere heard from our most considerate and virtuous citizens . . . that our governments are too unstable." The problem, for Madison, was to control faction within society, and the most dangerous type of faction is that which includes a majority. Unfortunately, the "smaller the society, the fewer probably will be the distinct parties and interests composing it; the fewer the distinct parties and interests, the more frequently will a majority be found of the same party; and the smaller the number of individuals composing a majority, and the smaller the compass within which they are placed, the more easily will they concert and execute their plans of oppression." The solution is to enlarge the sphere, because if "you take in a greater variety of parties and interests," then "you make it less probable that a majority of the whole will have a common motive to invade the rights of other citizens . . . The influence of factious leaders may kindle a flame within their particular States, but will be unable to spread a general conflagration through the other States."

Nor was the opposition to the Constitution less concerned than Madison about order and stability within society. Again, disagreement was fundamentally over means, not ends. The anti-Federalists clung to the former ideas of local autonomy. They were, in fact, not more democratic than their opponents but more conservative. They were afraid of change: "If it were not for the stability and attachment which time and habit gives to forms of government, it would be in the power of the enlightened and aspiring few, if they should combine, at any time to destroy the best establishments, and even make the people the instruments of their own subjugation." The trouble was that the system created under the Articles was not yet sanctified by time: "The late revolution having effaced in a great measure all former habits, and the present institutions are so recent, that there exists not that great reluctance to innovation, so remarkable in old communities . . . it is the genius of the common law to resist innovation."[6] George Clinton agreed with

Madison on the dangers of faction: "The people, when wearied with their distresses, will in the moment of frenzy, be guilty of the most imprudent and desperate measures. . . . I know the people are too apt to vibrate from one extreme to another. The effects of this disposition are what I wish to guard against."[7] It was on the solution to the problem, not on the nature of the problem, that Clinton differed from Madison. For Clinton, the powerful central government created by the Constitution might too easily become a vehicle for popular tyranny. It was this same sentiment which led eventually to the adoption of the first ten amendments, the Bill of Rights, with their reservations of basic rights and powers to local units and individuals.

It would not do to carry the comparison between the American Revolution and other colonial wars of liberation, particularly those of the twentieth century, too far. But there is enough evidence to suggest certain basic similarities between the American experience and that of other emergent colonial peoples—enough evidence, at least, to suggest that the efforts of historians to impose on the American Revolution the classic pattern of the French and Russian revolutions have led to a distorted view of our national beginnings. A French Revolution is the product of unbearable tensions within a society. The purpose of such a revolution is to destroy society as it exists, or at least to destroy its most objectionable aspects, and to replace the old with something new. In contrast, a colonial "revolution" or war of liberation has as its

---

[6] Quoted in Cecelia M. Kenyon, *The Antifederalists* (Indianapolis, 1966), xcii. Miss Kenyon's introduction to this collection is an expansion of her provocative article, "Men of Little Faith: The Anti-

Federalists on the Nature of Representative Government," *Wm. and Mary Qtly.*, 3d Ser., XII (1955), 2–43. See also Stanley Elkins and Eric McKitrick, "The Founding Fathers: Young Men of the Revolution," *Pol. Sci. Qtly.*, LXXVI (1961), 200–216.

[7] Quoted in Kenyon, *Antifederalists*, xcii.

purpose the achievement of self-determination, the "completion" or fulfillment of an existing society, rather than its destruction. A French Revolution is first of all destructive; a colonial revolution, first of all constructive. In either case the process may not be completed. In the instance of the French Revolution, the re-constructed society may contain more of the old than the original revolutionaries desired. And in the case of the colonial revolution, the process of winning independence and the difficulties of organizing an effective national political structure may open the gates to change, may create a radicalism that carries the original society far from its former course; the result may be more destruction than was originally envisaged. Yet, the goals of these two revolutions are fundamentally different, and their different goals determine a different process of fulfillment. The unfolding of the revolutionary drama, the "stages" of revolution, will be quite different, if not opposite.

For John Adams, the American Revolution was an epochal event, a moment of wonder for the world to behold and consider. At times his rhetoric carried him beyond the confines of his innate caution, and he sounded like a typical revolutionary: "The progress of society will be accelerated by centuries by this revolution ... Light spreads from the dayspring in the west, and may it shine more and more until the perfect day."[8] But, as Edward Handler has noted, "The truth is that if Adams was a revolutionary, he was so in a sense very different than that produced by the other great modern revolutions."[9] Adams did indeed feel

that his revolution had a meaning for the world but it was not related to the violent re-structurings of society. Rather its message, for Adams, was that free men can decide voluntarily to limit their freedom in the interests of mutual association, that rational men can devise a system that can at once create order and preserve liberty. The American success was in contrast to the traditional authoritarian systems of the Old World: "Can authority be more amiable or respectable, when it descends from accidents or institutions established in remote antiquity, than when it springs fresh from the hearts and judgments of an honest and enlightened people?"

Most wars of liberation are not so orderly as that of the American Revolution. Most, at least in this century, have led to increasing radicalism and division within the liberated society. National unity has not been easily achieved. That the American emergence from colonialism had a different ending is significant. A firm basis for unity obviously existed within American society, which, naturally, suggests that the reverse, too, was true—that such tensions and divisions as did exist within American society were relatively minor and harmless. It is no wonder that historians determined to find an internal social or political revolution of the French variety within the American Revolution have encountered such difficulties. Nor is it a wonder that the Revolution has become so beclouded with historiographical debates and arguments. The problem has been in our approach. We have been studying, it would seem, the wrong revolution.

---

[8] Quoted in Edward Handler, *America and Europe in the Political Thought of John Adams* (Cambridge, Mass., 1964), 102.

[9] *Ibid.,* 101. Elsewhere Handler comments that "Adams' experience had nothing in common with the concept of revolution as a total renovation of

existing institutions previously condemned as denials and perversions of the natural order" and that "nothing affords more certain indication that the Americans underwent a special kind of revolution than the peculiar breed of revolutionary typified by Adams who carried it through." *Ibid.,* 106–107.

RICHARD B. MORRIS (b. 1904) who taught at Columbia University is recognized as one of the outstanding scholars of American Colonial history. In this selection Morris finds that the American Revolution served as a model for many of the rising new nations that came into being in the 1950s and 1960s. What are some of the analogies he sees between the American Revolution and the modern anticolonial movements? What other analogies does he see in terms of social changes and reforms between the American Revolution and present-day revolutionary movements?*

Richard B. Morris

The Revolution and the Third World

In ritual or in substance, all the emerging nations of our time have paid obeisance to the American Revolution. As the first successful decolonization movement of the modern world, it serves as an object lesson even for emerging nations who have obtained their independence not through overt rebellion, as did the Americans, but through that piecemeal liquidation of empires by which the Great Powers have in most cases abdicated colonial rule since the Second World War.

If the American Revolution had done nothing more than to pioneer that historic movement of peoples from colonialism to national independence, it would still have enormous relevance for the emerging nations. The fact is, however, that the Revolution provided more than a set of guidelines for revolutionary tactics and strategy; it led to a total transformation of American society, and thus it has special pertinence in an age of revolutionary social change.

At first glance it might seem incredible that there should be any affinity in spirit between a superpower like the United States and the young nations rising phoenix-like from the ashes of colonialism, handicapped by poverty, illiteracy, overpopulation, and landlordism. Many striking analogies may be demonstrated, however. At Independence the United States was both young and relatively weak. The Chinese called the youthful

*By permission of Richard B. Morris, *The Emerging Nations and the American Revolution* (Harper & Row, 1970), pp. 1–12 and 32–35.

United States "The New People," while Europe's tradition-bound statesmen considered America not only young, but crude, undeveloped, and even primitive. Few if any of Europe's statesmen had faith in the lasting powers of a republic which extended its sway over so vast a territory as did the Thirteen States. Instead, they confidently expected that the centrifugal forces of sectionalism would soon rip it asunder. Even if America managed to survive as a political entity, Englishmen assumed that economic imperatives would once again attach the erstwhile insurgents to the mother country, and that the Thirteen States would resume a subordinate and dependent commercial role in the temporarily aborted relationship of Metropolis and Colony.

How like the posture assumed today by the Great Powers toward the young nations that have just emerged or are in the process of emerging from colonialism. Because so many Americans are not heedful of their revolutionary past it may come as a shock to many of them to have so powerful and affluent a nation as their own compared with Nigeria or Kenya, with Burma or Indonesia. Striking dissimilarities there are, to be sure, and they seem too obvious to need spelling out, but it is the appropriateness of the analogy in certain areas which should command our attention.

All of the devices to which the emerging nations have resorted in achieving independence for themselves can be discovered in that first anticolonial revolution waged by Thirteen Colonies against a powerful world empire. In that revolutionary process the Americans, like latter-day revolutionaries, utilized the weapons of noncooperation, civil disorder, provisional congresses, and finally war itself, even before issuing their declaration of independence. The Patriot or Revolutionary forces drew unity and inspiration from a charismatic leadership and fought a long and bitter war to a successful conclusion against seemingly hopeless odds.

First of all, though, the American Revolution determined the ritual observed by most later revolutions. Virtually all of the nations recently emerging from colonial status have felt obliged to justify their revolutions by declarations couched in language very similar to that utilized by the Americans in 1776. Even the Democratic Republic of Vietnam in its proclamation of September 2, 1945, made an open and intended levy on Jefferson's Great Declaration.

Secondly, in the use of sustained guerrilla operations over a period of years the American Revolution bears comparison with recent so-called "wars of national liberation." Except for climactic battles like Saratoga and Yorktown, the Patriot operation depended on maintaining a fighting force in being through mobility, withdrawal, and surprise counterattack. Operating with lightning speed from inaccessible bases which they changed frequently, Marion, Pickens, and Sumter, leaders of irregular forces, struck blows in rapid succession at isolated British and Tory camps, garrisons, and convoys in the lower South. Theirs indeed was a tactic of terror, which William Cullen Bryant has captured in his "Song of Marion's Men." The same kind of tactic has been exploited by such modern revolutionaries as Mao Tse-tung and the late Che Guevara.

If so many of the emerging nations have capitalized on peasant unrest, it should be remembered that despite the elitist character of its leadership, the American Revolution was a mass movement that drew support from farmers and workers, and that originated in mass meetings and demonstrations, escalating to town riots, mobbism, tarring and feathering, and vigilantism. Even before mobbism came to focus upon antiministerial grievances, mobs during the early 1760's had erupted on the frontiers of Pennsylvania and the Carolinas, exploiting violence and intimidation to redress a variety of grievances when the colonial governments proved weak and unresponsive. By the year 1765, however, demonstrations had as their objective the redress of imperial grievances. The nucleus of pre-Revolutionary radical mob action was, originally, the Sons of Liberty—groups making their appearance in New York and New England, but soon springing up in virtually every colonial town. In New York, a center of such agitation, the leadership of such groups was quickly assumed by affluent merchants like Isaac Sears, John Lamb, and Alexander McDougall. Significantly, all three were shipowners as well as traders and thus had close relations with the seamen, who nursed long-standing grievances against the British government. Similarly connected were shippers like the Browns of Providence and John Hancock of Boston.

The grievances of the maritime workers sprang principally from the inequitable and irresponsible impressment practices of the Royal Navy. Indeed, of all working-class groups, the seamen felt perhaps the most oppressed and exploited. Rootless, they had the least stake in the status quo. Accustomed to settling matters by brawn rather than brain, they proved the hard core of the "muscular radicals" so cleverly manipulated by affluent merchants and shrewd lawyers.

Joining the seamen in dissent were the

"mechanics," a catchall term covering master employers along with their journeymen wage workers, both sharing a common economic resentment against the new tax measures of the British government and a common desire to have a larger voice in domestic politics. The mass demonstrations conducted by these groups carried either a symbolic purport, as with the raising of the liberty pole, or a design to implant terror in the breasts of those charged with the enforcement of the law. They had precise targets on which to mete out retribution. In Boston they burned the home of the collector of customs and sacked the residence of Lieutenant Governor Hutchinson, a symbol of royal authority. In Albany they pulled down the house of the stamp collector, and in New York City a crowd knocked down the residence of a British officer, who had provocatively announced that he would "cram the stamps down" the people's "throats with the end of my sword." Without romanticizing these mass demonstrations, it seems fair to assert that in their beginnings they were subject to purposeful discipline, and, with some exceptions, not given to looting or committing arson indiscriminately. When the "Mohawk braves" hurled the 342 chests of tea into Boston Harbor in the action that triggered the Revolution, they made sure that none of their company stole any of the tea for himself. Generally speaking, the leadership and discipline of the rioting mobs were so effective that they could be utilized as vigilante groups to enforce the nonimportation agreements which the town merchants adopted.

In short, the demonstrations cannot be dismissed as meaningless acts of a mischief-bent riffraff, but must be viewed as purposeful protest designed to articulate a political position or to intimidate the authorities responsible for the enforcement of detested parliamentary laws. And nobody can deny that they achieved their aim. Like the activists of our own day, the radical leaders revealed themselves to be extremely touchy about preserving undiminished their own civil liberties while remaining disgracefully indifferent to the civil rights of their opponents. There is perhaps no better example than the raid that "King" Sears staged on the newspaper office of his archenemy, the Royalist and later secret turncoat Rivington, whose printing press Sears and his cohorts seized. It should be noted that Patriots of sounder judgment like Alexander Hamilton and John Jay made no secret of their disavowal of Sears' rash action. What concerned these young New York Patriots was that, when the "multitude" acted with unrestrained passion to punish a detestable character, they might be naturally led to "a contempt and disregard of all authority." John Jay was equally concerned that the provisional revolutionary machinery set up by the state of New York would exert its powers with vigor to suppress "licentiousness," and he remarked that "the tenderness shown to some wild people on account of their supposed attachment to the cause" not only was of disservice to that cause but diminished the dignity and authority of provisional governments.

In the main the elite who directed the Revolution kept the checkrein on mob violence. Even the attack of a Philadelphia mob in the fall of 1779 against the residence of the Patriot lawyer James Wilson, in whose house a number of profiteering merchants and speculators had taken refuge, could be put down to a purposeful, if dangerously unruly, effort to discipline businessmen who refused to abide by the schedule of prices set by a price-fixing committee acting under the authorization of a mass meeting in the Statehouse yard. If anything, this incident highlights the tendency of popularly chosen conventions, associations, and committees to usurp or encroach upon the governmental functions of constituted bodies. This phenomenon had its origins in the pre-Revolutionary agitation, burgeoned notably in the price- and wage-fixing conventions of Revolutionary years, and was continually utilized in the post-Revolutionary years as an institution for channeling a wide variety of socioeconomic and legal grievances, which may be said to have climaxed with Shays' Rebellion. What diverted the American Revolution from the path of tumult and even anarchy was the evolution of governmental mechanisms to express the will of the people.

A recent scholar has referred to the "crisis of legitimacy" that confronts all post-revolutionary societies, the need to create new bonds of loyalty to replace the old. The Americans resolved that crisis with great facility. They insisted upon the legality of their revolution, and fought for the rights of Englishmen as they believed them to be guaranteed by the British Constitution, and for the rights of man as they understood them to be guaranteed by Nature and Nature's God. Step by step they trimmed down Parliament's authority over the colonies until the King was the sole remaining tie. This, too, they deftly sundered. The Declaration cites "a long train of abuses" suffered by the colonies, and, taking a leaf from Tom Paine's *Common Sense*, presents the "history of the present King of Great Britain" as a "history of repeated injuries and usurpation." Denouncing as "unfit to be the ruler of a free people," "a prince whose character is thus marked by every act which may define a tyrant," the Great Declaration goes on to declare "these United Colonies" to be "free and independent states" and then to absolve them from "all political connection" with Great Britain. Thus the "crisis of legitimacy" was ingeniously resolved.

In the conduct of its diplomacy the American Revolutionaries were perhaps no more scrupulous than the leaders of emerging nations today. To win its fight for freedom America appealed to England's traditional enemies and counted on foreign aid to sustain the cause. Thus the American Revolution inevitably became part of a burgeoning world war, fought not only at Trenton, Saratoga, and Cowpens, but waged within the sight of the cliffs of Dover, at Gibraltar, off the Cape of Good Hope, in Caribbean waters, and along India's Coromandel Coast. In this larger involvement the Americans were reluctant participants. Their courtship in Europe had as its primary purpose military aid in the form of supplies and money, and, secondly, commercial alliances. They were disinclined to get involved in balance-of-power politics, and resisted being dragged into wars which they felt were no concern of theirs. In short, they were neutralists or proto-isolationists like so many leaders of the new states of today who quite cynically exploit the Cold War to their own advantage but want no part in a conflict between the rival Great Powers. That capacity for ingratitude which recent nations have manifested on so many occasions may well be matched by President Washington's Proclamation of Neutrality, wherein he gave classic formulation to the Great Rule of Nonentanglement in words that might have been voiced by a Nehru of India or a U

Nu of Burma. America then waged a quasi-war against France to bring to an end an uneasy military alliance which no longer served America's interest.

Not only in its disposition toward nonalignment was Revolutionary America akin to the emerging nations of Asia and Africa today, but also in its adherence to a one-party system. Since most Americans regard a multi-party system as a hallmark of a democratic state, they might profit by the reminder that, despite factionalism, there was only one party in America for some fifteen or sixteen years at the least, and that was the party of the Revolution. Antifederalism could hardly be elevated to the level of a nationally organized and structured party. The opposition provided by the Tory party the virtuous Revolutionaries proceeded to smash, hunting down or forcing its active members into exile. Those Loyalists who were sufficiently chameleon-like to escape patriotic censorship stayed and made their peace with the party of the Revolution. In time they became good Federalists. In short, there were factions but no parties in America. Before the country could afford the luxury of party divisions a national consensus had to be built. Thus, the Constitution takes no account of parties, and the first President denounced the substituting "for the delegated will of the nation the will of a party." Out of the power struggle between Jefferson and Hamilton, exacerbated by the divisions in America touched off by the French Revolution, a two-party system did emerge. But it was still necessary in 1804 to adopt the Twelfth Amendment to the Constitution providing for the separate designation on the ballot of a President and a Vice President to prevent the embarrassment of having a Vice President elected from a party opposed to the

President-elect as had occurred in the 1790's.

If nationalism is the yeast which produces the revolutionary ferment of emerging nations, the analogy from the world of the present to young America is by no means strained. The American nation was born of revolution, and from its infancy it possessed characteristics which set it apart from the nations of the Old World. Goethe caught that essential difference in his *Poems of Wisdom* when he wrote:

America, you fare much better
Than this old continent of ours
No basalt rocks your land enfetters
No ruined towers . . .

In its emergence America was destined to fix the character of much of modern nationalism. Leaders like Washington and John Jay were concerned about establishing a national character. To start, the common tongue, the English language, had to be Americanized— Noah Webster saw to that. Even before Webster the process was going forward. "You speak American well," the French traveler Chastellux reported to be a common remark as early as 1782. Education had to be made more available and pragmatic, the divisive force of religious intolerance mitigated, and the penal code modernized to fit a more humane society. The statesman John Jay did more than coin a phrase when he observed in 1797, "I wish to see our people more Americanized, if I may use that expression; until we feel and act as an independent nation, we shall always suffer from foreign intrigue."

Accordingly, when the Irish Free State compels its children to study Gaelic, when Israel adopts Hebrew as its official language, when the Vietnamese require all foreign signs removed and replaced by those in the Vietnamese language,

and when fanatical Indian patriots riot to make Hindi, not English, the language of instruction, we must bear in mind that they are taking the same basic steps in building national character that Americans themselves assumed without a venerated national tradition, with but few national myths, and with heroes chosen from an immediate past.

There is a dynamic of revolution which pervades all societies that have undergone a revolutionary experience, not least the American. If China has been in fierce competition with the Soviet Union in exporting its brand of Marxist-Leninism to the underdeveloped nations, and if Fidel Castro wants Latin America to bear the stamp of Fidelismo, the sense of revolutionary mission has not been confined to the Marxist-Leninist nations of the twentieth century. That sense of mission inspired the French Revolutionary leaders, and perhaps in a perverted sense the values and institutions of their revolution were transplanted to adjacent lands by a bold and imaginative Corsican adventurer. But even earlier that sense of revolutionary mission gripped America's Founding Fathers. In a closing *Crisis* letter Tom Paine voiced it with naive candor. "To see it in our power to make a world happy," he observed, "to teach mankind the art of being so—to exhibit on the theatre of the universe a character hitherto unknown, and to have, as it were, a new creation intrusted to our hands, are honors that command reflection and can neither be too highly estimated nor too gratefully received."

From its inception the American Revolution was pitched on a moral and even evangelical plane. The didactic character of the American Revolution has for better or worse permanently stamped itself upon American diplomacy. Stripped of its sense of mission the American

Revolution would have lost much of its world significance, while America's intervention in world affairs in the twentieth century would have assumed the character of a naked power grab. That America now ventures to shoulder global responsibilities of awesome dimension is attributable in no small part to the rearing of the American people during the infancy of the Republic. . . .

Although America stands as the classic example of a nation which enjoyed a phenomenal degree of economic growth since its establishment, it is seldom realized how great a spur to development the casting off of the shackles of colonialism proved. On balance, the entire mercantilist program of external control of trade embraced under the rubric of Parliament's Navigation Laws was disadvantageous to the economy of the mainland. Yet some historians play down the trade laws as an issue between colonies and mother country and would minimize the hardships imposed upon the colonial economy by the trade laws. If the colonists complained comparatively little about the Navigation Laws before 1763, it may well have been because they were so loosely administered. Powerful and articulate segments of the colonial population considered the strict enforcement of the acts after 1763, along with the revenue measures, as a serious grievance.

The anticolonial stance of the Americans represented a protest against the permanent debtor status assigned the colonies in the imperial economic scheme. In that respect it is not unlike the anticolonialism of emerging nations seeking to free themselves from economic dependency upon one or another of the Great Powers. What Jefferson felicitously called "the pursuit of happiness" was a concept embracing a variety of freedoms, including social mobility, freedom of occupational choice, freedom from monopolistic restraints, security, and a more abundant life, including a fair sharing of the nation's resources.

That America has achieved these goals for most of its citizens cannot be denied, nor can one controvert the fact that in some measure these achievements stem from the liberative effect of the American Revolution on the economy. The federal principle in the new Constitution gave America an instant common market, still unmatched in the world to date. Emulated by the Common Market nations of Europe, it serves as an example to Latin America and to the new states of East Africa now engaged in setting up their own common market. The sound fiscal policies inaugurated by Alexander Hamilton made abundant credit available to business, while the government's land programs encouraged the farmer just as the innovative and inventive climate of America spurred the manufacturer.

Whether one would date the take-off into a self-sustained economic growth with the adoption of the Constitution, or with the 1840's, or perhaps with even a later period, America did manage to win economic as well as political independence. Without the former the latter would have proven a hollow gain indeed. That sustained rate of growth and that degree of affluence which America did achieve still makes the United States the envy of the older nations whose economies it has surpassed. And if it may be said that the revolutions which have swept the underdeveloped world are a response to rising expectations, then the United States through the image of affluence it has projected is as much responsible for these insurgent movements as are dread subversives reared on the gospels of Marx, Lenin, and Mao.

To sum up the durable contribution of the American Revolution and its relevance to today's revolutionary world, it should be acknowledged at the start that the American War for Independence was a revolution of enormous consequences for the world. On the occasion of Great Britain's recognition of American independence, Edmund Burke declared:

A great revolution has happened—a revolution made, not by chopping and changing of power in any of the existing states, but by the appearance of a *new state*, of a *new species*, in a *new part of the globe*. It has made as great a change in all relations, and balances, and gravitations of power, as the appearance of a new planet would in the system of the solar world.

The Founding Fathers shared Burke's opinion of the uniqueness of their revolution which, to them, culminated in the adoption of the Constitution. In the Fourteenth *Federalist* James Madison paid tribute to the drafters of the Constitution who "accomplished a revolution which has no parallel in the annals of human society. They reared the fabrics

of government which have no model on the face of the globe."

As the first great revolution of modern times, the American Revolution was both a war of decolonization and a movement of broad social change and reform. Waged to establish an independent nation, sovereign and equal with all the nations of the earth, it constituted at the same time a movement to support the rights of man, of all men, and women too. And, in that wider sense, the American Revolution, with its egalitarian overtones, has enormous relevance to the revolutions of the emerging nations of later times and, not least of all, to our own time.

General Washington was indulging in no mere rhetorical effusion when, in his notable Circular to the States issued from his headquarters at Newburgh on June 8, 1783, he observed that, "according to the system of policy the States shall adopt at this moment, they will stand or fall, and by their confirmation or lapse, it is yet to be decided, whether the Revolution must ultimately be considered as a blessing or a curse; a blessing or a curse, not to the present age alone, for with our fate will the destiny of unborn millions be involved."

SUNG BOK KIM (b. 1932), an American Colonial historian, teaches at S.U.N.Y.-Albany and is best known for his book, *Landlord and Tenant in Colonial New York*. In this essay, Kim compares the French and American revolutions and concludes that the former had a greater impact on world history. In what ways did the emphasis on private property and traditional civil liberties prevent the American Revolution from having a greater impact on modern revolutionary movements?*

Sung Bok Kim

The Revolution and the Modern World

On November 25, 1783, when the British troops under Sir Guy Carleton completed their withdrawal from New York City, Governor George Clinton of New York gave a public dinner at Fraunce's Tavern at which George Washington and his generals were present. After dinner, they raised thirteen toasts, three of which touched on the cause of liberty in the world: "the Vindicators of the Rights of Mankind in every Quarter of the Globe," "May America be an Asylum to the Persecuted of the Earth," and "May the Remembrance of This be a Lesson to Princes (of the World)." The international character of the Revolution which the toasts invoked was underscored by other Revolutionary Americans

as well. Thomas Paine declared in *Common Sense*, that "the cause of America is in a great measure the cause of all mankind" and that "we . . . have it in our power to begin the world over again." Thomas Jefferson struck much the same note: "We feel that we are acting under obligations not confined to the limits of our own society. It is impossible not to be sensible that we are acting for all mankind." John Adams opined that the Revolution was fought "for future millions, and millions of millions," and hoped that it would "spread liberty and Enlightenment everywhere in the world." Underlying these declarations were the profound beliefs that the entire world was "overrun with oppression"

---

*From Sung Bok Kim, "The American Revolution and the Modern World," in *Legacies of the American Revolution*, Larry Gerlach, *et al.*, eds. (Logan, Utah, 1978), pp. 221–238.

and that "freedom hath been hunted round the globe." Nurtured on ideas of the Enlightenment that presupposed the unity of mankind in reason, impulses, and natural laws, the Revolutionary Americans were optimistic that oppressed people abroad would be inspired by their examples and would eventually rise up against repressive regimes. This optimism was not mere wishful thinking, but had been consecrated by their own experience in the last decade of the colonial period. The colonists regarded their campaign against British imperial policies as an episode in a world-wide struggle then under way—in Ireland, Scotland, Spain, France, Turkey, Poland, Corsica, England, and Russia—between liberty and tyranny. It was this sense of camaraderie with international freedom fighters and "absorption in affairs outside their continent" which "played a central role in the colonists' own conversion to active revolution." The American Revolution was a chapter of what Robert R. Palmer has called a "great" Atlantic revolution.

For the Revolutionary generation, the independence of America from Britain would have been "a matter but of little importance, had it not been accompanied by a revolution in the principles and practices of governments"; the struggle for liberation should be merely a precondition for building a new foundation of freedom. The outbreak of the War for Independence was followed rapidly by the making of new constitutions in the states based on republican principles. Republicanism as a theory was nothing new; it was as old as the Roman Republic. What was new and revolutionary is that the Americans took theoretical republican ideas out of the ivory tower and salon and turned them into an effective revolutionary instru-

ment and a workable governmental institution. Speaking of the ideas contained in the Declaration of Independence, Thomas Jefferson refused to make even a modest claim to originality: [I did not] "try to find out new principles, or new arguments, never thought of . . . , but to place before mankind the common sense of the subject." John Adams, the author of the Massachusetts Constitution of 1780, said of the document: "It is Locke, Sidney, Rousseau, and de Mably reduced to practice." On another occasion, when talking about the American system of government, he said "the principles of Aristotle and Plato, of Livy and Cicero, and Sidney, Harrington and Locke; the principles of nature and eternal reason; [are] the principles on which the whole government over us now stands."

Nevertheless, it would be terribly wrong to imagine that the Founding Fathers merely borrowed ideas from others. There were a number of areas in which the Founders made distinct contributions to political theory and procedure. The most important was the invention of the "constitutional convention" as the means of making, unmaking, and remaking a written constitution, a method which had never before been tried by any other nation. The resultant constitution, embodying the sovereignty of the people, created and defined the powers of government and spelled out the "inalienable" rights of the people. The governments emerging from the constitutional conventions were hamstrung with checks, balances, restrictions, and prohibitions, while the rights and liberty of the people were jealously guarded. Having escaped from "a long train of abuses and usurpations" by the British government and impressed with the prevalence of European autocracy, the Americans were determined to make their government limited and moderate. They feared power regardless of where it was located and who wielded it because they understood the inevitable tendency of its possessor to abuse it.

The most dramatic illustration of this fear of power was the incorporation into the new state constitutions of various bills of rights—giving such things as religious toleration, freedom of press and assembly, freedom of person under the protection of *habeas corpus*, and trial by juries, and subordination of the military to the civilian authority—with the view to placing permanent restraints on the government of their own creation. The Revolutionaries seem to have agreed with James Lovell, a Massachusetts orator, that free people were not those who merely had escaped from oppression "but those who have a constitutional check upon the power to oppress." The process of adopting bills of rights began, it will be remembered, at the very time the United States was engaged in a war with mighty Britain and the state governments needed power and vigor to cope with both internal and external enemies. The significance of this unremitting concern for personal freedom takes on special meaning given the suspension of basic civil rights in such subsequent national emergencies as the Civil War and the First and Second World Wars. It was this institutionalization of liberty during the Revolution that probably prompted Lord Acton to declare: "In the strictest sense the history of liberty dated from 1776 'for never till then had men sought liberty knowing what they sought.' "

At the very inception of the nation, then, Americans were committed to a government whose supreme goal was to secure the fundamental liberties of the people—a truly revolutionary doctrine.

They had no intention of replacing a monarchical tyranny with an elective tyranny whether exercised by a majority or a minority. Nowhere was this attitude revealed better than in the movement to create a new federal system of government. The critical problems during the Confederation period were numerous, but the seeming majoritarian licentiousness and accompanying social and economic disorder in various states which led to the impairment of minority rights particularly distressed the Founding Fathers. Seasoned in what John Adams called "the divine science of politics—the art of discovering the forms and combinations of power in republics," the Founders distributed the power among the different branches of the government so that neither the majoritarian interest nor the minority interest would predominate. This arrangement may seem undemocratic to the modern citizen long accustomed to a majoritarian democracy. But the Founders thought otherwise. James Madison, a chief architect of the Constitution, was convinced that "if *all* power be suffered to slide" into either party "liberty will be subverted" and that "it is of great importance in a republic not only to guard the society against the oppression of its rulers; but to guard one part of the society against the injustice of other parts."

Indeed, the uniqueness of the American brand of federalism lies in the fact that it not only allowed for the rise and interplay of the divergent political, social, and economic forces or factions that were inevitable in such a heterogeneous society as America, but also made such diversity the essential guarantor of equilibrium and liberty for all members of the society. In the United States federalism was not the tool of a class or estate or order as it had been for the corporate localities dominated by oligarchic or privileged families in Switzerland and Holland, but a representative process in which every class, faction, and local jurisdiction was supposed to have a meaningful voice. For this democratic imperative, federalism did not presuppose the destruction of the states as intermediate political units, although it did subordinate and bypass them to derive its power directly from the people. That Americans did not establish a powerful unitary or national form of government but instead created a federal form encumbered by an intricate network of checks and balances and limited by a bill of rights was another measure of the people's fear of power and preoccupation with civil liberty.

Fear is inherently a negative force. It makes a man timid, immobile, blind, desperate, mad, and even worse, brutally destructive—the traits which Aristotle spelled out in detail twenty-five centuries ago. Harold Laski, a distinguished English political scientist and a laborite, noted that "a government built upon fear is driven into tyranny." The American Revolutionary experience, however, provides a convincing rebuff to this time-honored pattern of human behavior. Though gripped with fear of the British oppression, the colonists did not lash out against their internal subversives (Tories) with blind fury. Nor did they wholly destroy the inherited institutions: the die-hard republicans in Connecticut and Rhode Island retained their colonial charters as state constitutions well into the nineteenth century. When Americans became dissatisfied with the existing state-dominated system of the Confederation, they built another system on top of it rather than on its extinction. The aggrieved states rightists, known as Antifederalists, though fearful

of the extension of the central power, willingly submitted to the new national political settlement. In the hands of the Revolutionary generation, the fear of power, cushioned by "the wisdom of their greatest men," was made into an innovative force of liberty with the result that the transformation from British rule to independence, from the state constitutions to the federal system, in Alexis de Tocqueville's words, "proceeded hand in hand with a love of order and legality."

The Founding Fathers were hopeful that the political achievements of the Revolution—namely, the doctrine of national independence, the constitutional convention, the limited constitutional government, republican federalism, and the bills of rights—would awaken every nation in the world and that a spirit and blessings of liberty would gain ground everywhere. They were certain that their government was the finest, "the world's best hope," and, being derived from and supported by the people, was the "strongest Government on earth." These were the achievements, hopes, and convictions which our forefathers bequeathed to us all.

What kind of reception did modern history accord to the legacies of the American Revolution? Let us for a moment look around the globe. To me, most of its living space looks like a graveyard for liberty. In the Western Hemisphere authoritarian regimes, whether military or civilian, are in the majority. The same is true in Africa, Asia, Eastern and Central Europe, and Asia Minor. Some countries, like the Philippines, may have constitutions patterned after the American or British model, but they are no more than paper declarations without any bearing on actual practice. Some leaders, like Indira Gandhi of India, invoke the "inspiring words" of the Founding Fathers, but do so only for public relations on ceremonious occasions or during press conferences. Countries like monarchical Spain may call themselves "free nations," but the language is meaningful only in relation to the Communist nations. In these countries the government, by means of the most advanced techniques of thought and social control, systematically suppress dissenters. It is only in a handful of countries on both sides of the North Atlantic, in Japan, and in Australia and New Zealand that freedom maintains its lonely existence. Even there, the future of democracy seems uncertain.

To be sure, some leaders of the emerging nations seem to have been inspired by the principles of national self-determination embodied in the Declaration of Independence. For instance, Ho Chi Minh, who had been trained primarily in Marxism-Leninism, "knew more" about the historic document than a young American officer operating in Indochina in 1945, and was "deadly serious about it." In August of that year, when the Vietminh seized power, Ho read to 500,000 people assembled in Hanoi the Declaration of Independence of the Democratic Republic. Its opening words were: "All men are created equal. They are endowed by their Creator with certain inalienable Rights . . ." These words are, of course, Jefferson's. Yet, a national aspiration for independence was the only thing he had in common with the American Revolution. In the Third World, the securing of independence has not developed simultaneously with the equally arduous—and probably more difficult—task of securing and practicing constitutional guarantees of civil liberties as it had in America's revolutionary experience. It may be, as will be

argued later, that other priorities existed there. From the contemporary perspective, we can therefore state that the legacies of the American Revolution are rejected by most people and linger on in only a few countries.

The picture, however, changes when we turn our attention to the dawn of modern history. The American Revolutionaries' successful efforts to put politics on an entirely different plateau and their bold republican language enthralled the discontented in the Old Society, heightened their hope for a new political order, and fortified their faith in the infinite progress of humanity. Richard Price, a nonconformist minister in England, wrote in 1776 that he would turn to the United States "as now the hope and likely soon to become the refuge of mankind" and that Americans were "inspired by the noblest of all passions, the passions for being free." A few years later Price observed that the American example already had liberated one country (by which in 1785 he probably meant Holland or Ireland) and would soon liberate others. Henry Grattan, a leading Irish Parliamentary reformer, urged his countrymen that "before you decide on the practicability of being slaves forever, look to America." One observer of the Irish situation noted in 1776 that "all Ireland is America mad" and three years later that "It is now too publicly known to be disguised any longer, that Ireland has much the air of Americanizing." Aleksandr Nikolaevich Radischev, a Russian reformer, addressing the American people sometime during the years 1781–1783, wrote "Thou were and art invincible: Thy leader, Washington, is Liberty" and "your example has set a goal for us—we all wish for the same. I have no part in your glory, but since the soul is subject to no one, allow at least my ashes to rest in your soil!" In 1777, Benjamin Franklin, United States emissary in France, wrote home that "all Europe is on our side of the question, as far as Applause and good Wish can carry them. Those who live under arbitrary Power do nevertheless approve of Liberty, and wish for it; they almost despair of recovering it in Europe; they read the Transactions of our separate Colony Constitutions with Rapture. . . . Hence 'tis a common observation here, that our Cause is the cause of all Mankind, and that we are fighting for their Liberty in defending our own." Many European writers voiced their idealization of America so frequently that the repetition of their examples would be tedious.

If the Irish became "America mad," a host of French philosophers became American enthusiasts. The Marquis de Condorcet, in his prize-winning essay *The Influence of the American Revolution in Europe*, asserted: "it is not enough that the rights of man be written in the books of philosophers and inscribed in the hearts of virtuous men; the weak and ignorant must be able to read them in the example of a great people. America has given us this example." On another occasion, he said that Thomas Jefferson was "entitled to the eternal gratitude of mankind" for his authorship of the Virginia Bill of Rights. Curiosity, excitement, and debate about the American constitutional ideas were more intense in France than anywhere else. The American state constitutions were published there not once but on at least five different occasions between 1776 and 1786. Thomas Paine's *Common Sense* was quickly translated into French. This is understandable, since France was an ally of the United States and, more important, was the most vibrant center

of the Enlightenment despite having the most absolute of the ancient regimes. The frequency of publications of American books and the avid reading of them, as reported by Franklin, may tell us about the popularity of the writings but not necessarily reveal their influence on French opinion.

However, the initial course of the French Revolution is a concrete manifestation of that influence. When the Estates-General was about to be convened, Brissot, a future Girondist leader who had just returned from an American tour, published *A Plan of Conduct* for the deputies. In this tract, he called for a special constitutional convention for the purpose of drawing up a constitution for France, denying the Estates-General the power to do so on the grounds that the body did not represent the people. He admitted that "we owe [the idea of a constitutional convention] to the Free Americans . . . and this device . . . of the Free Americans can perhaps be very easily adapted to the circumstances in which France now finds itself." Another example of the American influence is the Marquis de Lafayette, who led the revolt of the Estates-General against the aristocracy and the king. Lafayette first participated in the American war not from a love of liberty but from a venturesome spirit and desire to weaken England. Then, during his service in the Revolution as a Continental army officer and through his close association with George Washington, he developed an incurable affection for the "American principles." The very day he was elected vice-president of the National Assembly of France (July 11, 1789), he proposed to the adoption of a declaration of the rights of man which he hoped would imitate the American model. The committee charged with drafting the declaration obliged his wishes. The committee explained before the Assembly the philosophical genesis of the draft declaration:

This noble idea, conceived in another hemisphere, should by preference, be transplanted among us at once. We have cooperated in the events which have established liberty in North America; she shows us on what principles we should base the conservation of our own; and the New World into which hitherto we have borne only a sword, teaches us today to guard ourselves from the dangers of carrying it to our own hurt.

It should also be noted that during the hectic summer and fall of 1789 the so-called "American party" under the leadership of Lafayette held their meetings at Thomas Jefferson's house in Paris to discuss a new constitution for France and consulted the American minister about the various forms of a parliamentary system. Finally, Condorcet's advocacy of unicameralism for the French legislature was directly "inspired" by the Constitution of Pennsylvania of 1776.

With these observations I am not suggesting that the American Revolution and its revolutionary legacies led directly to the French Revolution, as one French historian argued sometime ago. Such an argument is as absurd as saying that the old ideas of the Enlightenment and the English opposition to them caused the American Revolution. The basic and immediate causes of the French Revolution were French in origin, relating to serious financial and other domestic political problems exacerbated by the American War for Independence. The effect of the American Revolution upon the French Revolution was contributory at best. The successful implementation of the Enlightenment in the United States brought into sharper relief the anarchronisms of the absolute monarchy and the resurgence of aristocracy and encouraged the French intellectuals to reexamine their ideas and assumptions in terms of practicability. Condorcet was emphatic: "America has proved that a country can prosper even though it harbors neither persecutors nor hypocrites."

Nonetheless, once the French Revolution came under the sway of Jacobin leadership, it began to lose almost every trace of the American ideological flavor. It ceased to be the search for constitutional system and even Maximilien Robespierre's "despotism of liberty" and of "Republican virtue." The Jacobin dictatorship of Public Safety (1793–1794) represented the transformation of the Revolution into a mass social movement primarily directed against France's traditional social hierarchy and for liberation from abject poverty and acute human misery. The poor are always under the crushing weight of necessity. Robespierre, overwhelmed by the poor's cry for vengeance upon the nobility and scarcity, subjected his revolutionary government to "the most sacred of all laws, the welfare of the people, the most ir refragable of all titles, necessity," that is, necessity of "dress, food and reproduction of their species." Meanwhile, dissenters were crushed in the name of all absorbing *General Will* which, in actuality, meant nothing but the will of the republican sans-culottes. Thus, the "Rights of Man" became the class rights of the dispossessed. Ironically, however, the fury of the proletariat unleashed the reign of terror and soon made the Revolution to devour its own children. Equally ironic is that the Revolution, from the Jacobins to Napoleon Bonaparte, far from changing the political spirit of the old state, made the new state more absolute and the exercise of its power more arbitrary than ever before.

The French Revolution, as far as its Jacobin phase was concerned, constituted the antithesis of everything the American Revolution promoted except for the abolition of monarchy. The Jacobins promised an instant happiness through the expropriation of the aristocratic estates and were obsessed with such social questions as poverty, scarcity, and inequality of wealth. The American Revolution promised no such socio-economic program, but guaranteed to citizens only the right to engage in the "pursuit of happiness." The French created an absolute and unitary state in the place of the old regime, while the Americans worked to preserve the foundation of civil freedom and limit government.

It was the Jacobin model of the French Revolution with its preoccupation with the social questions, not the American model with its preoccupation with civil liberties, which inspired and affected almost all subsequent revolutions. To be sure, the American Revolutionary creed, particularly its constitutional formulations, would be adopted by many countries. The Belgian revolt against the Hapsburg monarchy invoked some phrases of the American Revolution, and some democratic elements in Belgium in 1790 even considered molding their government in the image of certain American state constitutions. The abortive Polish Constitution of May 3, 1791, reflected the attempts by the Polish gentry to reorganize the government in the spirit of the Federal Constitution of the United States and the French Declaration of the Rights of Man and Citizen. Thaddeus Kosciuszko must have perceived his leading an insurrection against Russia for the independence of Poland in 1794 in the light of the American Revolution in which he had participated side-by-side with Washington and his dear friend Jefferson. The American idea of a written constitution as the basis of public law would have a continuing impact on the constitutional history of Switzerland. In Russia, the Northern Society, a moderate wing of the Decembrist Movement of 1825 advocated a constitutional scheme similar to the American Federal Constitution. In the 1830s and 1840s the English reformers and the radical Chartists attacked the suppression of freedom and the corruption of the nobility, monarch, and church by invoking the principles of the American Revolution. Henry Hetherington, the publisher of the popular but illegal *Poor Man's Guardian*, soon after the House of Lords rejected the Reform Bill in 1831, reminded his readers that the American Revolution was "the best precedent and guide to the oppressed and enslaved people of England in their struggle for the RIGHT OF REPRESENTATION FOR EVERY MAN." The American Declaration of Independence appeared on the English political scene again and again. The Chartists warned of the American example of dealing with tyranny. The English Chartist Circular, dated November 6, 1841, observed: "America is not only a phenomenon in the history of the nation, but an example worthy of emulation of all who invoke the sacred name of liberty—who long to see her blessings diffused and her cause triumphant over the dark friends of despotism, vice, and wretchedness." Of all the revolutionary movements of 1848, the Hungarian uprising seems to have been very much stirred by the principles in the American Declaration of Independence which Louis Kossuth, one of the Hungarian patriots, characterized as the "noblest, happiest page of mankind's history."

But the importance of the message of the American Revolution, which is fundamentally bourgeois and political in character, waned as modern history became afflicted more and more with the social questions of poverty and scarcity. We cannot blame the Founding Fathers for not addressing themselves to these questions because plentiful land and benign civil constitutions in the American colonies had overcome poverty and because American colonial society had been spared from the entrenched feudal nobility and privileged class. As Tocqueville perceptively put it, "The great advantage of the Americans is that they have arrived at a state of democracy without having to endure a democratic revolution, and they are born equal instead of becoming so." This was precisely the reason why Americans with Jefferson could hold as "self-evident" the notion that "men are created equal," a notion which eighteenth-century Europeans could not accept so easily.

The nonsocial American Revolution could not be an example for many Eastern and Central European countries to follow, for they had yet to liberate themselves from such feudal oppression as serfdom and racking landlords. The French model, therefore, became the blueprint for social revolutionaries. Furthermore, the spread of the French influence to most of Latin Europe, the Low Countries, Switzerland, and West Germany, was accelerated with the march of the French conquering armies proclaiming in the name of the French nation "the abolition of tithes, feudality, and seigneureal rights." Through direct or indirect agency of the French Revolution, feudalism was abolished from 1789

to 1848 from Gibraltar to East Prussia, and from the Baltic to Sicily. The persistent influence of the Gallic revolution is suggested by the fact that political organizations like Young Italy, Young Poland, Young Switzerland, Young Germany, Young France, Young Czechs, and Young Turks adopted a tricolor of some kind in the image of the French revolutionary flag. The present Irish, Yugoslav, Rumanian, Syrian, South African, Mexican, and other Latin American tricolors point to the same inspiration.

Indeed, most of the nationalist movements from 1820 on were closely bound up with social struggle. José de San Martin, the Argentinean liberator, fought not only for independence but also for social and economic changes. The Democratic Society of Poland, founded by Polish emigres in Paris after the failure of the November Uprising of 1830–31, declared in 1836 that the elimination of feudal exactions and social injustice in Poland was the precondition for bringing about "a free and harmonious development of national forces." Sun Yat-sen, the father of Modern China, upheld the principle of social equality as one of the three major goals of his revolution. Jawaharlal Nehru, the Indian Nationalist leader, believed that a real revolution should affect the "whole fabric of life and society" as did the French and Russian revolutions—and not just political life as did the American Revolution. It was this "real" revolution he tried to apply to his country. In 1954 Gamal Abdel Nasser of Egypt asserted that he had "no alternative" but to carry out political and social [class] revolutions together and at the same time.

In Industrial Europe, too, the social questions continued to occupy the center stage of revolutionary ferment. The industrial development produced a horde of workingmen subject to bourgeois exploitation, which, in turn, deepened their miseries and threw them into despair. Karl Marx, emerging as their spokesman, rejected the entire constitutional, economic, social, and cultural systems based on the sanctity of private property and traditional civil liberties. He preached a class revolution to obtain freedom for the proletariat from the fetters of scarcity.

This ideological scheme, like Jacobinism, posed a serious challenge to the American republicanism. The American system with its worship of private property and its guarantee of free-play of capitalistic interests was anathema to the socialists who worshipped a collective ownership of productive means and the historical inevitability of a revolution in which "one class overthrows another." In 1873, Peter Lavrov, a Russian Populist (Narodnik) writer, while commemorating the centennial of Pugachev's Rebellion, commented on the achievements and influence of the American Revolution. As much as he was impressed with them, he did not seem wholly persuaded with their relevance for American society of the Gilded Age characterized by the rule of money, corruption, and growing social inequality. He believed that the splendid achievements of the "heroic" Revolution were now "exhausted" due to the emergence of the social evils, for which the American "constitutions and codices" appeared to be impotent and that "the social question smashed, destroyed and buried the political creations of the revolutionary period." Lavrov's view with respect to the American conditions seems to hold true not only of the contemporary European society, but also of the world in the subsequent decades when the social problem aggravated. The ir-

relevance of the American Revolutionary heritage for the socialistic movement was clearly signalled when American socialists, gathered in the Masonic Hall at Indianapolis one summer day in 1901, sang the "Marsellaise" instead of "Yankee Doodle" or the "Star Spangled Banner" after they had just finished founding the Socialist Party of America.

The political and constitutional practices on the part of the ideological right and center in modern history also seem to have little relationship with the American system of government. All of them were deficient in a balance built on the principle of separation of powers and tempered by the popular sovereignty. These governments were either too strong or unstable at the center. Typical of the former were Imperial Germany and Japan, distinguished for their authoritarianism. Typical of the latter was France, where fourteen constitutions came and went from 1789 to 1875, one constitution for every six years on the average. Such a record would defy an attempt to locate the origin for each of them. The countries of limited monarchy, like Belgium, turned to the British constitutional arrangement for guidance. After the First World War, many of the monarchical constitutions in Europe were replaced by those modelled largely after the American constitution, but the new constitutions were mistrusted by the people living under them. Fifteen years after the fall of the monarchical governments, half of Europe would live under some form of dictatorship.

Modern history has shabbily dealt with the legacies of the American Revolution. The record is due to no fault of the Founders of the American Republic. Rather, it was the deepening social and economic malaise of pre-modern and modern society which dulled people's sensitivity for the classical political liberties and enhanced their concern for equality and necessity.

It would be remiss not to say something about the record of the United States regarding its Revolutionary heritage. Americans still live under the Constitution created almost two centuries ago, but no longer live by its original spirit. Local township government, the matrix and mainstay of our democracy, is no longer what it used to be, having badly atrophied under the heavy hand of the state and federal governments. The government in Washington, D.C., has become so powerful that one sensitive historian recently described its executive branch as the "Imperial Presidency." Its huge and expensive bureaucracy seems to have acquired a life of its own unsusceptible to the feelings and opinions of the people. Even the behavior of elected officials has been such as to warrant a loss of faith in representative system.

In the conduct of foreign affairs, the record is no better. America has argued for the principles of open door and national self-determination, but has often failed to live up to those lofty ideals whenever they came into conflict with its own interests and security considerations. It is true that the United States, from Woodrow Wilson to Harry S. Truman, has liberated many people from both domestic and foreign tyrants and given them democratic constitutions. Yet in these instances, America seems to have been motivated by considerations other than its Revolutionary principles. Being the richest nation, enjoying an unprecedented influence in international affairs and holding vast investments abroad, protecting its stakes has become the main obsession of our "security managers" since the Second World War. In 1948,

President Truman, disturbed by increasing Communist insurgency in the Mediterranean area, declared: "We cannot allow changes in the Status Quo." This passion for order has often led to intervention, overtly and covertly, in many parts of the world. During our 1965 intervention in the Dominican Republic, the commanding U. S. admiral explained as he took over the Dominican occupation: "our troops will remain until all revolutionary movements have been stamped out." America inflicted terrible pain and destruction on the Vietnamese people in a vain attempt to "save" them from Communism, although they were fighting for their independence. The United States has become the Metternich of the mid-twentieth century, a posture which runs afoul of its Revolutionary heritage.

Yet, no nation has been more critical and scrutinizing of its own conduct in the light of its national creed than has the United States. No nation has tried so hard in reconciling the gap between its creed and the sordid realities of racism and foreign adventurism than the Americans. There have been many Jeffersons and Lincolns who, suffering from heavy guilt feelings about the black Americans' plight, worked for equal justice. There have been many anti-imperialists like Lincoln and Ulysses Grant who vigorously condemned the immorality of the Mexican War, like Mark Twain and Andrew Carnegie who warned of the betrayal of the Revolutionary heritage by the annexation of the Philippines, like William Fulbright and George McGovern who denounced our activities in Vietnam for the same reason. There have also been many Archibald Coxes and John Siricas who displayed courage to defend the Constitution at a critical moment. We are entitled to the comfortable thought that, through these great men, our Revolutionary legacies have been kept alive, affecting our life and modern history alike, and that this country, without a history of social revolution, has provided an asylum for fifty million or more people escaping from that perennial albatross of mankind, scarcity, which all the modern social revolutions have yet to overcome.

America may not have become a place where Hegel's *Geistes-Geschichte* (Spirit-History) of the world lodged, but it has been a nation of an "abounding strength and vitality." Ultimately, the vindication of the American Revolution does not have to be found in its approval or duplication by other nations, but rather in how well it has worked for and how strongly it will continue to inspire the people of the United States of America.

GUIDE TO FURTHER READING

The Revolution has appealed to American historians not only because it gave birth to the United States but because it is considered the first of the great revolutions of modern times. A voluminous literature has arisen over its causes and consequences as well as on the separate subject of comparative revolutions. This selective bibliography barely scratches the surface of the numerous publications devoted to these two topics. For a fuller listing, see John Shy, comp., *The American Revolution* (Northbrook, 1973), and the pertinent entries in Frank Freidel, *et al.*, eds., *The Harvard Guide to American History* (2 vols: Cambridge, 1974, rev. ed.).

The beginning student should first become familiar with the trends of historiography regarding the Revolution. To identify major schools of interpretation, the following five essays should prove helpful: Wesley F. Craven, "The Revolutionary Era," in John Higham ed., *The Reconstruction of American History* (New York, 1962), 46–63; Merrill Jensen, 'Historians and the Nature of the American Revolution," in Ray A. Billington, ed., *The Reinterpretation of Early American History* (San Marino, 1966), 101–127. George Athan Billias, "The Revolutionary Era: Reinterpretations and Revisions," in George Athan Billias and Gerald N. Grob, eds., *American History: Retrospect and Prospect* (New York, 1970), 34–84; Jack P. Greene, "Revolution, Confederation, and Constitution, 1763–1787," in *The Reinterpretation of American History and Culture*, William H. Cartwright and Richard L. Watson, eds., (Washington, 1973), 259–295; James Kirby Martin, "The Human Dimensions of Nation Making; Merrill Jen-

sen's Scholarship and the American Revolution," in James Kirby Martin, ed., *The Human Dimensions in Nation Making* (Madison, 1976), 9–22.

The historiography of the Revolution began with contemporaries who witnessed the event. Two of the best Patriot histories were written by Mercy Otis Warren and David Ramsay. Warren's *History of the Rise, Progress, and Termination of the American Revolution* (3 vols: New York, 1967, rev. ed.) was published originally in 1805. Ramsay's *The History of the American Revolution* (2 vols: New York, 1967, rev. ed.) was first issued in 1789. Both these historians viewed the Revolution as an epic struggle to protect human liberty. Loyalist historians, of course, saw things differently. Thomas Hutchinson believed that Whig politicians in Massachusetts were motivated by a lust for power, and that they had conspired to gain independence. See the third volume of his work, *The History of the Colony and Province of Massachusetts-Bay*, Lawrence S. Mayo, ed., (3 vols: Cambridge, 1936) which was written in 1781 but published later. Peter Oliver was more emotional and pictured the Whig leaders as unprincipled demagogues who deliberately aroused the passions of the people in his *Origin & Progress of the American Rebellion*, Douglass Adair and John A. Schutz, eds., (San Marino, 1961).

The Patriot interpretation of the Revolution remained dominant throughout most of the nineteenth century. American history as a whole during that period was seen as a never-ending struggle by mankind to preserve and expand liberty. George Bancroft believed

195

this drive for liberty was part of God's master plan for America, and that the Revolution was but one step in that direction. See his monumental *History of the United States of America from the Discovery of the American Continent* (10 vols: Boston, 1834–1874).

The imperial school of historians which emerged at the turn of the century, arose in reaction to Bancroft's highly nationalistic interpretation. These scholars argued that the Revolution, to be properly understood, had to be viewed as an integral part of the history of the British empire. George L. Beer traced the beginnings of the British mercantilist system in *The Origins of the British Colonial System, 1578–1660* (New York, 1908) and in *The Old Colonial System, 1660–1754* (2 vols: New York, 1912), and proclaimed that the policies of the mother country were remarkably fair. Charles M. Andrews reached somewhat similar conclusions in *The Colonial Background of the American Revolution* (New Haven, 1931), and in the last volume of *The Colonial Period of American History* (4 vols: New Haven, 1934–1938). Two of Andrews' students continued to write along the lines of their mentor: Leonard W. Labaree, *Royal Government in America* (New Haven, 1930) and Lawrence H. Gipson's massive *The British Empire Before the American Revolution* (15 vols: Caldwell, Idaho and New York, 1936–1970). Gipson in a single-volume work, *The Coming of the Revolution, 1763–1775* (New York, 1954), summarized many of his views.

In the 1960s and 1970s, another generation of historians produced studies that might be called neo-imperialist in nature. Members of the more traditional imperial school, like Gipson, were often too favorably inclined oward Britain and pictured the American colonists as selfish, self-centered, and shortsighted. The current crop of neo-imperial scholars are less interested in taking sides and more concerned with the complexities of the imperial relationship. In writing about politics, they focus on the following aspects: the informal structure of authority behind formal public institutions; the continual struggle for power among Britain's officials, agencies, and

institutions; and the personal rivalries, political factions, and lobby interests (both British and American) that helped shape imperial policies. When discussing ideology, the neo-imperialists are more sensitive to the crucial role that ideas played in precipitating the Revolution.

The following historians may be said to be of the neo-imperialist persuasion: Thomas C. Barrow, *Trade and Empire* (Cambridge, 1967); Michael G. Kammen, *A Rope of Sand* (Ithaca, 1968); Stanley N. Katz, *Newcastle's New York* (Cambridge, 1968); and Dora Mae Clark, *The Rise of the British Treasury* (New Haven, 1960). Many of the essays in *Anglo-American Political Relations, 1675–1775*, edited by Alison G. Olson and Richard M. Brown (New Brunswick, 1970) fall into this category. See also Michael G. Kammen's book, *Empire and Interest* (Philadelphia and New York, 1970).

Certain British historians viewed the Revolution from quite a different perspective than did American scholars. Sir Lewis Namier analyzed the internal workings of eighteenth-century British politics to determine to what degree King George III and Parliament were responsible for bringing on the Revolution. In two seminal studies, *The Structure of Politics at the Accession of George III* (London, 1929) and *England in the Age of the American Revolution* (London, 1930), Namier discovered that "interests," and "connections," tended to dominate political affairs in Parliament, thus making it difficult, if not impossible, to agree upon empire-minded policies.

The Namierist school of historians in England and America fleshed out certain implications of his thesis. Among the more important works in this field are the following: Richard Pares, *King George III and the Politicians* (Oxford, 1953); Eric Robson, *The American Revolution in Its Political and Military Aspects, 1763–1783* (London, 1955); George H. Gutteridge, *English Whiggism and the American Revolution* (Berkeley, 1942); John Brooke, *The Chatham Administration, 1766–1768* (London, 1955); Ian R. Christie, *The End of North's Ministry, 1780–1782* (London, 1958); John Derry, *English Politics* and the American Revolution (London, 1976); P.D.G. Thomas, *British Politics and the Stamp Act Crisis* (New York, 1975); Bernard Donoughue, *British Politics and the American Revolution* (London, 1964); John Brooke and Lewis Namier, *Charles Townshend* (London, 1964); Colin Bonwick, *English Radicals and the American Revolution* (Chapel Hill, 1977); Ian R. Christie, *Crisis of Empire* (New York, 1966); Charles R. Ritcheson, *British Politics and the American Revolution* (Norman, 1954); and Franklin B. Wickwire, *British Subministers and Colonial America, 1763–1783* (Princeton, 1966). In John Brewer's, *Party Ideology and Popular Politics at the Accession of George III* (Cambridge, New York, 1976), there is a sharp critique of the Namierist approach. Jack P. Greene has published a historiographical survey that includes not only Namierists but other British historians writing on Anglo-American relations prior to the Revolution. See his "The Plunge of the Lemmings: A Consideration of Recent Writings on British Politics and the American Revolution," *South Atlantic Quarterly*, 67 (1968), 141–175.

The Progressive historians, another major category of American scholars, believed that economic and social forces were primarily responsible for bringing on the Revolution. They began to write during the Progressive era, and many of them postulated a dual revolution: an "external" revolution based on a clash of economic interests between Britain and the American colonies; and an "internal" revolution within American society arising from a conflict between lower and upper classes. The major works presenting this interpretation or some version of it are: Carl L. Becker. *The History of Political Parties in the Province of New York, 1760–1776* (Madison, 1909); Charles A. Beard, *An Economic Interpretation of the Constitution of the United States* (New York, 1913); Charles A. Beard and Mary R. Beard, *Rise of American Civilization* (New York, 1927), Vol. I; Arthur M. Schlesinger, *The Colonial Merchants and the American Revolution 1763–1776* (New York, 1918); and J. Franklin Jameson, *The American Revolution Considered as a Social Movement* (Princeton,

1926). A thoughtful critique of this first generation of Progressive historians is in Frederick B. Tolles', "The American Revolution Considered as a Social Movement: A Re-evaluation," *American Historical Review* 60 (1954), 1–12.

The Progressive tradition was carried on by a later generation of scholars, most notably by Merrill Jensen and his students. Jensen's interpretation, stressing an internal revolution, was set forth in two works: *Articles of Confederation* (Madison, 1940) and *The New Nation* (New York, 1950). Jensen has modified his thesis somewhat in the article appearing in this book, in which he argues that the Revolution was a democratic movement, not in its origins but in its results. He held to this modified interpretation in his later works: *Founding of a Nation* (New York, 1969); and *The American Revolution Within America* (New York, 1974).

The first generation of Progressive historians had assumed that the Revolution was a sweeping social movement—one that broadened opportunities for the common people in terms of their political rights, economic standing, and social status as a result of a conscious commitment to greater democracy. Among the current generation of Progressive historians, however, such advances in opportunities were seen more as the result of unplanned historical circumstances. Two of Jensen's students made major contributions along these lines, Jackson Turner Main concluded in two studies that there were greater opportunities for the people to hold important political offices. See his "Government by the People: The American Revolution and the Democratization of the Legislatures," *William and Mary Quarterly*, 3d Series, 23 (1966), 391–407; and *The Upper House in Revolutionary America, 1763–1788* (Madison, 1967). James Kirby Martin in *Men in Rebellion* (New Brunswick, 1973) argued that the transfer of power in the top echelons of government took place among the political elite, and that even though the people eventually benefited from the process, it was not necessarily because Revolutionary leaders had wanted it so.

The coming of World War II witnessed

the rise of a new school of scholars—the Neo-conservative historians—who revised the Progressive tradition which had stressed the more radical side of the Revolution. The Neo-conservatives held that the Revolution was primarily a conservative movement—a defense of American rights and liberties against British measures. During the 1950s, this interpretation emerged as the prevailing view.

The Neo-conservatives emphasized consensus and continuity among social groups in revolutionary America and downplayed internal class conflict and discontinuity. Daniel J. Boorstin's chapter in *The Genius of American Politics* (Chicago, 1953) and Clinton Rossiter's *Seedtime of the Republic* (New York, 1953) both stressed the unity among the American people at the time of the Revolution. Louis Hartz in *The Liberal Tradition in America* (New York, 1955) concluded that the Revolution was a conservative movement whose main aim was to preserve the world's freest society, one unaffected by Europe's feudal institutions. Robert E. Brown in *Middle-Class Democracy and the Revolution in Massachusetts 1691–1780* (Ithaca, 1955) repudiated the claim of the Progressive historians that American colonial society had been undemocratic because high suffrage requirements had prevented many of the people from voting. Brown showed that voting rights were widespread among white adult males in Massachusetts, most of whom owned enough property to qualify for the right to vote. The Revolution, according to Brown, was a fight by middle-class freeholders in America to defend a democratic social order that was being threatened by British encroachments. Somewhat the same point of view is presented in Robert E. Brown and B. Katherine Brown's *Virginia, 1705–1786: Democracy or Aristocracy?* (East Lansing, 1964).

During the decade of the 1960s, two groups of historians emerged to challenge the Neo-conservative interpretation. One consisted of intellectual historians, many of whom viewed the Revolution as a radical ideological movement. Bernard Bailyn, the foremost member of this group, argued that the true revolution

took place in men's minds. Americans came to accept in intellectual terms the revolutionary implications of their divergences from European norms that had arisen as a result of different experiences in the New World. Bailyn's pioneering article, "Political Experience and Enlightenment Ideas in Eighteenth-Century America," *American Historical Review* 67 (1962), 339–351, explored the role of Enlightenment ideas in rationalizing the changes that had already taken place. His brilliant introduction to *Pamphlets of the American Revolution, 1750–1776*, Vol. I (Cambridge, 1965) broke new ground in relating the body of American revolutionary thought to the anti-authoritarian ideas in English Whig thought of the mid-seventeenth and early eighteenth centuries. This study, expanded and republished as *The Ideological Origins of the American Revolution* (Cambridge, 1967), stressed the significance of radical Whig ideology in bringing about the Revolution, and portions of this work are reproduced in these pages. In his *Origins of American Politics* (New York, 1968), Bailyn delved into the question of why the Americans had been so receptive to the English intellectual tradition of anti-authoritarianism.

Bailyn's work had a profound impact, and was followed by a rash of books—many by his students—which showed the influence of English Whig radical ideology on the Revolution. Gordon S. Wood's *The Creation of the American Republic, 1776–1787* (Chapel Hill, 1969) stressed republicanism as a radical ideology and showed the changes American political thought underwent from the signing of the Declaration of Independence to the writing of the Constitution. Richard D. Brown viewed the Massachusetts Committee of Correspondence in the context of radical Whig thought in his *Revolutionary Politics in Massachusetts* (Cambridge, 1970), and Pauline Maier explored crowd behavior and violence in the pre-Revolutionary period from the same perspective in her book, *From Resistance to Revolution* (New York, 1972).

Bailyn's work was not without its critics. Jack P. Greene put greater emphasis on the prerogative tradition rather than on opposition Whig thought as the source of American dissent in *The Quest for Power* (Chapel Hill, 1963). Greene expanded his argument in "Political Mimesis: A Consideration of the Historical and Cultural Roots of Legislative Behavior in the British Colonies in the Eighteenth Century," *American Historical Review*, 75 (1969), 337–367, and Bailyn responded in an extended reply. Many of the "New Left" scholars and "new social historians" also attacked Bailyn's interpretation. Generally speaking, these scholars questioned the existence of a republican world view that was so powerful and pervasive as to motivate the Americans to rebel against Britain.

Bailyn was not alone among the intellectual historians to take up the subject of the antecedents to the Revolution. Caroline Robbins' The *Eighteenth-Century Commonwealthman* (Cambridge, 1959) provided some of the background for Bailyn's emphasis on the English tradition of anti-authoritarianism. Other works which should be consulted in this regard are: J.G.A. Pocock's *The Machiavellian Moment* (Princeton, 1975); Richard Buel's "Democracy and the American Revolution: A Frame of Reference," *William and Mary Quarterly*, 3d Series, 21 (1964), 164–190; Joyce Appleby's "The Social Origins of American Revolutionary Ideology," *Journal of American History* 64, (1978), 935–958; Garry Wills, *Inventing America* (New York, 1978); and Morton White's *The Philosophy of the American Revolution* (New York, 1979).

Edmund S. Morgan, a distinguished intellectual historian, wrote widely about other aspects of the Revolution. In *The Stamp Act Crisis* (Chapel Hill, 1953) produced with his wife, Helen, Morgan claimed that the colonists were consistent in their denial of Parliament's right to impose taxes for revenue. Contrary to what Progressive historians had written earlier, the colonists remained faithful to this principle throughout the decade 1765–1775. Morgan synthesized many of his ideas in *The Birth of a Republic, 1763–1789* (Chicago, 1977, rev. ed.). His essay, "The Puritan Ethic and the American Revolution," *William and Mary Quarterly*, 3d Series, 24 '(1967), 3–43, discussed the fear Americans

had about their own degeneracy in terms of luxury and corruption. Morgan's many essays on the subject were collected in a volume entitled *The Challenge of the American Revolution* (New York, 1976).

The second group of scholars who contested the findings of the Neo-conservatives, beginning in the 1960s, were the "New Left" historians. For the most part, they viewed the Revolution as a radical movement and focused their studies on the lower classes and upon a more precise economic interpretation of the causes of the conflict. Jesse Lemisch's two essays are representative of this approach: one is reprinted in this volume, and the other is "Jack Tar in the Streets: Merchant Seamen in the Politics of Revolutionary America," *William and Mary Quarterly*, 3d Series, 25 (1968), 371–407. Following the same approach are Staughton Lynd's essays in *Class Conflict, Slavery, and the United States Constitution,* and Eric Foner's biography, *Tom Paine and Revolutionary America* (New York, 1976). The collected essays in Alfred F. Young, ed., *The American Revolution: Explorations in the History of American Radicalism* (DeKalb, 1976) are equally pertinent, though they reveal how diverse the views of this group of scholars are. For recent interpretations of economic causes of the Revolution, see Marc Egnal and Joseph A. Ernst, "An Economic Interpretation of the American Revolution," *William and Mary Quarterly* 3d Series, 29 (1972), 3–32; and Joseph A. Ernst, *Money and Politics in America, 1755–1775* (Chapel Hill, 1973).

Along with the "New Left" critique of the Neo-conservatives, mention should also be made of the work of a number of scholars who called attention to the way evangelical religion had helped to mobilize the lower classes in the revolutionary movement. See three articles by Rhys Isaac, "Religion and Authority: Problems of the Anglican Establishment in Virginia in the Era of the Great Awakening and the Parsons' Cause," *William and Mary Quarterly*, 3d Series, 30 (1973), 3–36; "Evangelical Revolt: The Nature of the Baptists' Challenge to the Traditional Order in Virginia, 1765 to 1775," *ibid.,*

31 (1974), 345–368; and "Dramatizing the Ideology of Revolution: Popular Mobilization in Virginia, 1774–1776," *ibid.*, 33 (1976), 357–385.

For the connection between the Great Awakening and the Revolution, see William G. McLoughlin, "The Role of Religion in the Revolution," in Stephen G. Kurtz and James H. Hutson, eds., *Essays on the American Revolution* (Chapel Hill, 1973); Alan Heimert, *Religion and the American Mind: From the Great Awakening to the Revolution* (Cambridge, 1966); and Richard L. Bushman, *From Puritan to Yankee: Character and Social Order in Connecticut, 1690–1765* (Cambridge, 1967).

During the 1960s, yet another major group of scholars—the "new social historians"—began writing about the Revolution. Their work was characterized by methodological innovations such as quantification techniques and research in non-traditional sources like wills, deeds, tax lists, and town and church records. Robert A. Gross' work, *The Minutemen and Their World* (New York, 1976), from which a selection in this book is drawn, is a case study of one community during the Revolution.

One question to which the "new social historians" directed their studies was whether the distribution of wealth was becoming more or less equitable as the Revolution drew near. In *The Social Structure of Revolutionary America* (Princeton, 1965), Jackson Turner Main had already demonstrated that there was a growing gap between the rich and poor before the Revolution and that that event had halted the growing trend. Quantitative studies of certain regions and urban areas appeared in general to support the contention that there were growing inequalities in wealth prior to the Revolution. See James A. Henretta, "Economic Development and Social Structure in Colonial Boston," *William and Mary Quarterly*, 3d Series, 22 (1965), 75–92; Allan Kulikoff, "The Progress of Inequality in Boston," *William and Mary Quarterly*, 3d Series, 28 (1971), 375–412; James T. Lemon and Gary B. Nash, "The Distribution of Wealth in Eighteenth-Century

America: A Century of Change in Chester County, Pennsylvania, 1693–1802," *Journal of Social History*, 2 (1968), 1–24; Gary B. Nash, *The Urban Crucible* (Cambridge, 1979); Gary B. Nash, "Urban Wealth and Poverty in Pre-Revolutionary America," *Journal of Interdisciplinary History*, 6 (1976), 545–584; Gary B. Nash, "Poverty and Poor Relief in Pre-Revolutionary Philadelphia," *William and Mary Quarterly*, 3d Series, 33 (1976) 3–30; Aubrey C. Land, "Economic Base and Social Structure: The Northern Chesapeake in the Eighteenth Century," *Journal of Economic History*, 25 (1965), 639–654; and Kenneth A. Lockridge, "Social Change and the Meaning of the Revolution," *Journal of Social History*, 6 (1973), 403–439. These studies were less successful, however, when they sought to link such widening economic inequalities with the causes of the Revolution itself.

The "new social historians," among others, have paid particular attention to specific social groups—blacks and women—to study how they were affected by the Revolution. Linda DePauw in a penetrating overview, "Land of the Unfree: Legal Limitations on Liberty in Pre-Revolutionary America," *Maryland Historical Magazine*, 68 (1973), 355–368, concluded that the Revolution failed to bring about many advances in terms of legal and human rights for these two groups. But there is considerable disagreement about what the Revolution meant to black slaves, slave owners, and the slave trade. For differing views on these issues, the following works are pertinent: Benjamin Quarles, *The Negro in the American Revolution* (Chapel Hill, 1961); Herbert Aptheker, *The Negro in the American Revolution* (New York, 1940); Winthrop Jordan, *White Over Black* (Chapel Hill, 1968); David Brion Davis, *The Problem of Slavery in the Age of Revolution, 1770–1823* (Ithaca, 1975); Duncan J. MacLeod, *Slavery, Race, and the American Revolution* (New York, 1974); Robert M. McColley, *Slavery and Jeffersonian Virginia* (Urbana, 1964); Gerald W. Mullin, *Flight and Rebellion* (New York, 1972); Edmund S. Morgan, *American Slavery American Freedom* (New York, 1975);

John Hope Franklin, "The North, the South, and The American Revolution," *Journal of American History*, 62 (1975), 5–23; Donald L. Robinson, *Slavery in the Structure of American Politics, 1765–1820* (New York, 1971); and Sidney Kaplan, *The Black Presence in the Era of the American Revolution, 1770–1800* (Washington, 1973).

The role of women in the Revolution has a more limited literature, though the recent growth of women's studies is rapidly changing that situation. Four earlier works are useful: Mary S. Benson, *Women in Eighteenth-Century America* (New York, 1935); Julia C. Spruill, *Women's Life and Work in the Southern Colonies* (Chapel Hill, 1938); Elizabeth Cometti, "Women in the American Revolution," *New England Quarterly, 20* (1947), 329–346; and Elizabeth T. Ellet, *The Women of the American Revolution* (3 vols.; New York, 1848–1850; reprinted 1969). Typical of the more recent analytical work being done on the changing status of women in revolutionary times are: Joan Hoff Wilson, "Illusion of Change: Women and the American Revolution," in Alfred F. Young, ed., *The American Revolution* (DeKalb, 1976); Mary Beth Norton, "Eighteenth-Century American Women in Peace and War: The Case of the Loyalists," *William and Mary Quarterly*, 3d Series, 33 (1976), 386–409; Nancy F. Cott, *The Bonds of Womanhood* (New Haven and London, 1977); Linda Kerber, "Daughters of Columbia: Educating Women for the Republic," in Stanley Elkins and Eric McKitrick, eds., *The Hofstadter Aegis* (New York, 1974); and Linda Kerber, "The Republican Mother: Women and the Enlightenment—An American Perspective," *American Quarterly*, 28, 2 (Special Issue, 1976). See two works now in press: Linda Kerber, *Daughters of Columbia* (forthcoming, University of North Carolina Press); and Mary Beth Norton, *The Revolutionary Experience of American Women, 1760–1800* (forthcoming, Little, Brown and Company).

With the coming of the Bicentennial, greater attention was paid by historians to yet another important group in the Revolution—the Loyalists. The most helpful earlier works on this subject are Moses Coit Tyler's *Literary History of the American Revolution* (2 vols: New York, rev. ed. 1898); Claude H. Van Tyne's *The Loyalists in the American Revolution* (New York, 1902); and Leonard W. Labaree's "The Nature of American Loyalism," in American Antiquarian Society *Proceedings*, 54 (1944), 15–58. William H. Nelson produced the best general analysis of the subject in *The American Tory* (New York, 1961), suggesting that the Loyalists might best be seen as cultural minorities who looked to Britain for support against surrounding Whig majorities. Two works by Wallace Brown, *The King's Friends* (Providence, 1965) and *The Good Americans* (New York, 1969) show that the Loyalists were not always members of the upper class. For the number of Loyalists in America, see Eugene F. Fingerhut's "Uses and Abuses of the American Loyalists' Claims: A Critique of Quantitative Analysis," *William and Mary Quarterly*, 3d Series, 25 (1968), 245–258. The ideology of the Loyalists is discussed in Bernard Bailyn's *The Ordeal of Thomas Hutchinson* (Cambridge, 1974); Mary Beth Norton's *The British-Americans* (Boston, 1972); William A. Benton's *Whig-Loyalism* (Rutherford, 1969); and Robert M. Calhoon's *The Loyalists in Revolutionary America, 1760–1781* (New York, 1973).

The Revolution, it should be remembered, was a military conflict, and the struggle often reflected the relationship between war and society. John Shy, for example, has resorted to a strikingly original approach to determine whether or not the Revolution was revolutionary by analyzing the effects the war and military service had upon America's social structure. See his essays in *A People Numerous & Armed* (London, New York, 1976). His book, *Toward Lexington* (Princeton, 1965), on the other hand, is a work on the role that the British army played in the coming of the Revolution.

For the American side of the military struggle and its aftermath, see the following recent studies: Don Higginbotham, *The War of American Independence* (New York, 1971); the pertinent chapters in Russell F. Weigley's

Towards an American Army (New York and London, 1962) and his *American Way of War* (New York, 1973); the sketches in George Athan Billias, ed., *George Washington's Generals* (New York, 1964); and Richard H. Kohn, *Eagle and Sword* (New York, 1975). For the British side, see Piers Mackesy, *The War for America, 1775–1783* (Cambridge, 1965); William Willcox, *Portrait of a General* (New York, 1964); Ira S. Gruber, *The Howe Brothers and the American Revolution* (New York, 1972); the essays in George Athan Billias, ed., *George Washington's Opponents* (New York, 1969); Paul H. Smith, *Loyalists and Redcoats* (New York, 1964); R. Arthur Bowler, *Logistics and the Failure of the British Army in America, 1775–1783* (Princeton, 1975); and David Syrett, *Shipping and the American War, 1775–1783* (London, 1970). Among the general accounts of the war are: Willard M. Wallace, *Appeal to Arms* (New York, 1951); John R. Alden, *The American Revolution, 1775–1783* (New York, 1954); Howard H. Peckham, *The War for Independence* (Chicago, 1958); and Marshall Smelser, *The Winning of Independence* (Chicago, 1972).

There is an on-going debate regarding the role of law and lawyers in the coming of the Revolution as well as the part played by presumably lawless elements—the Patriot mobs. Milton M. Klein in "New York Lawyers and the Coming of the American Revolution," *New York History*, 55 (1974), 383–408, and John P. Reid in numerous articles and two books, *In a Defiant Stance* (University Park, 1977) and *In a Rebellious Spirit* (University Park, 1979), emphasize the attention paid to legality by the American revolutionaries. Richard M. Brown in *Strain of Violence* (New York, 1975) stresses the more violent and extra-legal character of the Revolution. Following the lead of three British scholars —George Rudé, E. J. Hobsbawm, and E. P. Thompson—American historians have written about mob activities within a more conceptual context. Gordon S. Wood in "A Note on Mobs in the American Revolution," *William and Mary Quarterly*, 3d Series, 23 (1966), 635–642 concludes that mobs on the eve of the Revolution were concerned mainly with defending American constitutional rights against what they considered arbitrary British moves. Pauline Maier in "Popular Uprisings and Civil Authority in Eighteenth-Century America," *William and Mary Quarterly*, 3d Series, 27 (1970), 3–35 holds that mobs played a constitutional role. But Jesse Lemisch, in "Jack Tar in the Streets: Merchant Seamen in the Politics of Revolutionary America," *William and Mary Quarterly*, 3d Series, 25 (1968) 371–407, feels that mobs were more violent, less middle class and less rational than Maier assumes them to have been. James H. Hutson's "An Investigation of the Inarticulate: Philadelphia's White Oaks," *William and Mary Quarterly*, 3d Series, 28 (1971), 3–35 is a rebuttal to Lemisch's arguments.

There are a number of key articles relating to specific aspects of the Revolution that should not be overlooked: Rowland Berthoff and John M. Murrin, "Feudalism, Communalism, and the Yeoman Freeholder: The American Revolution Considered as a Social Accident," in Stephen G. Kurtz and James H. Hutson, eds., *Essays on the American Revolution* (Chapel Hill, 1973); Edwin G. Burroughs and Michael Wallace, "The American Revolution: The Ideology and Psychology of National Liberation," *Perspectives in American History*, 6 (1972), 167–306; Richard B. Morris, "We the People of the United States: The Bicentennial of a People's Revolution," *American Historical Review*, 82 (1977), 1–19; Richard B. Morris, "Class Struggle and the American Revolution," *William and Mary Quarterly*, 3d Series, 19 (1962), 3–29; Clarence R. Ver Steeg, "The American Revolution Considered as an Economic Movement," *Huntington Library Quarterly*, 20 (1957), 361–372; Milton M. Klein, "Democracy and Politics in Colonial New York," *New York History*, 40 (1959), 221–246; Cecelia M. Kenyon, "Republicanism and Radicalism in the American Revolution: An Old-Fashioned Interpretation," *William and Mary Quarterly*, 3d Series, 19 (1962), 153–182; and Robert W. Weir, "Who Shall Rule at Home: The American Revolution as a Crisis of Legitimacy for the Colonial Elite," *Journal of Interdisciplinary History*, 6 (1976), 679–

700. All of the essays in the Kurtz and Hutson volume listed above are pertinent, as are those in Elizabeth H. Kagan, comp., *Leadership in the American Revolution* (Washington, 1974).

Biographical studies not only reflect the spirit of the times but reveal the human dimension of the Revolution. The following are but a few of the studies of some of the more important revolutionary leaders: Douglas S. Freeman, *et al.*, *George Washington* (7 vols: New York, 1948–1958); James T. Flexner, *George Washington* (4 vols: Boston, 1965–1972); Marcus Cunliffe, *George Washington* (Boston, 1958); Dumas Malone, *Thomas Jefferson and His Time* (5 vols: Boston, 1974–); Merrill Peterson, *Thomas Jefferson and the New Nation* (New York, 1970); Page Smith, *John Adams* (2 vols: Garden City, 1962); Peter Shaw, *The Character of John Adams* (Chapel Hill, 1976); Irving Brant, *James Madison* (6 vols: 1941–1961); Ralph Ketcham, *James Madison* (New York, 1971); Carl Van Doren, *Benjamin Franklin* (New York, 1938); John C. Miller, *Sam Adams* (Boston, 1936); Broadus Mitchell, *Alexander Hamilton* (3 vols: New York, 1957–1970); John C. Miller, *Alexander Hamilton* (New York, 1959); Richard R. Beaman, *Patrick Henry* (New York, 1974); Clarence R. Ver Steeg, *Robert Morris* (Philadelphia, 1954); George Athan Billias, *Elbridge Gerry* (New York, 1976); Charles Page Smith, *James Wilson* (Chapel Hill, 1956); and David F. Hawke, *Paine* (New York, 1974).

Finally some mature scholars have written overviews of the Revolution. In this regard the following works are of significance: John R. Alden, *A History of the American Revolution* (New York, 1969); John C. Miller's two books, *Origins of the American Revolution* (Boston, 1943) and *Triumph of Freedom, 1775–1783* (Boston, 1948); Richard B. Morris, *The American Revolution Reconsidered* (New York, 1976); Ian R. Christie, *Crisis of Empire* (New York, 1966); Dan Lacey, *The Meaning of the American Revolution* (New York, 1964); and Page Smith, *A People's History of the American Revolution* (2 vols: New York, 1976).

The writings of scholars who viewed the Revolution from the perspective of comparative history are more limited because of the complexity of the subject. To gain some idea of the problems involved, three essays should be read first: Lawrence Stone's "Theories of Revolution," *World Politics,* 11 (1966), 159–176; Peter Amann's "Revolution: A Redefinition," *Political Science Quarterly,* 77 (1962), 36–53; and Robert R. Palmer's "The Revolution" in C. Vann Woodward, ed., *The Comparative Approach to American History* (New York, 1968). Palmer's *The Age of Democratic Revolution* (2 vols: Princeton, 1959–1964) remains the classic work on the subject. Hannah Arendt in *On Revolution* (New York, 1963) and Crane Brinton in *The Anatomy of Revolution* (New York, 1938) offer different views from Palmer's. The work of a French scholar, Jacques Godechot, *France and the Atlantic Revolution of the Eighteenth Century,* Herbert Rowan, trans. (New York, 1965) is more in keeping with Palmer's ideas. Seymour M. Lipset, a political sociologist, compares the American Revolution to modern-day anticolonial revolutions in *The First New Nation* (New York, rev. ed. 1979) as does Thomas C. Barrow in the essay reprinted in this volume. Richard B. Morris, *The Emerging Nations and the American Revolution* (New York, 1970) should be read in its entirety. J.R. Pole in *Political Representation in England and the Origins of the American Republic* (New York, 1966) and William H. Nelson in "The Revolutionary Character of the American Revolution," *American Historical Review,* 70 (1965) 998–1014, approach the problem of comparative history from a different point of view than did the authors of the works cited above.

For works of European scholars writing on the Revolution, besides those previously mentioned, see Friedrich Gentz, *The Origins and Principles of the American Revolution, Compared with the Origins and Principles of the French Revolution* [John Q. Adams], trans. (Philadelphia, 1800); Carlo Botta, *History of the War of Independence of the United States of America,* George Alexander Otis, trans. (3 vols.: Philadelphia, 1820–21); and N. N. Kolkhovitinov, *Russia and the American Revolution* (Tallahassee, 1976).